CHURCHILL'S PRIV

Eric Morris

CHURCHILL'S PRIVATE ARMIES

Hutchinson
London Melbourne Auckland Johannesburg

This edition first published in 1986 by Hutchinson Ltd, an imprint of
Century Hutchinson Ltd., Brookmount House, 62–65 Chandos Place,
London WC2N 4NW

Century Hutchinson Australia (Pty) Ltd.
PO Box 496, 16–22 Church Street, Hawthorn, Melbourne, Victoria 3122

Century Hutchinson New Zealand Limited
PO Box 40–086, 32–34 View Road, Glenfield, Auckland 10

Century Hutchinson South Africa (Pty) Ltd.
PO Box 337, Bergvlei 2012, South Africa

ISBN: 0 09 161920 3

Printed and bound in Great Britain by
Anchor Brendon Ltd, Tiptree, Essex

For Pamela

Acknowledgements

I have a personal debt of gratitude to so many people who have helped in writing this account. First to the veterans, the men who served in the Special Forces. It was not possible to include all their stories in the account, but there are so many who shared their experiences with me.

To the citizens of Maaloy and Vaagso in Norway who contributed so much to my research, welcomed me into their homes and for all their kindness and hospitality, my heartfelt thanks. Dr Otto Pedersen, an old friend, helped to arrange my visit to Vaagso and Maaloy.

The Reverend Joe Nichols, friend and mentor, kindly allowed me to use material from the late Colonel Newman's journal, which is in his safe keeping.

I began this book while on the staff of The Royal Military Academy Sandhurst, and completed it in my new employment in industry. Colleagues and friends, both in the War Studies Department at Sandhurst and in my present company have been on hand with help and advice. I am particularly indebted to John Hunt, Librarian, and his staff at Sandhurst for searching out the books and documents.

Century Hutchinson have been patient and forbearing whilst I coped with the transition into industry. My thanks to James Cochrane for his inspiration and support and to Paul Sidey whose immaculate editing has improved the original manuscript beyond measure.

Three ladies coped with the transcription of tapes, interviews, correspondence and manuscript: Dorothy Fox, Liz Cain and Anne Johnson all did a magnificent job.

Last and by no means least, thanks to my wife Pamela and my family who have shown patience and sympathy and given their full encouragement, especially during the hard times.

Contents

Part Four Mountbatten's Tenure

Part Five St Nazaire

'THE SAUCIEST RAID SINCE DRAKE'

List of Illustrations

The Prime Minister, in characteristic pose with the Tommy Gun, a weapon favoured by the early formations of his 'Private Armies'. (Imperial War Museum)

Dunford Slater and some of his officers pose with their Naval colleagues for the War Correspondent. (Imperial War Museum)

In August 1941, the Commandos exercised before the King at Scapa Flow. (Imperial War Museum)

King George VI is greeted by Admiral of the Fleet, Sir Roger Keyes. (Imperial War Museum)

The early version of the Higgins boat. (Imperial War Museum)

Commandos, having landed from their assault craft, are mustered in an orderly fashion and await fresh instructions. (Imperial War Museum)

Casualty evacuation was no easy thing at Sör Vaagso especially when German snipers controlled the high ground. (Imperial War Museum)

Before the Commandos withdrew from Sör Vaagso, everything of value was put to the torch. (Imperial War Museum)

Lt General Sir Alan Brooke was appointed Commander in Chief of the Home Forces after the evacuation of the BEF from Dunkirk. (Imperial War Museum)

Major Frost and his paratroopers prepare to board their Whitley Bombers for the highly successful Bruneval Raid. (Imperial War Museum)

The second raid on the Lofotens ended with the complete destruction of the local industry at Stamsund. (Imperial War Museum)

The Lancastria, pressed into service as a troop ship, was instrumental in the evacuation of the Independent Companies from Norway. (Imperial War Museum)

The landing at Spitzbergen was a gentle affair. (Imperial War Museum)

Lord Louis Mountbatten inspects members of 3 Commando. (Major Jack Churchill and Imperial War Museum)

Anthony Dean-Drummond. (Anthony Dean-Drummond)

Lieutenant Colonel Dunford Slater with members of his Commando on the voyage home. (Imperial War Museum)

Major Jack Churchill, claymore at the ready, leads his troops ashore during an exercise in Scotland, 1941. (Major Jack Churchill and Imperial War Museum)

Major Jack Churchill, second in command of the newly raised 5 Commando. (Major Jack Churchill)

Major Jack Churchill removes a shell fragment from the barrel of one of the captured 75mm guns on Maaloy. (Major Jack Churchill and Imperial War Museum)

List of Maps

Introduction

Any self-respecting army today will include special forces in its order of battle. Some are just for show. But in a turbulent and violent world, such élite units, besides being symbols of national pride, are required to demonstrate a prowess and military skill of a higher standard than more conventional battalions.

Some special forces, such as those of Israel and South Africa, are used, often in the full glare of international publicity, as the avenging arm of their nation's counter to insurgence, conducting penetration raids deep into enemy territory. Others are used in a more paramilitary function to counter the threat of terrorism from within the country. The success of the Special Air Service Regiment in its intervention during the Iranian Embassy siege in London readily comes to mind. Airport alerts, real and practice, against a terrorist threat continue to demonstrate the very special skills needed to respond to extreme situations.

Special forces also figure prominently in the order of battle for the more orthodox war. Much attention has focused in recent years on the Soviet Union's *Spetsnatz*. In the event of a European war, their function is the assassination of senior officers, the elimination of headquarters and communication centres, and the general disruption and destruction of installations deep behind the lines.

Member states of the North Atlantic Alliance have their own special forces deployed into the order of battle.

Outside Europe, special forces have figured prominently in the Lebanon and the Gulf War between Iraq and Iran. Sometimes special forces fail, as did Delta Force in its abortive rescue attempt of Americans held hostage by Iran.

The Falklands War was dominated by special forces. When the Argentinians invaded in March 1982, their forces were spearheaded by the *Buzo Tactico*, a unit styled on the SAS, and their élite naval infantry, modelled on the Royal Marine Commandos.

Their opponents were a tiny, company-sized garrison of Royal Marines, who although heavily outnumbered and armed only with small arms and light mortars, downed two helicopters, knocked out an armoured personnel carrier, and even crippled a frigate before they were ordered to surrender.

The Argentinians have never revealed their own casualties from that particular action.

In the return match (the campaign to liberate the Falklands), it was the SAS and SBS who helped pave the way to success. Their role varied from deep penetration patrols engaged in intelligence gathering, to a cold-blooded attack on the airfield at Pebble Island, and the capture of the garrison on South Georgia without a shot being fired.

In subsequent operations, battalions of the Parachute Regiment and Royal Marine Commandos showed what can be achieved by élite formations which outmarched and outfought a numerically far superior enemy possessed of all the advantages.

Many nations in the Western and free worlds send their best to be trained by Britain's best, and the vast majority of the special forces units are based on the British models.

To trace the origin of these formations we need to look back to the early months of the Second World War. Then it was the Prime Minister, Winston Churchill, who goaded his military chiefs into accepting the need for a special force to counter the German threat. The field army had suffered its worst defeat since the American War of Independence, and was in no position to defend the homeland, let alone carry the fight to the enemy. Neither was the Prime Minister too abashed to demand that his reluctant generals emulate the German success in storm troopers, parachutists and Blitzkrieg.

Churchill's Private Armies examines the events of these years from the first, tentative steps in the raising of independent companies to wage guerrilla warfare in Norway, to the spring of 1942 and the brilliantly audacious commando raid on St Nazaire.

These were the formative years of the special forces. It was not a very auspicious beginning.

Churchill's Private Armies is not a regimental history, neither is it a campaign history. The book examines the reasons why special forces were created, and why indeed there was so much opposition to their continued existence. In this first volume we look to the European theatre of operations and measure the performance of the special forces in battle, and the ways in which volunteers were chosen.

Times change, but even in those early days the leaders dedicated to the concept of special forces were able to identify the vital qualities for their soldiers.

Lieutenant Colonel Charles Newman kept a journal for much of the war, and when it came to choosing those men who were to form his 2 Commando listed his requirements; Newman believed that he was creating a special service, not just one of many branches in a service. There was room only for the best and the keenest of men. In his eyes it was a privilege and an honour to be allowed to serve in a commando:

All ranks must be alert and individualistic: able to think quickly and act quickly for themselves;

Officers and men would be closer than in the normal unit, and each officer must have the complete understanding and confidence of his men;

Such a condition of mutual respect and friendship was present in every section and every troop. The Commando was a large and happy family;

It was the natural desire to be always extremely fit and able to overcome obstacles that the enemy would not expect one to, to get there before the enemy would ever expect you;

Covering 7 miles in the hour and 10 miles in two hours and fit to fight at the end of it;

Marches of 30 miles and feet good at the end of it;

Hills covered at march and run speed in full fighting order;

Going straight across country, taking all obstacles in one's stride;

Rivers, marshes, shrubs, fences, anything;

At all times, however tired, just doing a bit more and still keeping the brain alert and spirits up, were among the many ideals.

To live rough: hard living wherever one found oneself;

Living off the land;

Every man able to forage for and cook his own meal;

To understand a map like the back of your hand and to memorize any route to be covered by night or by day;

To be able to move swiftly across country by night;

To have night sense and night confidence;

To be able to deal with one's own wounded without medical aid;

To be able to signal: every man must be an expert signaller in Morse, Semaphore and WT;

To be able to climb any cliff or mountainside either with or without ropes;

To be able to swim in uniform and battle order;

To handle any small boat and be trained in seamanship;

To be able to live on board a man-of-war;

To be conversant with nautical terms;

Have rudimentary navigation and feel that the sea is the natural home of the commando from which all offensive action must start.

To be highly expert in all forms of fieldcraft;

Woodcraft, scouting, camouflaging, stalking;

Animal sense and animal movements;

To be trained in taking in and storing all one sees and making a good report later.

To appreciate every situation in a military sense before committing oneself;

To be able to drive any vehicle, train, cycle or animal;

To be able to cross at speed any normal barbed wire defences;

To be highly expert in street fighting by day and by night;

To be able to overcome any obstacle, walls, houses, move over roof tops;

To be highly trained in all forms of unarmed combat;

To be quick in dealing with any form of unexpected situations;

To be proficient with all types of arms both ours and those used by the enemy;

To be able to fire artillery;

To be expert in sabotage and handling high explosives; all ranks must be highly trained in demolitions;

To be good shots;

And above all to be proud of No. 2 Commando, its badge and what it stands for.

Such was the ideal underlying all ensuing commando training.

In the war years the special forces fought an entrenched and conservative-minded military bureaucracy who opposed their creation, resented their existence, challenged their need and obstructed their deployment whenever the opportunities presented. The private armies were hastily disbanded once their immediate need had been fulfilled.

They were misused and abused through sustained conflict where their zeal and quality compensated for firepower but produced heavy casualties.

I am talking about the Second World War, although these comments could equally refer to the Falklands.

Even today there are those schools of thought, within and without the military, who question the need and the role of some of the special force units. Throughout their history special forces have always enjoyed privileged access to status and resources. This has caused inter-organizational tensions and produced a kind of military class war where resentments run high. It was rampant in the early war years and today, in a time of economic entrenchment, it is once again prevalent.

Eric Morris
Winchester May 1986

PART ONE

EARLY DAYS

CHAPTER ONE

Something Special

The War Office telegram ordered Captain J. M. T. F. Churchill, First Battalion The Manchester Regiment, to report for special duty to Quebec Barracks, Bordon in Hampshire.

Bordon has a long and venerable military lineage. The Romans had a fort there since it was on the road from Colchester to Silchester. In later years the army had become associated with the area because its heather, gorse and woods of silver birch were quite unsuited to farming. In Victorian times the War Office purchased land from the Commissioner of Her Majesty's Woods, Forests and Lands on which to build a new and permanent barrack complex. Quebec Barracks was completed in time to house the first troops to return from the Boer War. The Canadians used the camp during the Great War and thereafter the Royal Engineers arrived to learn to drive trains. A branch line connected Bordon with a neighbouring camp at Longmoor and thence to Southern Railway's station at Liss.

A reluctant and half-hearted Imperial General Staff, at the instigation and subsequent hounding of Winston Churchill at the Admiralty, had taken the decision to raise a battalion of ski troops. A signal had been dispatched throughout the army, at home and abroad, calling for volunteers from men who could ski. Churchill had answered that call.

He found Quebec Barracks without difficulty. The original South African vintage huts had been demolished in 1937 and were now replaced by an imposing brick-built barracks. Churchill was impressed, but not half so much as he was with the sign outside

3

the main gates. This read 'Fifth Battalion The Scots Guards'. Neither the original signal, nor the telegram had said anything about joining the Guards!

There were scores of officers milling about outside the Orderly Room all wrapped up for warmth in greatcoats, sheepskins and astrakhans. Churchill looked about him, every cap badge in the British and Indian army seemed to be represented, and all worn by officers. Then it dawned on Churchill, the army was about to form a battalion of ski troops entirely composed of officers!

The Second World War spawned some very odd formations, and none was more bizarre, as we shall see, than the Fifth Battalion The Scots Guards. Though the War Office fought its own campaign to retain control of the military establishment, it allowed restless and amateur spirits to find free rein for both their energies and their aspirations in the plethora of special forces that emerged in the early part of the war. This was particularly the case in the early years, that time of the 'Strategic Defensive', when the Axis swept all before them and the military hierarchy in Whitehall were stumped for an answer. In the subsequent years, when the initiative rested securely on the Allied shoulders, no new special formations were created, and none survived the immediate peace.

If the British record of special forces is a strange affair, the Germans in contrast present a completely different picture. By the time that Hitler came upon the scene, the small, thoroughly professional army had already reached its conclusions on the value of such formations. Restricted in size and armaments by Versailles, surrounded by powerful and unfriendly neighbours, the Germans since the early Twenties had shown a healthy interest in guerrilla war. Their officer corps had studied T. E. Lawrence's campaign and their verdict was that an elusive band of saboteurs, highly trained, motivated and disciplined could cause mayhem behind the lines of a conventionally armed enemy. Such bands, operating free from the encumbrances of bases and supply lines, and without the support of heavy weapons, could through their own mobility and ingenuity cause considerable confusion and damage.

The Germans, in line with Blitzkrieg, applied the doctrine of total war to guerrilla warfare, a concept which ultimately received the support of the Fuhrer.

The study was taken further under an officer called von Hippel, who had himself won considerable distinction as an elusive foe of the British in German East Africa. Von Hippel proposed the infiltration of élite formations into enemy territory in advance of war; ready to seize vital points and targets as soon as hostilities began.

The intention was to create a 'Corps of Raiders'. Élite formations of young men possessed of specialist knowledge were to be recruited from those who had foreign language skills gained from working abroad. Independently minded young men, who had left the depressions of the Weimar Republic to seek their fortune in Latin America or Africa and now attracted home by the appeal of National Socialism and the call of the Fatherland, were an obvious choice. Trained to carry out operations for which conventional units were unsuited, these formations were not to be wasted in ordinary battle.

The first such formation, raised under the cover of No. 1 Construction Company and including Sudeten Germans, and Volksdeutsche from Eastern Europe amongst its numbers, was ready for war in the early summer of 1939. The unit came under the control of the Abwehr, Germany's counter-intelligence and intelligence department, but this did not mean that they were spies.

The construction company helped open the door to Blitzkrieg in Poland. The industrial complexes of western Poland presented a rich prize for Hitler if they could be captured largely intact. The Poles were equally appreciative of their value, and since they were mostly concentrated in a salient, were determined to destroy such resources if they could not be defended. The special forces were infiltrated into the area from a base in Breslau in the last days of August, and come the first of September emerged to contest the factories from the Poles. They were eminently successful. The construction company handed over largely intact a number of invaluable industrial concerns to the advancing Wehrmacht and thence slipped quietly back into Germany.

The Germans made no special or public recognition of their contribution. Poland had been a proving ground, the real test would come should there be battles in the west. The Abwehr had no intention of broadcasting the success of such an élite special formation to the British and French.

In October 1939 a second company was raised from recruits drawn from Palestinian, Baltic and Romanian Germans. The two companies were amalgamated and given 'regimental status' as Bau-Lehr Battalion zbV Nr 800. Their depot was in Brandenburg-Havel.

The men called themselves the 'Brandenburgers'.

The German army had always prided itself on the toughness of its training. For conventional formations the programme was a physically hard, often brutal regime which produced a superbly prepared soldier. For specialist formations such as the Brandenburgers, having completed the basic training common to all, they went on to even harder and more exacting tests. Indeed their training course reads like a testament to such contemporary units as the Special Air Service.

Trained to attack by land, sea or air, parachute training was also undertaken as a matter of course, when in Britain it had not even reached the stage of a War Office minute. Boatsmanship on assault craft, skiing and language initiative tests were taught whilst British soldiers learned to parade in columns of four. The Brandenburger learned fieldcraft, camouflage and survival techniques which would allow him to operate, alone if necessary, behind the lines, while the British expeditionary force watched the French frontier and waited for the enemy to strike first.

The Brandenburgers, as befitted their role, became expert marksmen, learned all the skills of silent killing and unarmed combat, and the techniques of making explosive devices from the most innocent of ingredients. Besides an all-round capability, each man learned one skill to a specialist level. The result was that by the time that Churchill reported to Britain's special forces, the Brandenburgers were just about reaching the peak of fighting efficiency and physical fitness in readiness for the forthcoming offensives.

In the light of history, it must be seen as a blessing in disguise that the only British special force – The Fifth Battalion The Scots Guards – was never called upon to fight. This is not because of any lack of resolve or fighting spirit, though, like so much of the army in those early days, they were poorly equipped and woefully undertrained for what was to prove to be in any case the wrong war. There were enough officers in the Fifth Battalion to service the needs of every junior command appointment in an infantry division. The wisdom of concentrating so many leaders, and potentially great leaders in a single formation, and thence to hurl it into battle defies description.

Hindsight is an exact science, but considerations such as these must have been understood at the time. So why was this battalion formed?

In the winter of 1939/40 while Lord Gort's expeditionary force marked time in the trenches of the 'phoney war', Allied strategists, fearing deadlock on the Western Front, looked as they had before to Europe's flanks. In the Great War Churchill's enthusiasm had taken the Allies south to the Dardanelles and to disaster. In 1940 Churchill directed the Cabinet's attention northwards.

The Allies were interested in Scandinavia for two reasons. The first was Germany's dependence on iron ore from Sweden's mines, concentrated in the Gulf of Bothnia at the very head of the Baltic.[1] In the summer months the ore was shipped by sea direct to Germany. In four of the winter months the Gulf and much of the Baltic was frozen and so the ore was moved overland by rail to Narvik; situated at the head of a fjord on the west coast of Norway, it was ice-free all the year round. Steamers sailed south through the Leads, that strip of territorial water formed between the mainland and island necklace, thence via the Skagerrak to German home waters. In wartime, and with Norway neutral, such traffic was immune to hostile interdiction.

The Norwegians could not help but be aware of their own predicament, a neutral sandwiched between belligerent great powers. They were nevertheless determined to protect their interests and their territorial integrity from whatever threat. The Germans were anxious to protect their lines of communication through to the Swedish ore. The British were equally determined to close down the German supply line; with or without Norwegian co-operation. In the face of Norwegian defiance, it would at least mean blockading and mining Norwegian waters. If necessary, Winston Churchill was prepared to advocate occupying Narvik, and hang international laws, conventions, and the sovereign integrity of neutrals.

The second reason for Allied interests in the northern flank was Finland, and this soon subsumed the first. Stalin had signed the treaty with Hitler, but by all accounts put little faith in its durability and was anxious to safeguard Leningrad and his Baltic flank against any possible attack from his temporary colleague. In the interests of 'forward defence', Moscow leaned on the Baltic States and thereby assumed strategic control over Latvia, Lithuania and Estonia. Stalin had demands to make on the Finns too but these prickly neighbours he approached with a little more care. The Russians invited the Finns to cede territory in exchange for territory. On a 'knock-for-knock' basis the Finns would have had the better of the deal in square mileage and while the terms enhanced Soviet security, Finnish defence would not have been compromised. National sentiment and ancient animosities made the Finns inflexible and the Russians lost patience. The Soviet Union threatened, cajoled and thence, on 30 November 1939, just 48 hours after cancelling their non-aggression pact, they invaded Finland.

To the utter astonishment of the watching Europeans the advance of the Red Army stalled at the Finnish defences. In the west, still bitter at Moscow's treaty with Germany and the cynical partition of Poland, sympathy lay not unnaturally with the Finns, now firmly cast in the role of victim to aggression. The rout of the Russians

7

was greeted with great enthusiasm, and public sentiment prompted Britain and France to contemplate sending 'volunteers' in an expeditionary force to this new theatre of war. Not only could Finland be helped, but an Allied presence in Scandinavia could stop the German iron ore supplies at source, and threaten Germany's sensitive Baltic flanks.

War correspondents, that new breed of newspaperman, flocked to the 'Winter War', after all, the Western Front had become tedious beyond measure. The newspapers carried graphic details of Russia's ill-prepared troops and photographs showed Red soldiers frozen to death in the snowy wastes.[2] The Allied governments thus needed little prompting to appreciate that their 'volunteers' must be skilled in winter warfare. This was no problem to the French who had in their regiments of Chasseurs Alpins excellent ski troops. The British army contained plenty of men who skied, but in those days skiing was the sport of the rich or the privileged, and those were officers.

Instead of taking a trained battalion, and teaching the soldiers to ski, which probably would have been the best course of action, the War Office in its wisdom decided to create a fighting battalion of experienced skiers. This scratch force was arbitrarily given the title 'The Fifth Battalion Scots Guards'.

In January 1940 the word was spread abroad, via that indomitable channel of communication, Part One Orders and men with skiing experience were asked to volunteer. Such an instruction however came as no great surprise to the army in either France or at home, security had been lax, and a ski battalion had been the subject of conversation in most officers' messes since well before Christmas.

Jack Churchill had answered the call. A Sandhurst graduate and pre-war regular officer, he had resigned his commission while still a subaltern, after ten years' service. Regimental duty in a succession of peacetime garrisons, where promotion was slow, proved tedious and stifling. Churchill spent an adventurous few years as a civilian especially after his small gratuity had been exhausted. He was a film extra and an Olympic archer; he played the bagpipes in Italian cafés and nightclubs as part of a novelty act; and he ended up as bodyguard and general factotum to a Siamese playboy in Paris. Churchill was a conformist, but also an eccentric. In the aftermath of the Munich Crisis with war looming, Churchill was recalled to the Colours and joined the Manchesters as second in command of a company. He crossed to France with the battalion taking with him his three 'toys of war', bagpipes, crossbow and sword – the latter being a very large claymore. After the first heady couple of weeks, soldiering on the Western Front in the Phoney War must have been deadly dull and for someone like Churchill, suffocatingly so.

Churchill's thirst for individual expression had already landed him in trouble. His battledress blouse sported French army buttons. He had done a deal with a French officer, for he rather admired their large silver buttons, and so he gave his brass regimental buttons in exchange. Such behaviour was frowned upon by the senior officers in the battalion, and Churchill found it hard to abide by their patterns of regimental behaviour. He had the additional burden of having to take orders from those officers, who in pre-war days were junior to him in the battalion. But he did not remove his buttons.

Churchill volunteered for special forces to escape the formalism and inaction of conventional soldiering. His was a common enough motive which was to inspire thousands of others to similar actions in the early years of the war, both at home and abroad. Neither was his departure from the battalion opposed, and this too became a common enough feature as special forces attracted so many kindred spirits and misfits of the regimental family.

---

[1] German dependence can be seen from peacetime figures which showed that in 1938/1939 German industry consumed 15,000,000 tons of iron ore. Of this, 11,000,000 came from Sweden, and 4,500,000 through Narvik in the four winter months.

[2] Winston Churchill in particular was especially scathing in his comment on the Russian War Machine. Hitler too probably held similar views since his invasion of Russia some two years later was influenced by the poor Soviet military performance in the Winter War.

CHAPTER TWO

The Fifth Battalion The Scots Guards

In anticipation of events, Churchill cancelled Christmas in England and instead decided to brush up on his skiing. The place to go was Montpellier and thence to the French Alps.

Churchill travelled first to Paris. He took the precaution of booking a seat on the night train, before treating himself to dinner in one of his old and favourite haunts. Despite the uniform, the restaurateur recognized him instantly; his Siamese patron had been a frequent and extravagant visitor. Churchill dined well, extremely well.

There were not many minutes to spare as Churchill scrambled aboard the night express at the Gare du St Nazaire. The doors slammed shut and then with great clamour and noise the train jerked into motion. Churchill, clutching his suitcase and a half-finished bottle of best claret, found a conductor who took him to his compartment, only to find it occupied. A major in the French army had already staked his claim. The conductor beat a hasty retreat.

'Pardon, Monsieur Major, this is my seat,' said Churchill in his schoolboy French, and he showed him his ticket.

'You were not here,' said the French officer, peering over the top of his evening paper.

'I don't have to be here,' responded Churchill. 'That's why I booked the seat so I don't have to be here. If you come early, anyone can get a seat, but if you book a seat – '

'No, I shall not move,' said the Frenchman dismissively.

'But you've got to move, it's my bloody compartment,' said

Churchill, his anger rising. He stomped off to find the conductor but the latter was not about to intervene on the side of an Englishman, and only a captain, against a French major. The conductor advised Churchill to find a seat towards the rear of the train, all the sleeping compartments having been taken and offered a receipt which would allow the young officer to obtain a refund on his ticket. Churchill was too angry to comply and instead sat on his baggage in the corridor outside his compartment.

His feeling of injustice burned deep. Regimental honour, national pride and an excellent claret cried out for revenge against such a Gallic outrage. With a bit of luck 'the bugger' would scramble into the bunk and go to sleep. Sure enough, the French officer who had presumably eaten a good dinner was soon abed. Churchill stepped into the compartment, reached up to the rack and quietly removed the major's bag. He shut the door, opened the corridor window and hurled the bag into the night. Churchill gathered up his own baggage and then moved as rapidly as he could to the furthest end of the train, where clambering over recumbent passengers, he eventually found an empty seat in a third-class compartment. At first, Churchill was afraid to sleep, lest the major woke up and put two and two together. But everybody else slept, and there was no sign of any irate, rampaging major, so Churchill fell into a deep sleep.

He was dead to the world through Montpellier and half a dozen other stations until the train came to a final shuddering stop across the Italian frontier. A border guard shook him awake.

'Christ Almighty!' exclaimed Churchill; 'I'm in Italy.'

He was immediately aware of his predicament. Italy was neutral, and he was in the uniform of a nation at war. He had neither permits nor documents which would allow travel in a neutral state. Instead of adventure and battle, internment and an inglorious future beckoned.

There was another cause for concern, for once the authorities saw his ID card and read the name, there was bound to be trouble. Churchill was not related to his famous namesake, but who would believe that?[1]

'I was very sleepy. I went to sleep. I meant to get off at Montpellier,' said Churchill with quiet, but resigned dignity.

The Italians couldn't have been kinder or more concerned. An officer appeared who not only spoke excellent English, but also could see the humour in the young officer's predicament.

'You wait here,' the Italian instructed. 'In a little while the train will be returning and you'll be okay.'

Churchill mumbled his thanks.

'Now,' continued the Italian. 'You mustn't say anything. We will arrange everything with the French border guards. After all,' he concluded, 'they should have found you in the first place!'

The plan worked a treat. Within a few hours, Churchill was at Montpellier where he changed trains and headed straight for Chamonix and the ski slopes. Christmas or not, he needed to put in much practice to qualify for the rumoured ski battalion.

The Fifth Battalion Scots Guards was the step-child of the House-hold Brigade; and it was treated as such. Lieutenant Colonel J. S. Coats MC, a distinguished skier and a well-known figure at the fashionable winter sports scene, was loaned by the Coldstream Guards to command the new battalion. Another well-known skier, Captain W. D. M. Raeburn, who was serving in Egypt with the Second Battalion Scots Guards, was flown home to be adjutant. Colonel Coats was lent a small skeleton administrative staff from the Guards' Depot at Pirbright and between them they had to process over a thousand volunteers. Most were able to report on 6 February but many many more drifted into Bordon throughout the rest of the month and this caused even greater confusions and strains. Coats was under pressure from the War Office. His orders were to have the battalion ready, equipped and in all senses prepared for war service overseas by 1 March. The orders were as preposterous as the battalion.

Amongst the volunteers were over 700 officers, many being senior captains or majors, with service and seniority who joined from commanding companies and squadrons in France and elsewhere. Coats needed 19 officers, namely four company commanders, an assistant adjutant, and 14 subalterns. Once the 'officer' selections had been made, the remaining officers were asked to assemble in the canteen (the Officers' Mess was far too small) where they were addressed by Coats. The colonel simply explained that since he could not accept them all as officers, he asked if they would care to resign their commissions and serve in the ranks in the battalion.

'Christ,' thought Churchill, 'Now that's a novel idea.'

King's Regulations, that august bible of military service and folk-lore does recognize such a process. It is called 'degazetting'. Under this rather tortuous bureaucratic process, the 'new rankers' were to be paid as officers, in their old ranks. They would retain their seniority and return to full commissioned service at the end of their tour of duty.

Coats and his adjutant explained the process patiently and succinctly, but there was uproar and pandemonium. The vast majority of the assembled officers clearly thought the suggestion to be an outrage and an insult. They demanded to be returned to their regiments without delay, and in this Coats and his staff acquiesced, albeit reluctantly. Nevertheless, 173 officers accepted the offer, some consumed by curiosity, some undoubtedly with good reasons for not wanting to rejoin their old units, the majority stirred by the prospect of early action. Churchill stayed, so did David Stirling, a subaltern in the Scots Guards, who was later to create The Special Air Service Regiment.

It was from this select band that Coats now chose the non-commissioned officers for the battalion, and some of the officers did make excellent platoon sergeants and corporals. Spencer Chapman became an NCO; he was already an accomplished and popularly acclaimed mountaineering figure and had been on a number of famous expeditions.[2] Where the system did fail, and by all accounts fail miserably, was in the selection of the warrant officers and the quartermaster sergeants. To find one's way around a company or battalion store took years of apprenticeship and experience, and in pre-war army establishments this was not officer territory. The administrative knowledge required by the new company sergeant majors and their staff was not going to be created overnight. Theirs was a unique skill acknowledged as such by that well known 'officer expression' that was an instruction, a dismissal, and an article of faith – 'Carry on Sarn't Major'.

Coats was now short of soldiers and the month was slipping by with little having been achieved. One hundred and eighty men came straight from civilian life; all had at least some experience of skiing or mountaineering, but they didn't have the faintest idea of soldiering. Seventy-two officer cadets were transferred from training units and selection boards.

So this strange assortment of 'gentlemen volunteers', which included seasoned expedition men, mountaineers and those who tracked the Himalayas and high peaks of the Empire, soldiers of fortune, and professional soldiers, stockbrokers and university undergraduates were settled into their new existence. Majors who had never been privates were under the instruction of captains who had never been corporals. Veterans of a dozen bush fire wars lived cheek by jowl with youngsters who found the army boot and laces a source of mystery.

Not every tradition and standard went by the board in this strange battalion. Coats, and indeed the War Office, had given an undertaking that status and privilege of the previous rank would be maintained at all times. Within a week of the battalion being formed, a company from the First Battalion Scots Guards reported to Quebec Barracks. They were to undertake the fatigues and menial duties around the camp so that Coats and his battalion could concentrate on their training 'undistracted by the cares of housekeeping'.[3]

Preparations and training for winter warfare largely took the form of lectures on arctic survival, avoiding frostbite, etc. There could be little practical training since Bordon was snow-free and in any case the battalion had neither skis nor weapons at this stage.[4]

Colonel Coats was still short of men, 429 other ranks does not make a battalion on war establishment. The Brigade of Guards again looked favourably upon their step-child. A company of recently trained Scots Guardsmen were despatched to Bordon from the Guards' Depot at Pirbright. None had ever seen a ski before, and of the remainder in the battalion, none of the civilians and only a few of the officer cadets had ever seen a rifle.

The new contingent from Pirbright were not officers, and most had no such aspirations so their arrival could have caused some difficulties amongst the 'gentlemen volunteers'.

Colonel Coats decided they should remain as a separate entity and so become Y Company with their own officers who had brought them from Pirbright. This was a sensible and pragmatic move but there is no evidence to suggest there was even the slightest friction amongst the assorted backgrounds and pedigrees of the battalion's rank and file. Neither do the records reveal the nature of the relationship between the Scots Guards of Y Company and those earlier arrivals on permanent fatigue, but then that is not difficult to imagine either.

On 2 March 1940, the Fifth Battalion Scots Guards held its final parade and passing out inspection. The salute was taken by Lieutenant General Sir Bertram Ferguson-Brooke, the major general commanding the Brigade of Guards. The battalion was pronounced ready for active service. All leave was immediately cancelled and a couple of days later, in the greatest secrecy, the battalion left Bordon for service overseas. They embarked on a troopship and headed out into the English Channel. Rumours were rife as to their destination. 'Guardsman' Churchill was convinced they were intended for the Caucasus, others favoured Scandinavia and some put their money on the North Pole.

The ship docked at Cherbourg, and the following day all was revealed when after a non-stop train journey across France, they saw the unmistakable and majestic peak of Mont Blanc, and the train finally pulled into the station at Chamonix. Although the guardsmen were forbidden to write home and tell their families where they were, their arrival in Chamonix was fully reported in the French Press, commented upon by Lord Haw-Haw on Berlin

Radio, and a paragraph in the *Daily Telegraph* escaped the censor's pen. The farce that was attached to such official secrecy was too much for one young ex-undergraduate guardsman. Churchill remembers the youngster being severely reprimanded when he wrote to his girlfriend from Chamonix, 'I must not tell you where we are for fear of endangering the fleet.'

Initially, it had been decided that the battalion would stay in the local hotels but should be responsible for its own catering. The hoteliers were delighted with this arrangement since the ski season was all but over and they had plenty of spare beds; however, their joy knew no bounds when within a very few days the men were using the restaurants too. For the battalion it was Hobson's Choice. Officers make very poor quartermaster sergeants, they make even worse cooks.

On the second day, training began in earnest. The battalion enlisted the help of the 199th Battalion of Chasseurs Alpins, the local and rather comfortable reserve unit. The French soldiers, who Churchill found were for some obscure reason called the 'Blue Devils', were ski instructors and mountain guides. Under the watchful eye of their instructors, the battalion's skills improved considerably. By common consent the French thought that Y Company, those soldiers who had never skied before, were among the best.

Such a pleasant sojourn could not last for ever, but most at least expected more than a week in which to savour the pleasures that Chamonix had to offer. It was not to be. On 9 March, Major Parvis, who acted as the battalion liaison officer, was called to the telephone at his hotel.

It was the War Office in London.

Parvis was ordered to have an officer standing by who could speak Hindustani, and London would telephone again with orders. There was no military telephone network, and this ruse was the best that the War Office could devise to counter German intelligence who doubtless listened in to all the conversations.

On the following day, Berlin Radio broadcast the news that 'The Fifth Battalion The Scots Guards would leave Chamonix by train at 7 o'clock on the morning of Monday 11 March.'

The Germans were wrong, but only by about ten minutes, and that was because the French train was late in arriving at Chamonix.

There was no disguising the fact. Guardsman Churchill and the others knew that the battalion was off to war. The Russians had indeed launched a new and massive offensive, and the Finns were hard pressed. The newspapers and radio were full of the news from the Northern Front. The Allies conferred and agreed that immediate action would have to be taken if the Finns were not to succumb to the Soviet onslaught.

France proposed an expeditionary force of 50,000 men and Britain planned to send a division.

The Fifth Battalion Scots Guards, as the army's specialists in winter warfare, were to spearhead the British contingent.

Their journey to war was one of the most boring and tedious that Churchill was to make in the whole of his wartime service. They travelled for four days without a break, across France and then over the Channel to Southampton where another troop train took them north to Scotland and the Clyde. At Gourrock Docks, the battalion boarded a Polish liner and waited for other contingents to join.

There the whole affair came to an abrupt halt. On 15 March, they were told that the Russian offensive had proved too much for the Finns, and their Prime Minister had flown to Moscow and accepted Stalin's terms.

It was all an anticlimax. The British expeditionary force to Finland was surplus to requirement, and the army did not need the services of an élite ski battalion, especially in springtime.

Within the week, the battalion had returned to Bordon, handed over stores and equipment, and been disbanded. Guardsmen became officers again and the military establishment breathed a sigh of relief that such nonsense was over. And to be fair, the 'guardsmen' themselves were for the most part only too anxious to return to their parent units. The prevailing view throughout the army was that there was some real soldiering to be done, but only by disciplined battalions ready to man the defences on the decisive Western Front.

But this episode was the first in what eventually would emerge as an oft-repeated pattern in the war. A special force would be created, usually to fill a gap in military capabilities. By the time such a force had acquired the necessary expertise the need had gone, overtaken by events.

Some forces clung to existence whilst their enthusiasts searched a new role to suit their talents, others mobilized the voices of the influential to argue their case, some disappeared from the scene.

There was no one to argue the case that the British army needed a battalion of ski specialists, not when the demand for young officers was so obvious and overwhelming. A fatigue party from Pirbright returned to Bordon to clean up after the Fifth Battalion Scots Guards, and to prepare Quebec Barracks for the new incumbents. The Guards Brigade coolly and clinically effected the demise of its own step-child.

Jack Churchill returned to France and the First Battalion The Manchester Regiment. Once again restored to the rank of captain, but with the French silver buttons still adorning the blouse of his battledress, he rejoined his old company. He had mixed feelings about the ski battalion, it had been too amateur by half and had it been tested in war, then its logistics and supply would have failed the fighting platoons.

Yet Churchill was the first to admit there was a free and easy relationship, an élitist air about the battalion that was particularly appealing. It had numbered men of the highest quality among its ranks, many destined to make their mark on the war, and only a few to survive. Perhaps in part, it was that the Fifth Battalion Scots Guards held out the prospect of early action, and this attracted men who preferred that to what conventional soldiering had to offer at the time.

What is not in doubt is that for men such as Churchill, and a host of others, the Fifth Battalion had given them a taste of a new kind of military existence.

---

[1] The Germans certainly didn't when, much later in the war, Churchill, by then a brigadier, became their prisoner.

[2] After the war Spencer Chapman wrote that most excellent book *The Jungle is Neutral*, an account of his experiences behind the Japanese lines in Burma.

[3] Regimental History, Scots Guards.

[4] The battalion was issued with rifles at the end of February. There were no other weapons.

CHAPTER THREE

Independent Companies: The First Guerrillas

'If guerrilla warfare is co-ordinated with the main operations it should, in favourable circumstances, present decisive opportunities to the main forces.'

On 7 April 1940, Germany invaded Denmark and Norway without warning.

Danish-speaking members of the Brandenburgers, disguised as Danish soldiers, seized the bridge across the Grosse Belt over which the invading Wehrmacht had to advance to reach the northern parts of the kingdom and secure the country with the minimum of resistance. Other tactical units from the Brandenburg battalion were used to spearhead operations in Norway. Troops disguised as Norwegian soldiers caused considerable confusion and panic.

After a couple of days the major ports and most of the southern part of Norway were secured by the Wehrmacht (Denmark succumbed without a struggle). However, the Norwegian armed forces and home defence units, seemed to be consolidating in the central regions of this large and extensive country, aided by a persistingly late winter and the primitive roads. Within these first days of the campaign, the War Office in London, moving with commendable speed, ordered that a special force of 3,000 volunteers were to be raised from the territorial army divisions then under training in England. The volunteers formed into ten independent companies for irregular warfare and were to be despatched to Norway.

Such a scheme might at first sight appear to have been a novel approach, but it had a solid precedent and most respectable pedigree. The Independent Companies was the first of several attempts made during the Second World War to revive the 'Light Infantry', a tradition which had first been established in the Peninsula War.

Perhaps the commandos and Wingate's Chindits were better-known examples, but they all trace their origin to Spain.

The 95th Rifles, later called the Rifle Brigade, were first formed in 1800 as an *experimental corps*. The soldiers were armed with a rifle, rather than the usual musket and taught a different form of tactics. Instead of standing and fighting in line or square, in a pitched battle, these green clad riflemen were taught to fight in open order, and encouraged to use the ground and available cover to their own advantage. Riflemen were allowed to judge a situation, to act independently and not simply to respond like automatons to a word of command. In their day such tactics were considered revolutionary in character, and since their operation required less formal discipline, there were those who opposed such developments.

The Rifle Brigade gained an enviable reputation in the Peninsula War where they were very successful; in no small part this was due to the firm base provided by the Line Infantry and the excellent quality of generalship and command right down to regimental level. The same cannot be said for Norway. It was the first clash of arms for the British army in the war and it fell to that campaign to reveal just how poorly prepared Britain was for war. Norway proved that no army can fight without air equality and shouldn't be deployed without guaranteed air superiority, no matter what their role.

Soldiers were sent to Norway who were barely trained in even the most rudimentary aspects of war. The campaign showed that the battlefield is merciless, it is no place for any man who has not been trained to take a pride in his stamina and endurance, and who can withstand mental and physical hardship.

Half-trained British soldiers came up against some of the best in the Wehrmacht – Alpine troops perfectly at home in those northern climes, where the ski and the snowshoe are essential. For the British expeditionary force in general and the independent companies in particular, the Norwegian campaign was a bloody shambles, outshone by our allies and outfought by the enemy.

Major Newman was in command of No. 3 Independent Company in Norway. He was a territorial army officer and had been for 16 years. He had spent the whole time in the Essex Regiment and he was a company commander at the outbreak of war, serving with the Third Battalion, which drew its recruits from Barking, East Ham and the outer suburbs of London's East End.

In February 1940, the battalion moved north with the 54th (East Anglian) Infantry Division to train in Northumberland. They were stationed at Wooler, a camp which had been expanded too rapidly to cope with wartime demands, and many of the soldiers were living under canvas. Conditions were bleak and primitive, and the training schemes little better.

It was in Berwick-on-Tweed that Newman had his first view of the First Battalion Scots Guards with whom he was to become so involved later. He had driven into the market town to see a farmer about buying some swill, a particular wool for soldiers' sweaters. The road was clogged with army convoys, as the First Guards Brigade drove north to a Scottish port. Newman guessed it had to be the overseas mission, rather than just another exercise, for all their vehicles were brand new and festooned with the full scale of equipment.

The Guards were off to Norway, to spearhead the British expeditionary force which together with French troops were to reinforce the Norwegian forces still fighting in the central part of their country.

Despite the spread and surprise of the German invasion, the Norwegian King Haakon had made good his escape from Oslo and raised the banner of resistance. The Allies responded because a Norwegian theatre of war had a very definite appeal. Besides the tangled issues of German iron ore and the use of Narvik, the country did seem to present an opportunity to outflank the enemy. Indeed for many years there had been 'informal conversations' between British and French military staffs on the advisability of occupying Norway should war occur with Germany. The French, with their memories of Verdun, had no desire to launch a frontal attack on the German Siegfried Line. Thus an outflanking movement through Norway, with the consequent occupation of the main sources of German ore supply, seemed far more likely to lead to a rapid and less costly decision.

The trouble was that the Germans had also learned from the Great War and were not about to let themselves be strangled into submission by another naval blockade.

The plain truth is that both sides planned to occupy Norway, and had convinced themselves that their reasons were sound enough to violate Norwegian neutrality. Both sides started to plan their operations at about the same time, though the Germans in the event were ready first. On 5 April 1940, the Allies gave the game away when Britain announced her intention to mine Norwegian territorial waters.

Hitler immediately issued the executive instruction for the invasion of Denmark and Norway to begin at 0515 hours on 9 April. German military preparations were accelerated – but in the greatest secrecy.

In London the decision was taken to postpone operations for three days – until 8 or 9 April, when the minelayers would commence operations, followed shortly by the deployment of an expeditionary force to protect the Norwegians from German anger!

The delay proved fatal to the prospects of success. It enabled the Germans to seize the initiative. Besides the main thrust into Oslo Fjord, in a series of brilliant coups the Germans captured and garrisoned the main west coast ports of Bergen, Trondheim and Narvik. The latter was 1,200 miles distant from German naval bases.

The sheer audacity of the German moves, and in particular the deployment of their fleet in defiance of the superiority of the Royal Navy stunned the British nation, its leader and people alike. Subsequent British counter-measures were slow, hesitant and bungled. They concentrated for the most part on the recapture of Trondheim and Narvik.

It was about a week after the Scots Guards had passed by, on a normal Saturday morning, that Major Newman received his call to arms. Colonel Gibson, the commanding officer, had been called away to division headquarters. The morning parade was over and the battalion had been dismissed, soldiers to their canteens and the officers to the Mess.

The colonel returned in time to join his officers for a drink. He singled out Newman and asked about his company, which he himself had commanded some years before.

Many of the soldiers had served under both men, and looked to their officers for guidance, not just in military, but in civilian life as well; but that is how it was in a territorial army battalion at the time. It was a family, whether in war or peace, cemented by regimental traditions and reinforced by the community beyond the Drill Hall.

It was just typical of 'Gibbo', Newman thought later. They had talked for quite a while, then the CO made his excuses and returned to battalion headquarters; within a very few minutes the duty runner appeared at the Officers' Mess. Major Newman was to report to the commanding officer immediately.

The colonel looked strangely stern as Newman marched in.

'Would you volunteer for a dangerous job?'

'Yes Sir.' Newman didn't know what he meant, but supposed that in war one did these things.

'You have been selected to command a composite volunteer force to be raised from the division to go to a place unknown, to carry out a job unknown, for an unknown length of time! Would you like to go?'

They discussed things for a little while and then Newman returned to the Mess. The other officers had gone into lunch so the anteroom was deserted as Newman pondered the future over a large pink gin. Odd snatches of conversation and the occasional laugh drifted through from the dining-room. Newman would have to say goodbye to his friends, some of many years' service. He looked around the anteroom. It might be temporary, but it was home. The photographs on the wall either side of the fireplace were a permanent reminder of summer training camps stretching back into pre-war days. Newman moved across to the table where all the magazines and newspapers were now restored to order after the lunchtime stampede, and idly leafed through the Regimental Journal.

The regiment and everything that it had meant to him over 16 years of part-time soldiering would be a thing of the past in this new appointment.

Newman shook such maudlin thoughts from his head. He had made the decision, although upon reflection he hadn't been given any choice. Newman knew that he was a good officer, but wasn't clear why he had been selected from the division.

Colonel Gibson hadn't been able to give him much of an idea of what it was all about. He had said that he thought the force might be used in mountainous country, which was some help. The newspapers were full of communiqués about Norway, so it wasn't too difficult to read between the lines and appreciate that the campaign was not going too well for the Allies.

Gibson had given him a free hand to choose one officer and 20 men from the battalion. Provided they volunteered, they could go with him as the battalion's contribution to the new force. Newman recognized this as a more than generous gesture on the part of his commanding officer. Other battalions asked to do the same, would doubtless *select* those to go, and the temptation to unload the poor and the weak, the misfit and the malcontent, could prove irresistible.

Together with attached personnel there were close on 1,000 men in that battalion. The word on Newman's mission was already out, and so the task of selecting 21 men from 1,000 was daunting. Newman's diary gives us an interesting insight into the criteria he

used to select men for a special operation. He chose Captain Tiny
Waterman as his other officer: Waterman played cricket for Essex,
was a good wing three-quarter at rugby, had a marvellous sense of
humour, and was strong. Sergeant Catly also appeared an obvious
choice. He had served with the regular battalion in India, had won
the North-West Frontier Medal and thus knew mountains. There
was a clutch of volunteers taken from the battalion's boxing team,
little Green the bantamweight ('tough as hell'), Stevens the middle-
weight ('strong as an ox'), and Brewster the light-heavy.

Private Finch from C Company with his reputation for being a
bit of a poacher, was a good man; his nocturnal pursuits showed
character.

Newman selected those with initiative, men of proven courage,
and at this stage in the war the measure was blood sports, but the
bottom line was a sure personal knowledge of the men. The
problem appeared to be to keep the numbers down to 20 men. The
Essex was a good battalion, yet it was stuck at home, under training,
conditioned by the tedious red tape of a slow moving bureaucracy.
Service life in England for the more energetically minded was not
just dull, it was stupendously dull, and here was a chance for action
under a good officer. Even at this stage in the war, to volunteer
and to select was a personal affair.

Later that afternoon, when the decisions had been taken and the
press of people clamouring for his attention had drifted away,
Newman sat alone in his office. There was a knock at his door, and
in answer to his call the regimental sergeant major, Newman's old
boxing trainer, and a personal friend, stood before him.

'Take me with you, sir?' he asked. Newman shook his head.
'Even as a private soldier?' pleaded the RSM.

'You're too old, RSM,' said Newman as gently as he could.
Ramrod stiff, the RSM came as close to pleading as the dignity of
his rank would allow, but Newman remained firm.

Finally there was 'his man' Shears. He had been Newman's
servant and confidential adviser for many years. It was Private
Shears who decided what his officer should wear, who always
somehow managed to make Newman's room, wherever they were
living, into an exact replica of his own at home, or as near as
possible. Family photographs on the bedside table, his shoes laid
out in order of seniority, Shears took great pride in the welfare and
appearance of his officer.

Shears had one particular advantage as Newman's batman. They
had the same waist measurement. Shears could fit Newman's
pouches and webbing belt with its holster, binocular case, etc., the
officers' 'Christmas tree' ready to wear with minimum fuss and

delay. This was a boon for any officer who, always pushed for time, left his personal administration to the last minute.

Bald as a coot, Shears was getting on in years, and Newman appreciated that his special force was best suited to the young. Newman wanted to take Shears; he was a judo black belt and handy to have around, but was he fit enough?

Newman resolved to at least ask him whether he wanted to come with him and forsake all the comforts and perks that went with the job of being an officer's batman in a battalion.

Shears was fussing about, when Newman returned to his room at the end of the day.

'Evening Sir,' said Shears. 'When do we go Sir?'

Well, that solved that problem, thought Newman.

After dinner, Colonel Gibson and Russell-Doyle, the second-in-command, took Newman and Tiny Waterman over to division headquarters. There they were given a full brief and further instructions on the new force and its role.

Though the Germans had secured southern Norway without too much trouble, the Allies were convinced that as the enemy advanced northwards there would be some splendid opportunities to harass their lines of communications. The rugged terrain, few roads and friendly populations were ideal conditions for the waging of guerrilla warfare. This was to be the mission of the ten independent companies to be raised from the territorial divisions. Five of these were to be despatched as soon as possible, as Scissors Force, under the command of Lieutenant Colonel Colin Mc V. Gubbins, newly promoted, and the army's leading exponent on guerrilla warfare.

Gubbins had spent the months immediately prior to the outbreak of war in GS(R), the tiny research department of the War Office. Despite its size, in the heady days between the Munich Crisis and the invasion of Poland, GS(R) became a forcing house of ideas on warfare. Gubbins had also seen service in Ireland during the 1920s where he had experienced at first hand the value of guerrilla warfare. It was these apsects of war that he developed and refined during his short stay in the War Office. Against him ranged the full panoply of the military establishment, conservatives to a man who regarded guerrilla warfare as a skill unworthy of the British Empire, just as the Admiralty of an earlier day dismissed submarines as un-British.

Gubbins persisted and despite opposition pursued his case most successfully when the opportunities afforded by the Norwegian Campaign were apparent. Success not only meant promotion out of the War Office and into command, but also a controlling voice over the size and composition of his 'guerrillas in uniform'.

An Independent Company numbered 300 men, infantry for the most part, but engineers and signals in support, together with some interpreters.

The company was organized into three platoons of three sections, each under the command of an officer. This created an early precedent of 'officer heavy' units among special forces. A number of regular officers would also be attached as advisers, and for the most part these were men with experience in mountain warfare.

On the Monday morning Newman moved the short distance to Ponteland Camp. Some tents had been hastily erected for mess and sleeping accommodation, and the resident tenants, 51st Anti-Tank Regiment Royal Artillery, surrendered a number of wooden huts for use as offices and stores. Over the succeeding days, while the units of the division sent their volunteers to the new formation, Newman drew up his training programme and objectives. His task was to create a force capable of living off the country, to out-manoeuvre the enemy by descending swiftly from its mountain fastness to deliver a paralyzing blow, and disappearing into the hills before the enemy could react. By such bold actions it was hoped that the local population would also rise in revolt against the oppressors. This was traditional guerrilla warfare, a harassing force in support of an army which, it was hoped, would have already secured a solid position in this mountainous seabound country. It was a situation and a tactic which Wellington and his Rifle Brigade would have recognized easily.

Newman was under no illusions though about the task that confronted him. His men were all willing volunteers but, drawn from the Territorial Army, their worth in terms of training and expertise was at best suspect. The territorial brigades of the British army in 1940 upon which the nation's reserves were founded, had had all too little opportunity to acquire the basic rudiments of soldiering. Whilst the French reserves were of an even lower quality, their German equivalents were better prepared for war.

For many years before the outbreak of war the British territorials had been denied equipment and starved of ideas. Then in the wake of the Munich Crisis of 1938 and rearmament, these brigades had been expanded too quickly. Led by officers and senior NCOs who knew too little for the positions they held, there was little sense or structure to their training. Even by the end of 1939 most brigades could perhaps claim to be a 'formed body of men'; but little else.

Training for the independent companies was hard and furious. Newman and the other commanders were compelled first to bring their men up to a required infantry standard, and then to teach them the skills of the guerrilla. The men for their part were keen and willing to learn. The result was that much was accomplished in a short period of time. Newman was ordered by Gubbins to ensure that his men, in true guerrilla fashion, could march and fight at night. Two or three nights a week, after a hard day of training, the platoons moved out to perfect the techniques of marching on a compass bearing in the dark.

Other aspects of the training caused less concern. The art of sophisticated slaughter, slitting throats, and furtive acts of vandalism in the name of sabotage presented no real problem to his many 'East-enders'. They were graduates in street survival where ingenuity was the order of the day. The men from the more rural areas found living off the land to be no problem either. The company had the right blend of skills needed in a guerrilla unit.

Towards the end of April, while Newman and his cohort toiled through the training programmes, in far away India 20 junior army officers received orders to report to Lahore immediately, and from there to proceed to Britain. Their instructions were to 'act as advisers to officers commanding battalions which might be required to operate in mountainous country'. The officers assembled at Lahore on 22 April, a number carrying fishing rods, and discussed the quality of fishing in Norway. It was apparent that either they were men of acute deductive ability, or that army security was as lax as ever. In any event none of the assembled officers took their instructions too seriously.

Lahore brought an issue of gas masks and a lecture on behaviour from a senior staff officer at army headquarters. At Karachi they embarked in *Cathay*, a new Imperial Airways flying boat designed to carry seventeen passengers. Three extra seats were quickly installed in the luggage space which was in the very rear of the plane behind the toilet. This noisy, evil smelling and dark compartment was soon labelled the 'black hole of Cathay' by the three most junior officers who occupied it.

However, their misery did not last for too long. At Alexandria the group changed to the larger *Champion*, and completed the journey to London in slightly more comfort.

The morning after their arrival, the officers reported to the War Office, where they were briefed on the present situation and future intentions. Everything had changed in Norway. Initially there had appeared to be a chance of preserving central Norway providing the two long mountain defiles leading north from Oslo were firmly held. The first intention had been to recapture Trondheim, a city of considerable importance both economically and historically. Its liberation from the hands of a small German garrison, would, it was thought, help to consolidate resistance in western and central Norway.

From such a firm base the independent companies could venture forth to wreak havoc on the enemy in the south. British forces were therefore despatched to Namsos in the north and Aandalsnes in the south, the plan being to close on Trondheim in a pincer movement.
 The operation should have worked. The Allies planned to have 13,000 men ashore to take a German garrison of about 2,000 at Trondheim. The landings were disrupted by enemy air attack, and from the outset losses were heavy. Morale slumped. A regular brigade fought well, but overall the operation was an unmitigated disaster. Poor staff work, inadequate clothing against the winter weather and no air defence against a dominant Luftwaffe, spelt failure. Territorial units were broken by the enemy, the weather and their first shock of battle. A retreat was ordered and central Norway abandoned, causing irreparable harm to Anglo-Norwegian relations.

Thus, the only British infantry left were those involved in the Narvik operation, and so the use of the Indian army officers as battalion advisers was now out of the question.

Instead they were to become attached officers to the independent companies. Eight from the group were ordered to stand by at 24 hours' notice, and the remainder given one week's leave, and tickets on the first available troopship back to India. Since they had been given a baggage allowance of only 80 pounds on the flight home, the eight spent a busy couple of days buying essential uniform and equipment. After the lean years, these young officers doubtless savoured this novel experience of sending their bills to the India Office for payment.

Two Indian army officers were posted to No. 3 Independent Company, under Newman's command. A couple of Norwegian interpreters arrived at about the same time. They were civilians who had been hastily pressed into military service, and looked very self-conscious, and ill at ease in their battledress.

Along with the new arrivals came tons of equipment. The independent companies were equipped on the most lavish scale. After the impecunious years, this stood in uncomfortable contrast. In addition to the normal articles of clothing and battledress, the men were issued with arctic boots (three sizes too big to enable them to wear three extra pairs of socks), rifles and 120 rounds of ammunition, leather jerkins, sheepskin coats, snow shoes, ice axes and skis, steel helmets, coils of rope, sleeping bags and blankets. Every man was issued with a large Norwegian rucksack into which he also packed spare clothes, rations, in this case a five-day mountain ration of pemmican, and his share of a 30-day reserve ration. The officers also had to contend with map cases, and revolver, field glasses and compasses.

On 29 April, Newman received the warning order for war, all local leave was cancelled and the men confined to barracks. The divisional commander paid them a quick visit. Amidst all the frantic activities, a parade had to be organized and the general then addressed the company.

Newman was not at all impressed with the speech. Most of it consisted of advice on how to escape if taken prisoner. He regarded it as defeatist talk, but had no intention of making an issue of it since he had suffered one rebuff a couple of days previously. He had challenged Gubbins's insistence on night compass marches. It seemed rather a pointless exercise for a unit about to embark for a campaign in the land of the midnight sun. At this particular time of year it was light for 24 hours a day. Newman had received a very sharp and public rebuke from the army's expert on guerrilla warfare for his pains.

The company assembled on the rifle range at Ponteland Camp and set off to march to the local railway station, a distance of about two miles. The unit was prepared to undertake guerrilla warfare in the mountains, when Ludgate Hill was probably the highest hill that any of Newman's East-enders had ever seen. It was a unit designed to fight without transport, to be self supporting and self sufficient.

The march from the range to the station nearly killed them. The men were loaded down with over 100 lb of cumbersome equipment on a warm spring day. Fortunately the 51st Anti-Tank Regiment, who had come down to see them off gave a helping hand. Newman ensured however that one item of supplies remained clear of any light-fingered gunner: the previous evening a paymaster had arrived under armed escort, with a final gift towards 'independence', in the form of a large sum of sterling and Norwegian krone. The money was to buy local supplies, hire guides and local transport. It was as well the gunners did not know, or they might have demanded payment for their porterage. Gunners have a reputation – they never do anything for nothing, and Newman was carrying over £4,000 which in those days was a very considerable sum of money.

The slowest of trains took the company through the night, past Edinburgh and Glasgow until a cold, chilly dawn found them on the quayside at Gourrock in the Firth of Clyde.

It was just six weeks since Churchill and the skiers of the Fifth

Battalion The Scots Guards, Britain's first special force, had embarked from this self-same quay.

At Gourrock they met other independent companies. No. 4 was raised from the 54th Infantry Division, all Liverpool and Merseyside men with scouse accents you could cut with a knife. No. 5 Company was there too, which was drawn from the 56th (London) Division. Men from such famous territorial units as the London Scottish, London Irish, and The Queen's Westminster.

No matter what their background or cap badge, the independent companies were comprised largely of young men, indifferently trained and, in their innocence, eager for the fray. None doubted their potential, but this was going to be 'on the job training'; assuming circumstances and the enemy would permit.

CHAPTER FOUR

Northern Deployments

'It is not an easy war to wage but it is interesting enough.'

General Auchinleck on the Norwegian campaign.

Tenders took the troops out to waiting transports, packets commandeered off the Liverpool-Belfast run. The *Royal Scotsman* carried
Newman's No. 3 Company while Nos. 4 and 5 Companies were
embarked on *Ulsterman*. Newman was greeted as he stepped on
board by Gubbins, who had been given the local rank of brigadier,
and his brigade major 'Tiger' Urquhart.[1] The brigadier was to sail
with the *Ulsterman* while Urquhart would remain with Newman.
There was a last-minute flap when it was found the convoy was
sailing with all the brigadier's personal kit on the wrong boat. A
hasty change, a few red faces and they were off. A bevy of
destroyers fussed around as escort and a cruiser took station ahead
and proudly led the way.

The transports were not very comfortable. Troops were crammed
four or five to a small two-berth cabin together with all their
personal equipment.

Schoolboys would have been in heaven. The ships had been
requisitioned at such short notice there had been no time for a
refit; as a consequence after the second day water became so scarce,
all washing was forbidden. Not that such an inconvenience worried
the soldiers. Once in the open waters off the west coast of Scotland
the convoy ran into a howling gale. The weather was so bad that
most were horizontal with seasickness as the packets pitched and
tossed like corks.

Newman spent most of the voyage fighting back nausea and
discussing operations with Urquhart.

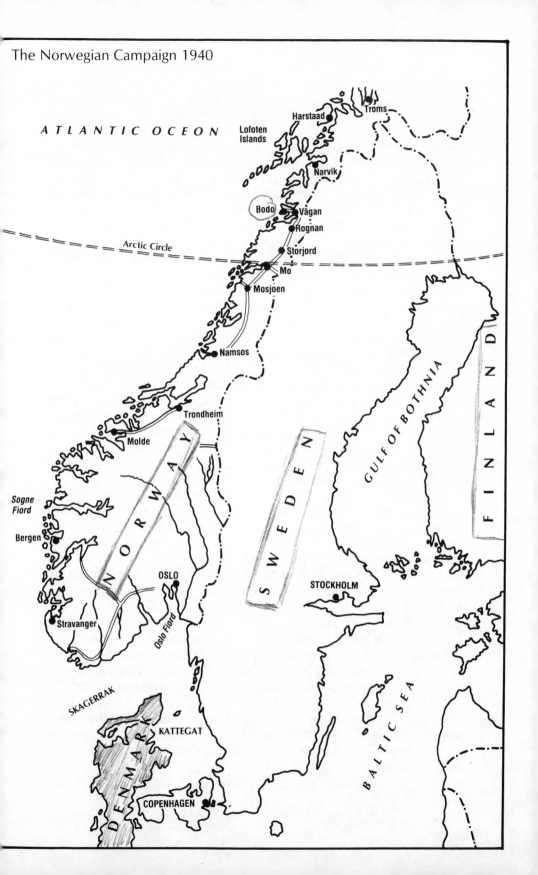

The Norwegian Campaign 1940

A T L A N T I C   O C E O N

Arctic Circle

Harstaad
Troms
Lofoten Islands
Narvik
Bodo
Vågan
Rognan
Storjord
Mo
Mosjoen
Namsos
Trondheim
Molde
Sogne Fiord
Bergen
OSLO
STOCKHOLM
Stravanger
Oslo Fiord

NORWAY

SWEDEN

FINLAND

GULF OF BOTHNIA

SKAGERRAK
KATTEGAT
DENMARK
COPENHAGEN

BALTIC SEA

Everything had changed again. Norway was a campaign where plans were redrawn far too lightly, but one must at least give the Allies some credit for persistence. Seemingly not in the least deterred by the disasters at Namsos and Aandalesnes, they continued with their operations against the German garrison isolated at Narvik in the north, more for face-saving reasons than any other. The German forces under General Dietl were 'marooned' on shore once the Royal Navy had steamed into the fjord with the battleship *Warspite* and sunk the enemy destroyers and transports. Deploying the surviving sailors alongside his Alpine ski troops, the energetic and forceful Dietl garrisoned the port and prepared his defences for a long siege. With the Royal Navy in seeming control of the waters they could do little else than wait for troops advancing through Norway from the south to effect a rescue.

The Allies were equally determined to salvage something from the campaign and despatched substantial forces to capture Narvik. The Guards Brigade was diverted to Harstaad, the nearest 'large' port to Narvik and capital of the Lofoten Islands. The weather, there was very deep snow late in the year, and the absence of proper landing craft delayed any immediate landing at Narvik.

The French despatched their own expeditionary force. Three battalions of Chasseurs Alpins, two battalions of Foreign Legion, and a Polish brigade of a further four battalions arrived in the Lofotens where the local commanders, with national sensitivities to protect, squabbled over the best way in which to capture Narvik and its German garrison.

Urquhart explained to Newman that the Scissors Force brigade was to be landed to the south of Narvik where it was to link up with the retreating Norwegians and fight a guerrilla campaign against the enemy. The plan was for Newman's No. 3 Company to be taken straight to Bodo to secure the port, whilst Nos. 4 and 5 Companies were to land further south at Mosjoen where they in all probability would be the first to be in contact with the Germans. Of the others in Gubbins's brigade, No. 1 Company had already landed at Rana and was deployed around a small town called Mo-i-Rana (Mo). The final unit No. 2 Company was to travel at a later date.

Urquhart expanded on the longer term picture. Once the German garrison at Narvik had been defeated, the enemy could no longer use that route for its iron ore shipments. If the Allies could stabilize the front at this narrow part of Norway between Bodo and Mo where neutral Sweden was nearest to the sea then the independent companies could come into their own as a guerrilla raiding force. In time the first five companies would be relieved by a second group still under training.

Newman took a less than optimistic view of the campaign. He could see the independent companies were no more than a scratch force to protect the southern flank of the Narvik operation and to deny the Germans the ports of Mosjoen Mo and Bodo. Neither did he share Urquhart's conviction on the immediate importance of Narvik – after all it was spring and the Baltic free of ice.

Newman concentrated on the more immediate issues; those that could affect his command. Bodo was important; besides being the chief port in that part of Norway, it was the seat of local government and the regional headquarters of the broadcasting company.

Where were the Germans in relation to Bodo? Urquhart didn't know. Perhaps Bodo was already in enemy hands. London bombarded the task force with a stream of signals which were as contradictory as they were confusing. The signals could not be queried because the force had been ordered to observe complete radio silence. The only maps they had of Norway were tourist folders provided by Thomas Cook, a most reputable firm of travel agents; but delightful, picturesque scenes of Norway and a small fold-out map showing one single road – was not the best way to plan a campaign.

Hindsight does suggest that a guerrilla war campaign could have been fought on terms more suited to the British forces. The coastline of Norway is covered by literally thousands of islands, and is broken by deep fjords which run miles inland; into these the mountains drop precipitously. The arctic highway north from Trondheim is almost amphibious in character, it passes for long stretches close to fjords and even today makes frequent use of ferries. Between Mosjoen and Bodo there was one main valley along which runs this single road, passable once the snow has melted. The road crosses a high snow field on the line of the Arctic Circle, which is between Mo and Bodo. At that time, the highway 'stopped' at Bodo. In terrain such as this, the British should have used their natural element, the sea and (from bases in the Lofoten Islands) launched small scale raids from coastal craft or submarines to hit an enemy line of communication which was long, exposed and vulnerable.

Although the Luftwaffe had air superiority, it would not have been possible for them to police all the fjords and islands. Even in today's world, rippling with the most sophisticated surveillance devices, the Soviets seem able to penetrate Norwegian fjords with impunity.

Perhaps it was all too late and even had a more intelligent use been made of the resources to hand, the Allies would still have been defeated. Some would maintain that the Allies had passed beyond the point of recovery. Earlier disasters and the Germans' firm grip on so much of the country weighted the scales heavily in favour of the enemy.

What is not in doubt is that this first deployment of a special force in battle set a precedent which subsequently was to become a tragic pattern. The independent companies, hand-picked men for a special role, were squandered in main force operations, where they lacked the numbers, fire-power and logistical support necessary for sustained conventional operations.

Within sight of that magnificent Norwegian coastline, high snow-covered mountains which sparkled in the most brilliant sunshine, the task force split. The *Ulsterman* moved in towards Mosjoen where the troops landed shortly after midnight on 9 May. The port was garrisoned by a company of French troops, élite Chasseurs Alpins, who were only too happy to explain the situation and hand over to the independent companies. It seemed that the Germans were still advancing northwards. Brigadier Gubbins borrowed a car and drove south to see the situation for himself, and to make contact with the retreating Norwegians. He found them at the village of Fellingfjord, some 25 miles from Mosjoen, dispirited, and close to disintegration. Their commander appeared to be convinced that, since the British withdrawal at Namsos, further resistance against the advancing foe was futile.

Gubbins ordered No. 5 Independent Company to move 12 miles south of Mosjoen where they were to dig in and defend the road. They were joined by a couple of weak Norwegian companies from the local *Landsvern* battalion. No. 4 Company was instructed to take over from the French and garrison Mosjoen. The Chasseurs embarked on the other troopship and sailed north to rejoin their regiment for the battles at Narvik. Gubbins kept No. 1 Independent Company at Mo where it could be held in reserve and garrison the harbour.

In the meanwhile one of the destroyers escorting Newman's group in the *Royal Scotsman* went ahead to explore Bodo fjord. It was with considerable relief that the message was flashed back: 'Proceed – Bodo not in enemy hands.'

The first sight of this little town nestling against a magnificent backdrop, was quite breathtaking. Newman's troops lined the rails and looked out on a landscape bathed in the strongest sunlight. The mountain peaks glowed brilliant white against a blue sky. In the fjord their ship manoeuvred around the thick ice, irregular and humped where it was starting to break up in the spring thaw.

Bodo itself did not amount to very much – quaint timber buildings clustered round a wooden jetty. There were a few more substantial brick buildings, a hotel and a cinema – the latter serving as the local community centre and meeting place.

The troopship was met by a small detachment of regular British infantry, which had been despatched from Harstaad, and the local inhabitants, who crammed onto the jetty to welcome the new arrivals. Dressed in thin, long plus-fours, boots with highly coloured, rolled-over socks and peaked skiing hats, the locals appeared remarkably fit. Appearances were deceptive. There was a high incidence of tuberculosis caused by people keeping cattle and livestock inside their houses during the long winter months. Neither was the welcome unambiguous. As elsewhere, the crowd contained a proportion of collaborators, those who supported Quisling, the leader of the Norwegian Fascist Party.

The regular company of infantry, from the South Wales Borderers, prepared to hand over and use the troopship to take them on to Harstaad and the main force. Their commander warned Newman to discount the many scares, tales of parachute landings, enemy ships in isolated fjords, etc. which were all the invention of a very healthy fifth column. He was, however, advised to use his discretion, for it was not all fanciful nonsense.

Amongst those who greeted Newman at Bodo were a couple of very dejected RAF officers. They had arrived two days before piloting their Walrus flying boats, to reconnoitre ground which would be suitable for a temporary landing strip. The nearest Allied aircraft were at Harstaad, which was well beyond fighter cover range.

The flying boats had been at anchor in the harbour for no more than a few hours when a Luftwaffe bomber appeared and sank one. The other was quickly towed into a small creek and carefully hidden. The next morning the bomber returned, made straight for the spot where the flying boat was hidden, and destroyed it with a well-aimed burst of machine-gun fire.

Newman's 'private funds' soon produced what lorries that were available to move the men inland. He kept one platoon in Bodo to guard the harbour and deployed a second, as advance guard, south to a village called Rognar which was at the end of the Bodo fjord. The remainder, together with his own headquarters, he established in a small unnamed hamlet about 12 miles inland from Bodo. The men were billeted in the odd-shaped Norwegian homes, where their kindly hosts fed them lashings of milk and cheese, very hard bread and extremely salted fish.

The company quickly settled to their new existence. But it did take some getting used to. In April the sun fails to set and the long summer of perpetual light had begun. But it would be late May before the snow melted in the villages, and July before the mountains above were clear. Soldiers found it difficult to sleep without the darkness. However, although the 'nights' were damp and cold, the 'days' in the valley were gloriously sunny and warm enough for men to strip to the waist and sunbathe in the snow.

The only signs of war were the sounds of aircraft; for the most part lumbering Junker 52 transports shuttling northwards towards Narvik. The Germans were reinforcing Dietl's garrison with men and supplies.

If life was fairly idyllic for Newman's troops, it was the very reverse for some of the other independent companies. On 10 May it fell to No. 5 Company to draw first blood on behalf of Scissors Force. The company had dug in south of Mosjoen, where, together with the Norwegians, they awaited the enemy in ambush. An Indian army officer, with bitter experience of the Pathan in the North-West Frontier, had picked the spot with care. The Germans had no idea there were any troops in the area, leave alone a disciplined force.

An advance guard of 60 cyclists were mown down in a very few moments. The first burst of fire killed many, and the next, shouting 'Heil Hitler', rode jinking through the dead to their own destruction. There were no survivors to the enemy and no casualties to Scissors Force.

That same day Norwegian coast watchers reported the movement northwards of an unescorted transport. Admiral of the Fleet, the Earl of Cork and Orrery, who was the senior naval officer (with his headquarters in the Lofoten Islands), received scores of such reports, most false and part of the Quisling tactic of misinformation. Though this one seemed authentic, the admiral had no warships immediately available to intercept; indeed a couple of destroyers had already been despatched to answer what proved to be a false alarm.

The transport was real enough. It was the Norwegian Narvik. packet *Nord Norge*, taken when the enemy captured Trondheim. Manned by a German naval crew, the ship sailed north, unescorted and carrying some 400 soldiers, including a reinforced company of 180 men from the crack 138th Mountain Regiment.

It was a bold stroke and fortune favours the brave. At 1900 hours, the enemy stepped ashore unopposed at the tiny port of Hemnesberger some 30 miles north of Mosjoen, in the Ranafjord. Shortly afterwards a couple of Dornier DO 18 flying boats landed further troops close to the town, before taking off and returning south.

The British light AA cruiser *Cairo* and the Tribal Class destroyer

Zulu appeared on the scene and promptly sank the *Nord Norge*. But it was too late. The damage had been done. At a stroke, the Germans had outflanked the Anglo-Norwegian defences at Mosjoen.

A platoon drawn from No. 1 Independent Company moved down to contest the landing but to no avail. Outnumbered and outgunned by trained mountain fighters, they were forced back along the road to the village of Finneid, where there was a Norwegian garrison.

It was something of a stand-off. The enemy had outflanked the defences at Mosjoen, but it was a small bridgehead. They might be the last word in mountain troops but they could do little until they were substantially reinforced. The flying boats shuttled reinforcements under the guardian eyes of the Luftwaffe's air superiority, but their capacity was strictly limited and they could make little impression on overall numbers.

Gubbins should have kept his nerve. He had sufficient Norwegian forces to seal the Germans into Hemnesberger, while he fought a delaying action against the main enemy advance to the south with his independent companies. The pressure would have then been on the Germans, who had two isolated pockets of unequal size, to rescue Hemnesberger and Narvik. Instead, convinced that his forces were threatened front and rear, Gubbins believed that Mosjoen was no longer tenable and ordered a withdrawal. The separate platoons of Nos. 4 and 5 Companies were widely scattered, and by all accounts it was Gubbins himself who conveyed his own orders. He moved unceasingly by car and bicycle, walking when the roads gave out and swimming where there were no boats in order to reach the isolated detachments. This was valiant behaviour indeed, but was it to be expected of a brigadier? Where was the staff who might have been better used while he concentrated on the big picture and *directed* the campaign?

The companies boarded small Norwegian steamers, transferred to destroyers and landed at Bodo where they joined with Newman.

No such arrangements were made for their Norwegian allies, who were forced to withdraw overland to Elsfjord, and thence by ferry to Finneid. They abandoned most of their equipment on the quayside at Elsfjord.

Brigadier Gubbins had surrendered 35 miles of most difficult mountain road between Mosjoen and Elsfjord. It was perfect ambush country in a situation tailor-made for guerrilla warfare. The Germans had a long line of communication along particularly bad roads made even worse by wet snow and a spring thaw. The Allied commanders failed to realize the German predicament. A determined stratagem which combined conventional defence with guerrilla raids supported by naval bombardment and carrier strike[2] could have caused havoc. Instead territory was surrendered and the Germans were allowed to move unhindered nearer to Narvik. Norwegian morale had plummeted, and the campaign now had that bad smell of impending defeat.

On that same momentous 10 May, the Western Front reeled under the hammer blow of a German Blitzkrieg. The *Evening Standard* carried the banner headlines:

NAZIS INVADE HOLLAND, BELGIUM, LUXEMBURG

The Brandenburgers once again had played a vital role in the early stages of the campaign. They were deployed in the van of the German Sixth Army to seize vital bridges into Holland. Bold action, helped by Dutch inaction, and no doubt treachery too, ensured success for their missions. Their task completed, the Brandenburgers were quietly withdrawn while Blitzkrieg rolled forward into the Low Countries. At this stage of the war at least the German High Command had no intention of wasting the assets of such a superbly trained special force in orthodox combat.

In London the Chamberlain government was forced to resign, and Winston Churchill, an advocate of the unorthodox in warfare, led a national government from a coalition of parties.

---

[1] Later to command the First Airborne Division at Arnhem. On 10 May 1945, he was to land in Oslo at the head of the British and Norwegian Forces for the liberation of the country.

[2] The carrier *Glorious* was patrolling off the Norwegian coast.

CHAPTER FIVE

Baptism of Fire

In the remote fastness of northern Norway the Allied commanders, unaware of the calamity that was about to engulf the Western Front, were still determined to capture Narvik, more for 'face saving' purposes than from any continued hope of reaching the Swedish ore mines. General Macksey, who was in command, had 20,000 troops available for the reduction of the Narvik defences, but his extreme caution delayed any real progress. Instead he blamed the Norwegians and the British territorial brigades for failing to hold the enemy advance from the south, an operation for which he would have to assume a much greater responsibility. Gubbins and his brigade of independent companies were insufficient as a harrying force and obviously needed considerable help; but this could only be achieved by weakening the attack on Narvik.

Yet more plans were made. On 12 May two battalions of French Foreign Legion landed at Bjerkvik to the north of Narvik. The Scots Guards were withdrawn and despatched south to Mo to garrison a new defence line in the Ranafjord. Brigadier Gubbins was given overall command in the area.

For the independent companies, all thoughts of guerrilla warfare were now cast aside and instead they were assigned the tasks of reinforcing detachments as a general reserve, and flankguards, in what was to become a long, difficult and bloody withdrawal, ostensibly to the main line of resistance at Ranafjord.

To a degree such a role did have overtones of the light infantry rearguards of the Peninsula War, but there were major differences.

The independent companies were now part of a south-facing defence line in a positional war, they were a considerable distance from reinforcements and supplies and they lacked the means of heavy fire support. This was a role for which they were never raised, and it is ironic that their instigator, creator and leader should now command them in a conventional rearguard action which was to see them dissipated.

Gubbins deployed Scissors Force, in anticipation of substantial and speedy reinforcements, and in readiness for the coming battle. Newman's company, rudely disturbed from its idyllic interlude was ordered south to Ragnar and Pothus, about 10 miles south of the head of the fjord on which Bodo stands and 40 miles away from the port. Their place in Bodo was taken by No. 2 Company newly arrived from England, while Nos. 4 and 5 Companies were redeployed to the head of Bodo fjord as reserve. It was still left to No. 1 Company to remain furthest south and nearest to the enemy.

Scissors Force was widely extended, and with indifferent transport on poor roads would be unable to concentrate to counter a single major threat.

Meanwhile, the German advance pressed relentlessly northwards to reach the small isolated hamlet at Finneidfjord, which was defended by a Norwegian battalion and the main elements of No. 1 Company.

The Germans attacked straight off the line of march, and they were good, too good. German infantry with light artillery support concentrated their main attack down the axis of the road and thus fully absorbed the attention and strength of the defenders. Mountain troops moved out onto the high ground and out-flanked the defence lines with relative ease.

Unable to withstand the pressure, the defenders abandoned their positions and fell back in relatively good order seven miles to the north and the village of Stein. Here No. 1 Company joined forces with the recently arrived Scots Guards.

The ease with which the Germans pushed aside the defence and the relative pace of their advance now thoroughly alarmed the generals still thwarted by the enemy resistance at Narvik. The remaining battalions of the 24th Guards Brigade were ordered south from Harstaad. The Irish Guards and the South Wales Borderers were to take ship for Bodo and thence continue south to Mo by road. The brigade commander, Fraser, was to assume the area command from Gubbins upon his arrival.

The Allies were moving troops within their own perimeter, but the line of communications was still cruelly exposed. The skies over Norway belonged to the Luftwaffe and this lesson was yet again to be rammed home to a bunch of British generals who still did not understand the meaning of air superiority.

The Irish Guards were crammed into a solitary unarmed transport which was quickly discovered by the Luftwaffe. Two bombs hit the freighter. The first sliced into a stateroom where Brigadier Fraser and his staff who, either unconcerned or unaware of the air raid, were briefing the commanding officer of the Irish Guards and his senior officers. All were either killed or seriously wounded. The second struck the forward hold and destroyed all the support weapons and three light tanks. The freighter limped back to Harstaad, the Irish Guards now commanded by their adjutant, a young captain.

The brigade's third battalion, the South Wales Borderers also failed to reach the front at their first attempt. They were embarked in HMS *Effingham*, a fast but dated 10,000-ton cruiser for the 200-mile voyage south.

The captain of the *Effingham*'s solution to running the Luftwaffe gauntlet was to sail at speed and close in-shore through those narrow waters. The ship was a prime target with an inadequate air defence, and 24-hour sunshine which permitted no respite from attack. The cruiser ran aground and became a total loss. Escorting destroyers collected the sailors and guardsmen, and returned them to Harstaad.

General Auchinleck, regarded as the Indian army's most outstanding officer, had by now arrived and assumed command at Narvik from the hesitant and floundering Macksey. The new commander ordered a renewed effort to force the issue at Narvik. He decided that the Bodo area was to be held at all costs, and Mo for as long as supply by road appeared feasible against Luftwaffe interdiction.

The two battalions, now minus almost all their heavy weapons and stores, were shipped to Bodo in fishing smacks and a succession of small inter-island steamers. Though less likely to attract the attention of the Luftwaffe, it proved a protracted process and their piecemeal arrival, rather than as formed units, was to have a serious effect on the coming battles.

Though they had never met, Auchinleck had no choice other than to confirm Gubbins in command of the southern front. Fraser was still recovering from his wounds and no other brigadiers were to be placed at risk on such a hazardous voyage.

Gubbins issued instructions that no efforts were to be spared to complete the landing strip at Bodo. Somehow the Luftwaffe had to be challenged for command of the air. This was easier said than done. The ground was so soft with the advanced spring thaw, that it needed to be dug out and completely resurfaced; but there was no engineer unit with the appropriate skills and equipment. The troops tackled the problem as best they could, even raiding the local houses for wooden doors to make a runway.

On 17 May, the Germans continued their advance northwards from Mo. Against them stood the Scots Guards and No. 1 Independent Company. Colonel Trappes-Lomax, who commanded the Guards, was under no illusions. He had the open flank of the mountains, no support from the sea and behind him, for both resupply and retreat, a long, bad road through the mountains bleakly exposed in the melting snow to the Luftwaffe.

Battle was fast and furious. Trappes-Lomax's guardsmen gave a good account of themselves, but up against Carinthian mountaineers and ski troops fighting in a countryside which was a mirror image of their own, the outcome was inevitable. The retreat was messy and there were casualties, nevertheless the bridge over the River Rana was blown and the battalion moved northwards.

No. 1 Independent Company had just about been fought out. After three weeks of near continuous fighting their numbers were depleted, and the survivors much in need of a rest. Brigadier Gubbins ordered Newman to relieve them.

Newman's company had enjoyed a busy and fruitful existence. They had spent their time preparing all the bridges for demolition and raising ski patrols from amongst the local population. They were sent out into the countryside to reconnoitre the mountain ridges and search for German paratroopers. Tasks well beyond the capability of Newman and his cohorts.

On 18 May Newman set out to meet Trappes-Lomax. A truck loaded with the supplies Newman considered the Guards would need most was to follow on behind. He had comandeered a little car and took Terry Liben who ran the support company with him. Radio communications had once again broken down so Newman carried with him Gubbins's plan of operations which he was to deliver and explain to the Scots Guards. The brigadier had selected three defensive positions across the 150-mile watershed that separated Mo from the head of Saltfjord and Bodo. On paper it looked good, but then plans always do. Unbeknown to Gubbins, Trappes-Lomax had already abandoned the first line.

The rugged, snow-covered mountains overshadowed the valley on each side, and it all reminded Newman of a Christmas card. The mess sergeant had prepared a picnic hamper, and as they drove south down the fertile valley from Rognan, the war seemed far removed. Every 10 or 12 miles they came upon little clusters of houses grouped around the point where the fast flowing river crossed and recrossed the road. Then, beyond a hamlet called Storjord, the countryside changed. The road climbed to a saddle at the valley's end, the trees became less frequent and more stunted in growth, and houses few and far between.

Quite suddenly at Viskiskoia, there were no more houses, just a river bridge and a few sad trees. Everything ceased except a solid stretch of ice and snow as far as one could see. It was the bleakest place on earth. The polar landscape was the snowfield, 20 miles of barren ice waste many feet thick in winter. A high moorland pasture in the few short summer months, it stretched as far as Krokstraad. A solitary track like a dark brown stain wound into the distance with banks of snow and ice about 12 feet high on either side.

Newman had never seen anything like it in his life. On they drove, mile after mile utterly alone. Frequently the car bottomed on the rutted snow, the wheels spinning madly. In such conditions, ten miles an hour was good progress. They passed a small monument denoting the Arctic Circle and then the track began to descend until, just as suddenly as it started, the icefield ended.

The village of Krokstaad, standing midst a thick belt of fir trees would have been a welcome sight had it not been for the human degradation that greeted them. Newman saw for the first time the meaning of an army in defeat. The houses and trees thronged with troops and their bivouacs. Norwegians, by the hundred and even more in long straggling files coming from the south. The road was a straggling mass of humanity. Soldiers led little short-legged ponies, straining at their crude bridles and hauling carts stacked high with stores of every description. There was no order and no command. Officers were indistinguishable from men, and all had the hang-dog expressions of an army in defeat.

Newman did not stop. There seemed no point. Their passing aroused no interest from the weary Norwegians. Instead, the two British officers pressed on, making even slower progress against this tide of humanity. Then they came upon the refugees. There were children, old men and women, which was to be expected; but there were younger men too, some still wearing the tattered remnants of uniforms.

Terry Liben condemned such behaviour, but Newman took a more tolerant view.

'Who can blame them,' he said. 'When your country has been overrun, your home destroyed, the first duty of any man is to protect his own loved ones.'

Liben couldn't agree and was about to launch forth when they spotted their first British soldier amongst the crowd. Newman wound down the window and beckoned the man over. He was a medic; a bedraggled and miserable private soldier in the Royal Army Medical Corps. 'Where's the Scots Guards?' enquired Newman.

'Further on. A fu----g hell of a mess.' And the man was away. He bolted into the crowd before Newman could even think of a rejoinder.

The two officers continued to make slow progress against the pressing mass of humanity. They came upon lines of dejected Tommies, mostly medics, unwilling to look the officers in the eye.

Then another tapestry unfolded to these newcomers to war. There was a shout and men dived for cover, an ambulance swerved out of control and ran into a ditch. Newman stopped the car and stared as a double line of dirt etched its way along the now empty road towards them. Comprehension dawned as an aircraft roared low overhead. The dust spouts passed by with a sound like gravel off a dustbin lid, and the single Luftwaffe fighter veered away.

Newman ran down to the ambulance. It was full of badly wounded Scots Guards packed two to a stretcher, and a very frightened orderly. Terry Liben organized a strong-arm gang and manhandled the truck back onto the road.

It was pointless to continue travelling by car. The Norwegian and British troops, the refugees and the rutted track were all too much. Newman parked off the road and removed the rotar arm, found a corporal and promised him a lift if he guarded the vehicle until their return. Then they tramped off in the opposite direction to the retreating troops. It was like trying to move against a football crowd.

About an hour later and a mile or so down the track, they came upon the headquarters of the Scots Guards, located in a broken down cottage.

Colonel Trappes-Lomax was sitting in his shirt-sleeves, planning the next move.

'Hullo! Who are you?'

'Newman, No. 3 Independent Company.'

'Never heard of you – what can I do for you?'

'It's what I can do for you, Sir.' Newman explained. 'I have been instructed to find your halting positions on the line of withdrawal, and build dumps of ammunition and food.'

'Well, tonight Krokstraad,' said Trappes-Lomax consulting his map. 'Tomorrow over the ice to Viskiskoia and that's about all I can tell you. My chaps have had a bad time and are damn tired. I must take them back as quickly as I can.'

Trappes-Lomax was right and Gubbins clearly wrong. The

blocking or defensive positions were hopelessly divorced from reality. There were never enough troops to cover all points, and they had no answer to the outflanking forays of the German ski troops. The British army in Norway lacked mobility off the road, heavy weapons and supporting artillery to repel attacks. This applied as much to the regular formations as to the so-called 'special forces'. Both suffered in equal measure through lack of preparation, and each was subjected to the paralyzing influence of the Luftwaffe against which they were impotent.

Newman jotted down the names and looked up. 'Right. I will make a dump at Krokstraad, and one or two further north if I can. You will find the dumps in clearings on the west side of the road, Sir.'

Trappes-Lomax pencilled a few comments on his map.

'Anything else I can do?' asked Newman.

'No – just too busy to talk much – must get on,' replied Trappes-Lomax. 'We'll probably see you later. Cheerio!'

Newman saluted and left the building. They quickly retraced their steps to the car and the corporal. The trouble with this perpetual daylight was that it was so easy to lose all track of time. 'God only knows where the supply truck is by now,' muttered Newman. He didn't raise his real fear, namely that it had gone through Krokstraad and onto the icefield.

The return was even worse. The mess on the road, snow and the cluttered congestion of the retreating army slowed their progress to a crawl. At one point they came upon the wretched ambulance again, stuck fast in the mud. Newman loaded the worst cases into the car and banished his companions to the wings where they clung precariously to the strap which straddled the bonnet.

By the time they reached the icefield, the Norwegians had begun to cross. The long columns of straggling troops reminded Newman of paintings depicting Napoleon's retreat from Moscow.

The overloaded staff car beat the supply truck into Krokstraad by half an hour and they established the first dump for the Scots Guards. This was left in the hands of Terry Liben while Newman pressed on with the wounded to Rognan, where he took his charges to an aid post and thence reported to the brigadier.

Gubbins wasted no time in issuing a crisp new set of orders.

Newman was instructed to take his company to Storjord, 25 miles south of Rognan, to dig a defensive position and establish a supply dump. There were only sufficient trucks for the supplies. The men marched, and on reaching their objectives dug their trenches.

Barely had the work been completed before a new set of orders arrived from Gubbins. Their line was to be established 12 miles further south. The men gathered their kit and their weapons and set off down the road. Newman, ever mindful of the Luftwaffe, ordered the platoons to be well spaced.

The company deployed into the new position as yet another motor-cyclist appeared. Gubbins ordered them on to Viskiskoia to cover the Scots Guards as they came across the ice belt; which they were scheduled to do in a day's time.

The Scots Guards beat them to it. Newman arrived with his advance party, as the Guards came off the ice and straight into the line. Despite their ordeal, Newman could not help but admire their demeanour and style. Trappes-Lomax had fought a brilliant delaying action, and brought his battalion through the potential death trap of the snow belt, seemingly unscathed.

'Tiger' Urquhart appeared on the scene. He ordered Newman to relieve No. 1 Company who gratefully continued the march on through to Storjord and a rest. Urquhart and Newman explored the mountainside for the best defensive positions.

The independent company was to be like the skirmishers of old. 'When your men arrive, get them up into the mountainside and ahead of the main position,' ordered 'Tiger' before dashing off again.

Newman's company appeared on the scene. They were neither in the best of order or humour, and they were exhausted by their long march. The prospect that marching was to be replaced by digging held little appeal. Newman and his officers were hard pressed to keep them awake, up the mountain and into their positions.

They were not left in peace for long. Within a very short while there were new orders. Newman was instructed to establish an ambush covering the road. He set off over the forward slopes, taking with him a young officer called Jacko Williams who would be responsible for the ambush.

Whilst in the midst of exploring a possible ambush site, they heard a truck approaching. A Norwegian army lorry passed along the road travelling south. This seemed very odd. Newman knew there was nothing in front of them but the Germans. Jacko hurried on over the crest of the slope to see where the truck had gone. That was the last Newman ever saw of him. What happened has never been resolved. He became a statistic of war under the heading of 'Missing believed killed in action'.

Newman chose Lieutenant Hopkirk and his platoon to man the ambush.

CHAPTER SIX

Rearguard

Hopkirk's platoon deployed into the ambush position. The prospect of action, the realization that nothing was between them and the enemy, had swept aside their tiredness and they moved with a new sense of purpose and vigour.

Newman joined the young officer, and they chatted quietly while he trained his binoculars on the road ahead. About a mile away he could see something moving towards them across the ice belt.

'Hold everything,' he ordered as the men scurried for cover and readied their weapons. 'It might well be the stragglers.'

The focus of attention was where the track breasted a slight rise in the ground.

'It's that Norwegian lorry coming back,' Newman said.

'What's that behind it?' queried Hopkirk.

Newman looked hard. 'Suffering hell!' he exclaimed. 'It's cyclists, Jerries – about a hundred or more!'

Hopkirk turned to his troops.

'For Godsakes hold everything Hoppy,' said Newman, placing a restraining hand on the young officer's shoulder. 'I'll give the order to fire.'

The cyclists came towards them in two long lines, cycling through the ruts, all slowly pedalling in what seemed to be perfect precision. Nearer and nearer they came, half a mile, 300 yards. How slowly they seemed to be moving. Newman quietly counted out the distance; he knew he mustn't let them get up to the bridge.

Two hundred yards.

'Ready Hoppy?' Safety-catches off. Newman could almost taste the tension around him.

One hundred and fifty yards.

One hundred yards.

'Fire!' shouted Newman as he blasted away with his service revolver. What a sight! Over the enemy went like ninepins, steel helmets rolled down the road.

The first burst of fire from a bren-gun shattered the windscreen of the truck. Newman caught a glimpse of a white face before it disintegrated into bloody pulp and the truck charged into the ditch. There were bicycles everywhere.

'Darned good shooting, Hoppy,' complimented Newman.

'Look!' exclaimed Hopkirk. 'There's one of them trying to cross the road into cover – quick give me a rifle.'

It was mad, discordant mayhem and not at all what the young officers imagined battle would be like.

'Look out!' someone yelled above the din. 'Jerry planes coming in low!'

Heinkels, three of them, swept in very low, flames dancing along the wing tips as lines of bullets chipped the bare rock outcrop into equally lethal splinters.

The fighters were followed by divebombers. In Norway the Luftwaffe still flew the Henschel which made a most demoralizing noise as it screamed down into the attack.[1]

Newman's company paid for its impertinence. Incessant waves of aircraft bombed and strafed their positions. Newman passed the word for the men to lie 'doggo' – there was no point in offering any defensive fire; such a futile gesture would simply betray the position.

The Luftwaffe probed further back and stung the Scots Guards into retaliation. One large guardsman stood on the lip of his slit trench, with a bren-gun at his hip.

'Come on you black bastards.' His bullets seemed to penetrate right into the guts of the plane, but it flew on regardless.

German ski troops were spotted moving round the mountain top, but they were well beyond the range of small arms.

The air attack lasted for a further hour and more. The planes gave them no respite, casualties began to mount, and after the first heady moments, it was now proving to be a most bitter baptism of fire. All the while the Germans infiltrated the mountain flanks; and then began to move down into a position from where they could threaten the defences. The sergeant major crawled up to Newman's slit trench.

'I've brought up the two-inch mortar Sir, what about it?'

'Jolly good, Sarn't Major,' replied Newman. 'Have a go behind that cluster of rocks up on the hill – there's a whole bunch of Jerries there.'

The mortar opened fire.

'Short.'

'Up fifty.'

'Good shooting.'

The mortar team was doing some good work, and already the enemy were scooting back from their nearest point. Newman left them to it while he made his way over to the Scots Guards. He needed to talk to Trappes-Lomax and find out the latest developments.

Battalion headquarters was in a small cottage which already showed the stains of war. Newman walked in to be greeted by Brigadier Gubbins and the indomitable Urquhart. He had no idea they were even in the area.

'Ah, Newman,' said Gubbins. 'This is Colonel Grahame, he is commanding the Scots Guards.' A rather tall, bespectacled officer emerged from the shadow.

'Urquhart will bring you up to date,' continued Gubbins.'We'll join you shortly.'

'Trappes-Lomax was relieved of command on the spot,' murmured Urquhart, leading Newman outside.

'Can I be permitted to ask why?' queried Newman.

'He crossed the ice belt too soon,' replied Urquhart, clearly discomfited. There was nothing to be said, but plenty to ponder. 'Poor sod,' thought Newman. 'It's bloody bad luck, and in any case – what else could he have done?'

'How are you getting on up there Newman?' said Gubbins as he stepped out into the daylight.

'Not too bad Sir,' he responded, 'though they seem to be working around our flanks.'

'Let's come up and take a look,' said Gubbins.

They moved off. The brigadier, Urquhart, Grahame; it was all a bit top-heavy and largely unnecessary, in Newman's opinion; but it was an opinion he chose to share with no one.

The bare mountainside was swept by German machinegun fire, whilst enemy mortars probed for the defences. The Luftwaffe seemed to have been taking a break, but it was still not the easiest of journeys to the little rock outcrop which served as Newman's tactical headquarters.

It was as good a place as any from which to observe the battle's progress. Newman showed the brigadier what was happening. The

Germans could be seen deploying in considerable numbers off the icefield and into the mountains on either side.

It took very few moments for Gubbins to take in the scene and reach the only conclusion which made any sense.

'We had better get out of it and back to Storjord before the buggers cut us off. Scots Guards first, then you Newman,' ordered the brigadier.

'Right, Sir,' responded Newman.

Brigadier Gubbins had taken the same decision which had earned Trappes-Lomax dismissal and disgrace.

Like the green-clad riflemen in Spain 140 years before, it fell to Newman's independent company of sharpshooters to skirmish as rearguard, and cover the retreat of the British army to the sea.

The long trek back to Storjord was a nightmare. They had extricated themselves from the hillside only with the greatest of difficulties, and there had been casualties. The company was exhausted, and now shocked and dazed, as reaction set in from their first experience of battle.

They marched 'all night' until at about 0730 hours the next morning the men stumbled into a temporary holding position, perhaps midway to Storjord. Gubbins ordered they should hold the position until 1630 hours before withdrawing on to Storjord.

Not that it was much of a position, a stand of trees, and a bridge over a small river, there were a dozen such nondescript spots on the road to Storjord. The Scots Guards took the right of the line as befitted their seniority while Newman's company dug in on the left hand side of the road. The men, Scots guardsmen and territorials, dug fast and furious. They needed no bidding on that score: the Luftwaffe had proved excellent tutors in fieldcraft. Once the trenches were ready and the sentries posted, the remainder fell asleep; with the prospect of yet another long trek ahead they seized the chance to take what rest they could. Some engineers pottered about fixing the demolition charges to the bridge, and then scurried away.

There was no quick follow-up by the Germans and, as if by common consent, both sides drew breath and licked their wounds, before the next round.

The men made good use of the lull. They fed and rested in turn, did their stint on sentry and checked their weapons.

Newman strolled across a meadow towards the foremost positions occupied by the company. With him was Captain Horton an Indian army officer who had been seconded to the unit. Horton was deeply critical of what he regarded as the rigid and hidebound attitudes of the army.

'Here we are, Sir,' the young officer continued, 'fighting a campaign in 24 hours of daylight; and yet what do we do? We march "all night", dig in at "daybreak" and repeat the process the next night.'

Newman could see no defence to Horton's criticism, and neither had he any desire to defend 'officialdom'. But he did feel it necessary to ensure that the younger officers had confidence in the men who governed the campaign and thereby their destiny. It was a dilemma which confronted many field commanders in the war, and particularly in the early days when the army was still largely in the grips of the peacetime regular officer. War presents an opportunity for officers to rise above the rank of major, which is as high as most regulars can go in peacetime armies.

In an expanded army the mediocre are promoted early in a war. 'It's probably why the British army always seems to start so badly,' mused Newman. Now, how to answer these all too frank comments?

The enemy rescued Newman from his dilemma. The dreaded Henschel droned into view. This nimble biplane would never have survived had there been any decent fighter cover, but with clear skies it could bomb with impunity. The soldiers called it the 'flying bedstead', but all the same, they had a healthy respect for its accuracy and the tenacity with which its pilots pressed home their attacks in the face of vicious small-arms fire.

Horton and Newman raced for protection, in this instance, stacks of trimmed timber logs – probably pit props. They dived for cover in the gaps between the stacks. It was all right for Horton, he was slight of build, but Newman was broad in the beam – too broad for the gap, into which he was now fairly wedged. When the enemy had finished, Newman had to be rescued. There was no shortage of volunteers to pull the company commander, feet first from his predicament. Out he popped like a cork from a bottle. Newman, red cheeked, very much on his dignity, looked up to the smiling faces that surrounded him. Men were laughing for the first time in days. Newman laughed too, and for once he felt a sense of gratitude to that 'blasted Henschel'.

Four o'clock came, and right on cue, orders for the continued march to the sea. Independent Company was to be first away while on this occasion the Scots Guards had the honour of the rearguard.

The bridge across the road blew with an almighty roar and Newman lost another man. A young corporal was skewered to the ground by a large chunk of flying girder – he was 400 yards from the bridge.

*

It was time to leave. Newman's rear echelon withdrew safely, but there was to be no such luck for the rifle platoons. Those in the front line were pinned down by enemy fire. The Germans had infiltrated unseen across the river and were now in a position to infiltrate the defences.

The Independent Company was able to extricate itself but with difficulty. It was a short but messy action in which more men died. Morale dipped for it all seemed so pointless. They had manned their trenches during a quiet day, with only a single air attack during which time the Germans had been able to outflank their positions. At 'last light', a period which is registered on a tidy-minded staff officer's clock, the rearguard moved and men died. Why couldn't they have pulled back earlier in the day? Newman tried to avoid Horton's accusing stare as the young officer doubled past at the head of Jacko Williams's old platoon.

The Henschels were particularly active during the 'night' march along the road to Storjord, though there were few casualties, except to men's nerves. It was a dreary trek and they were desperately tired. Some officers and men were close to breaking point.

Newman moved on ahead to attend the brigadier's O Group at Storjord. Gubbins appeared as dapper and neat as ever in stark contrast to his travel-stained field commanders. The brigadier issued new orders and attempted to impart fresh hope and confidence amongst his subordinates.

The command was to make a stand at Pothus – absent-mindedly, Newman looked at his map – a nondescript hamlet ten miles south of Rognan. A platoon had been based there earlier, three days before, but it seemed a lifetime ago.

The position was to be defended by a new formation called 'Stockforce'. Under the command of Lieutenant Colonel Hugh Stockwell of No. 2 Independent Company, it included the remnants of the Irish Guards, now led by their boyish captain, Nos. 2 and 3 Independent Companies. A Norwegian machinegun unit and a couple of mortars provided support. The Norwegians were also to furnish ski patrols along the mountain flanks.

Gubbins, fussy as ever, went on to outline the other forces that were available. In reserve at Rognan was a regular battalion of Chasseurs Alpins. Newman's company was ordered to join the reserve. The Scots Guards were to withdraw to Bodo and thence by sea to Harstaad, for a complete rest and refit.

At last there was a serious plan. Gubbins outlined future operations for the brigade and this too gave them fresh hope and confidence.

'There is to be no more retreat,' Gubbins emphasized. 'I intend to defend the Saltfjord area indefinitely and this will be our lodgement as a guerrilla sanctuary.'

Newman listened intently. This after all was what they had been sent to Norway to do.

'There will be more Independent Companies,' continued Gubbins. 'Better trained and better equipped than those of the original force. They will relieve you and take the fight to the enemy, whilst you rest, re-form and then rejoin the fray.'

It was a bold plan, of that there could be no doubt. Newman along with the others could not help but be impressed with Gubbins's vision of special forces.

Very little at this stage was said about the Germans or their plans and intentions. The enemy of course was determined to rescue its beleaguered garrison in Narvik, and this 'guerrilla sanctuary' lay athwart their route.

A sanctuary had by definition to be located in an area which was totally inaccessible or unknown to an enemy. It made little sense for the army's expert to talk in terms of sanctuary in an area which the enemy had to dominate. A 'fortress concept' as a patrol base was to be a recurrent theme in the fortune of special forces operating behind the lines. It worked only on rare occasions or for short periods.

The meeting broke up and the commanders rejoined their units. Newman drove a little way down the road to meet his own boys as they marched up to Pothus. They had made good progress and many had a smile for their CO as they acknowledged his greeting, but there were some gaps in the ranks. He learned that poor old Shears, his batman, had dropped out exhausted a few miles back. Newman had given firm instructions that those who fell by the wayside were to be left, but he couldn't abandon his faithful manservant. He jumped into a battered utility truck and headed south.

Newman came upon Shears together with a couple of other would-be guerrillas. Exhausted and resigned to their fate, they lay in the snow and awaited the arrival of the enemy. Newman gave them the rough edge of his tongue and the trio stumbled sheepishly into the back of the truck. None too gently he threw what kit they had left on top and returned to Pothus. The Luftwaffe were increasingly active, and on more than one occasion the lone vehicle was singled out as a tempting target for a divebomber's machine gunners. Somehow they survived a number of such attacks, and Newman even collected a few extra waifs; there were seven of them crammed into the utility.

A lorry with some wounded Scots Guards came by, into which

Newman transferred the exhausted men. The lorry drove off, and Newman was convinced he would never see Shears again, at least not on this campaign.

Pothus bulged at the seams with British and Norwegian soldiers. Most of the civilians seemed to have disappeared. Newman caught up with his company, now billeted in some empty huts. The cooks were organized and a hot stew washed down with a steaming mug of army tea laced with rum did wonders for morale.

Newman found an empty spot and lay down on the bare boards. Six hours of undisturbed rest, even on bare boards, was bliss compared to the events of previous days. The next morning Newman woke to find Shears standing there, bright as ever, with a mug of tea in one hand and shaving gear in the other, as if nothing had happened.

---

[1] On the Henschel 123 this was achieved by carefully adjusting the propeller speed, unlike its successor – the bat-winged Stuka Ju87 which had a siren fairing mounted on the port wing.

CHAPTER SEVEN

The Battle of Posthus

Posthus is small, too small to figure on all but the largest scale maps. Before the war it numbered fewer than 200 inhabitants. It boasted two bridges and these provided the focal point for the defenders. The main road, if it can be called such, crossed the river by a bridge just to the south of the village, while a side dirt road crossed a smaller bridge over a tributary stream on the eastern side of the village.

The Irish Guards provided the main force of defenders, three companies were deployed forward and the fourth was held in reserve near to battalion headquarters: 'three up and one back' – it was all copybook tactics imbued into generations of officers at the Staff College and Sandhurst.

In front of the Guards was No. 2 Independent Company. In true skirmisher fashion they held the outposts south of the main line of defence, and on both sides of the river. Sandwiched between the Guards, and in the village itself were the local forces in support, the Norwegian machinegun and mortar companies. Finally the reserve forces, which included Newman, were dug into a stretch of woodland behind or to the north of Posthus.

The German attack when it came was as sudden as it was swift, though the tactics they deployed were broadly similar to previous engagements. Regular infantry, many of them cyclists, pressed home the frontal attack along the axis of the main road and held the defenders' attention. Meanwhile, élite Carinthian Alpine troops, the edelweiss emblazoned on their combat smocks, probed for a weakness in the mountain flanks.

The Luftwaffe gave excellent air support to the attacking forces, and they seemed to know where most people were. While the bulk of the aircraft concentrated on the main battle, a number singled out the wood for particular attention. Incendiaries rained down on the reserve positions and made life increasingly uncomfortable for the troops. The enemy quartered the wood in a methodical fashion, and it was soon obvious to Newman that they were in search of bigger game than his increasingly demoralized company. Towards the rear of the wood they found what they were seeking. A Norwegian army arms dump went up in a great ball of fire. The immediate area and the sky above became a sea of flames, while ammunition exploded in every direction. Fortunately there were very few troops near by and casualties were low, but Newman was forced to move some of his men out of the wood and into the edge of the village, where they set to digging new slit trenches.

The German attack persisted into the late afternoon and Newman was ordered to send troops to reinforce the main approaches to the Posthus bridge. He despatched the support section, which came under heavy enemy mortar fire as it deployed forward. More names were added to the toll of casualties.

There was a lull in the fighting and the troops were able to eat some sort of meal. In the previous days, Newman had eaten a strange assortment of food, mostly bully beef and biscuits scrounged off the Guards. Living off the land, the guerrillas' original intention, had proved none too easy in this part of Norway.

The Germans renewed the battle, and it appeared that their main thrust was directed onto a high spur on the right flank, above the forward positions of the Guards. The Carinthians thrust aside the weak Norwegian patrols and penetrated the defences. Stockwell summoned Newman to his headquarters and ordered him to take his company and counter-attack the breakthrough. Newman returned to his command post and called his platoon commanders for new orders. He had barely started to outline the mission when a runner delivered a note from Stockwell.

'Cancel previous order – move off to left flank immediately – climb high ground covering the Posthus River and stop the enemy crossing upstream.'

There was little that Newman could do, other than fix upon an order of march and be prepared to respond to whatever greeted them on the hills above the village.

The company crossed the river by way of a hastily constructed army rope footbridge and Newman in the lead, began the steep climb. They met the remnants of No. 2 Independent Company and

Irish Guards coming off the hills, who told of numerous enemy having crossed the river and seizing the high ground.

Newman briefed his officers and the company deployed to skirmish up the mountainside. A runner arrived from Stockwell. The note was terse: 'Get some covering fire up the mountain.'

It was a hard climb. The men struggled with the slope and the need to maintain their tactical formations; while at the same time they expected to be greeted by a hail of fire from an enemy entrenched along the crest. Men floundered up through the snow, sweating more from fear than physical effort. Those in the front braced to throw themselves forward in a forlorn attempt to beat the bullets.

Nothing. The crest was empty, and not a German to be seen. The slit trenches on the reverse and forward slopes showed all the evidence of hurried evacuation. Newman deployed his company and gave them a moment or two to catch their breath, though his attention had already been drawn to the familiar sight of Stockwell's runner labouring up the mountainside.

The order was as brief as its predecessor. Now Newman was required to descend and to patrol the river bank on the edge of the village for German patrols which had infiltrated the defences.

Men cursed and fumbled with their equipment and webbing. The more enterprizing looted the abandoned Irish Guards' trenches, and they made their way back down the mountainside.

Some wag hummed 'The Grand Old Duke of York', just loud enough for Newman to hear, but not identify the miscreant. It seemed a fair comment on their contribution to the first day of the battle of Posthus.

Newman set up his command post and positions, on the lower slopes covering the bridge, and then despatched patrols along the river and in both directions. There were no enemy patrols nor indeed any signs or evidence to suggest there had ever been. Newman's company now effectively occupied the outpost line and there was a river between them and the main defence positions. It was late evening, and despite all the alarms and excursions, the defences were still intact as the sounds of battle died away.

Early the next morning, 26 May, the Germans finally outflanked the defences. They forced a crossing of the river, well to the south of the village, by means of home-made rafts.

For the new few hours or so, Newman's company were largely spectators to the battle. Lumbering Heinkel bombers, emboldened by the lack of resistance, dropped their bombs low over the trenches, while their machine gunners shot up the Irish Guards.

Such arrogant immunity was not destined to last. Suddenly a new sound penetrated the established noise of battle and Newman spied the most welcome sight of the campaign to date. Over the parallel ridge of mountains came a Gloster Gladiator.

The little biplane dived unseen on a Heinkel in the valley below, and there was a long burst of fire from its four Vickers-K machine-guns; the same guns which three years later and mounted on SAS jeeps were to wreak such havoc on the Luftwaffe and its airfields in the western desert. So rapid was their fire that it sounded like the tearing of canvas, and the Heinkel stumbled in flight, its glass canopy a shambles. A wing dipped and the bomber buried itself into the mountainside. British cheers echoed through the valley. It was a sound their commanders had not heard before in this awful campaign.

The Gladiator responded to its audience with a victory roll, then tore terrier-like into another Heinkel. It was the most wonderful sight to see just one plane having such a glorious time against the bombers, which broke off their attack and fled the scene, harried by the Gladiator.[1] After the departure of the Luftwaffe, the heart seemed to have been knocked out of the Wehrmacht, for the ground attack first slowed and then stopped for the present.

It took them a few hours, but the Germans regrouped and then renewed their attack in even greater force. On this occasion they achieved a major breakthrough and seized the high ground which Newman's company had been ordered to vacate. From there the enemy overlooked the main bridge and thereby made the defences in the village untenable. Stockwell ordered his own No. 2 Independent Company into the attack to restore the situation. They were sadly outnumbered and outfought. It was a brave enough attempt to attack up the hill but the Germans had the situation well in hand, and the British soldiers fell back in good order before their casualties mounted. The situation was now deteriorating rapidly and this was radioed through to Gubbins who was at the main force headquarters at Rognan. He ordered Stockwell to withdraw.

Nothing seemed to matter any more. Earlier Gubbins had been informed by the headquarters of the expeditionary forces in Harstaad that the decision had been taken to abandon the campaign and evacuate Norway. All those brave plans for a firm stronghold in the mountains as a sanctuary from which to launch guerrilla attacks counted for nothing.

Ironically, French troops, élite Chasseurs Alpins and Foreign Legionaires, were on the point of capturing Narvik. Eduard Dietl, the redoubtable German commander had broken out of the Allied perimeter. With a nucleus of his forces he prepared to make a stand in the mountains and wait until relieved by the troops coming up from the south.

It was about this time that a second special force abandoned its attempt to become involved in the Norwegian campaign. A number of officers from the disbanded Fifth Battalion Scots Guards had not been posted, or returned to their parent units by the time the Germans invaded Norway.

The group persuaded the authorities to allow them to raid the Germans in southern Norway. Their plan was to sabotage the railway line between Bergen and Oslo. A submarine was to convey them across the North Sea and land them ashore. The plan was then for the raiders to make their way northwards to link up with Gubbins's forces.

Unfortunately, the submarine struck a mine off the Norwegian coast, it was probably one laid by the Royal Navy in the early part of the campaign. Badly damaged it limped home across the North Sea. Not to be thwarted by such a mishap, the raiders persuaded the navy to provide another submarine. By the time they were ready to sail the decision to abandon Norway had been taken.

The young officers, convinced that there was a need for raiders, and perhaps by way of compensation, were allowed to establish a training school in the Scottish Highlands. They were led in this enterprise by Lieutenant William Stirling, brother of David and later to command the Special Air Service regiment.

Norway had become a side-show, but then it had never been anything else. The Low Countries had fallen, the French army, or the only bit that mattered was shattered, and the British expeditionary force locked into Dunkirk and the Channel Ports. Panzers secured the Pas de Calais and their crews gazed across the Channel at England.

In the south, Mussolini was preparing for war and his African Legions threatened Egypt and the Suez Canal.

In circumstances like these the Norwegian campaign was irrelevant, and the arguments in favour of withdrawal overwhelming, provided the navy had sufficient ships to service two evacuations and prepare to counter a new threat in the Mediterranean; and also provided the Luftwaffe allowed them to escape.

The Battle of Posthus had no significance except to those men and their families whose lives had been shattered by the experience and the cost. It has been estimated that the battle cost the British army 40 dead and perhaps 100 wounded. The guerrilla formations played their part, but not in the role for which they had been intended.

[1] The Gladiator was one of just three which had been despatched from the carrier HMS *Glorious* to the newly completed landing strip at Bodo. One later crashed upon take-off, but the other two were to put up a remarkable performance.

CHAPTER EIGHT

The March to the Sea

For an army to withdraw is one of the most difficult of all military manoeuvres to execute. It is an acknowledgement that the enemy has the whip hand, and morale is low. Withdrawal also requires that the forces break contact with the enemy in an orderly and discreet fashion if only to ensure that the subsequent retreat does not degenerate into a rout. It is at moments like these that unit discipline and cohesion are placed under the greatest strains.

The withdrawal from Posthus went wrong from the first. Newman never even received the orders, and was still holding his isolated positions, while other units beat a hasty withdrawal up the road. Word was sent from headquarters, but it took an exhausted, frightened and confused runner three hours to find Newman's company. Barely coherent, the man gasped out his message: 'Complete withdrawal to Rognan. All bridges will be blown. Last troops will leave Rognan by 1930 hours.'

The runner added a postscript for Newman's benefit. 'We're going to be withdrawn completely, Sir. It's all over here in Norway.'

Newman checked his watch and looked at the map. It was already past two-thirty and Rognan was 17 miles by road. He guessed that Bodo would be the main port for the evacuation. It guarded the entrance to the Saltfjord and lay on its northern shore. About 20 miles inland, the fjord divides into two long fingers, Rognan sits at the head of the southern inlet. The road from Posthus would be of little help since the bridges were blown and they were marooned on the wrong side of the river. Not for the first time in the annals of the British army had a rearguard been left in such a predicament.

Survival lay in a forced march across country and over the mountains to reach Rognan by the deadline; the alternative was annihilation or humiliation at the hands of the enemy.

Newman gathered his officers and senior ranks, and quickly explained the situation. He intended to move in column across country on a direct compass bearing to Rognan. Those who fell by the wayside would be left to the enemy.

The company quickly assembled and marched off to a punishing pace set by Newman. Officers and sergeants bullied, cajoled and even beat the men to keep up with the column. Within an hour or so they caught up with the war. Loud explosions were punctuated by sounds of heavy firing. It would seem that the rearguards had blown the bridges, but were in turn pinned down by the rapidly advancing Germans.

Newman's map reading and compass work was unsurpassed in its accuracy. Their cross-country route took them into Rognan by way of the lowest bridge in the town. This proved to be a single-plank wire suspension footbridge which spanned where the river was a mere 100 yards wide. The structure swayed perilously as the column crossed, platoon by platoon into the relative safety of Rognan. Newman could be proud too of the fact that his command was complete, not a single man had dropped out. Much of their equipment however, especially the heavier and more cumbersome items, was abandoned en route, and the line of march was littered with large packs, sheepskin coats and sleeping-bags.

Many were to rue such folly in the days to come.

Rognan was a hive of frantic activity. Every kind and type of small craft imaginable had been gathered in the little harbour to get the troops away. Newman marched at the head of the column to the jetty. It was no distance along a couple of streets where the raised wooden sidewalks were piled high with stores and abandoned equipment. The civilians had long since been evacuated and sappers were busy preparing the few warehouses for demolition.

The evacuation proved orderly enough. A couple of drifters ferried the company down the fjord to the northern shore at Fauske, a little village which the war had yet to touch. The men spread themselves through a few houses and looked to sleep. Newman commandeered an abandoned car, for past experience had shown the need for wheels when keeping in touch with an equally mobile force headquarters and the elusive Gubbins.

The house Newman occupied with his headquarters was warm and comfortable, and the woman who lived there made the weary warriors welcome. She refused to abandon her home but instead rushed out with a large basket, soon to return with dozens of eggs, hams and lashings of milk. It was the most marvellous feast; and with a sizeable stretch of water between him and the Germans, Newman allowed himself the luxury of relaxing into a deep sleep.

Meanwhile, the withdrawal from Rognan was completed more or less according to plan, but there was nothing to spare. The last boatload embarked as the Germans entered the village. A sapper lit the fuse which was to blow up the jetty, and scampered on board as enemy small arms fire splattered into the woodwork. It was at that moment the boat's engine chose to die. The heavily laden craft drifted out into deeper water while its 'engineer', a young soldier with no experience of marine engines, received all the moral encouragement he could handle from his frantic colleagues. They were still perilously close to the jetty and within range of increasingly well-aimed small arms, when the engine fired. A few moments later, with a little distance now between them and the shore, the jetty blew in the face of the enemy. Though straddled by timbers and debris, the little party mercifully emerged unscathed from this final assault, and beat a hasty retreat out into the fjord.

Newman's confidence was shared by Gubbins and his staff, who were convinced that the line had been stabilized, thus buying time and breathing space. A little sanity had been restored. There was now a deep fjord between the opposing forces, the only jetty destroyed, and all the available boats safely in Allied hands. The Germans could only advance by way of a long detour through the mountains, which at this point, so Gubbins was reliably informed by his Norwegian advisers, were sufficiently high and rugged to delay even the impressive alpine units.

The Germans attacked Rognan the next day, straight off the line of march. They had found a precipitous path around the cliff face at the head of the fjord. With outstanding energy and determination, their battalions of mountain specialists, marched 'all night' and deployed for battle.

Howling Stukas woke Newman from his slumbers as the Luftwaffe launched an attack on the defenders' positions along the northern shore of the Saltfjord. Now they had the skies to themselves. For a couple of days the Gladiators had performed miracles in the air and marvels for British morale. One or other had been in combat almost continuously, and perhaps as many as half a dozen Heinkels had been shot down. However, Messerschmidt 110s, Germany's new long-range fighter called *Zerstörer* (destroyer) arrived in strength, to destroy one Gladiator and force the other to flee to Harstaad.

No village or settlement along the Saltfjord was to escape the attention of the Luftwaffe. First they dropped leaflets on Bodo, which read in both English and Norwegian: 'Thank you for building the landing ground. We will not bomb it, we will take it.'

In the event they destroyed the airstrip as they destroyed everything else. In a series of raids which were to last through to the end of the campaign, Bodo and other villages along the Saltfjord were simply razed to the ground. The wooden buildings did reduce casualties however and the smoke pall acted as a cloak to help cover the evacuation of the soldiers, British and Norwegian, as well as the civilians.

Orders arrived. Newman was instructed to move down the fjord to a settlement called Vagan. He consulted his maps and measured the distance, tracing out the winding track with a bootlace and setting the length against the scale. It was 40 miles to Vagan and there was no way that his company could march that far. Square-jawed and determined, Newman called his officers and senior ranks together and explained the situation. They were to form up the company and march for Vagan. He would drive on ahead in the car to the nearest Norwegian unit and arrange transport.

There were units in and around the village, but none had transport, certainly none to spare a discredited ally. In the face of such rebuffs, Newman drove hard down the stone track that clung to the side of the fjord to Bodo and the Norwegian army headquarters.

The reception he received there was equally reserved, even frigid; and this was hardly surprising. The Norwegians were staring calamity in the face. Their country had been turned into a battleground, they had failed to preserve their neutrality, had been invaded by one great power, and now were in the process of being abandoned by another.

But Newman could be a determined and cussed man too when the occasion demanded. He stood his ground in a stormy interview with a Norwegian staff colonel and refused to go 'through channels', and use the liaison officers. The colonel relented, and agreed to half of what was requested. Newman settled for what was on offer, hastily signed a few forms, and drove back along the track with one small bus, and a couple of equally dilapidated trucks in convoy, driven by sullen and miserable Norwegian conscripts.

They came upon the company just a few miles outside Fauske. There was not enough room for everyone, so they ran a shuttle back and forth along the track, leaving the fittest men till last, until the whole company was safely ensconced in Vagan.

The orders were to get as much rest as possible, since they were to be held in reserve for a couple of days at least. No one needed telling twice – and the company crammed into the few small houses scattered along the shoreline.

For once the system was as good as its word, and the men were left in peace; even the Luftwaffe ignored their sanctuary. Newman, though, was disturbed at about four o'clock the next morning and ordered to force headquarters. There the final evacuation of the Norwegian 'mainland' was explained in more detail. The remaining troops were to be evacuated over a four day period which was to get under way the following day. Newman's company was to be rearguard, holding a blocking position at Mojores (about five miles down the fjord from Vagan) until D3, when it was to march the last 20 miles into Bodo and away.

Newman reconnoitred the position at Mojores on his way back to Vagan. It was on top of a high bleak and very exposed mountain overlooking the road, quite one of the most awful places Newman had seen. The prospect looked appalling.

The company arrived later the next day, climbed the mountain and took up their designated positions. Amidst that barren rock, the best that could be accomplished was shallow shell scrapes, and there they endured what Newman later was to admit was the worst 48 hours of his war. In part this was their own doing. Their inexperience, and the fact that they had moved so rapidly and marched so far in the preceding weeks, meant that most had lost their kit. Greatcoats, groundsheets, blankets and sleeping-bags had long since been dumped in the confusion. Gone were the sheepskins and leather jerkins. Many had just their battledress, and the blouse, though made of rough serge, had no weatherproof qualities.

The elements formed an alliance with the enemy and set about them without mercy. The icy mountain top afforded no protection to the bitter wind and the sleet. Squalls hit them so hard that the rain was horizontal. Casualties mounted from exposure and frostbite.

Newman tried to get the odd half-hour's sleep by taking it in turn to creep into cracks in the rocks, with two men lying on top to keep him warm. After a short while, the most exposed could stand the cold no longer, and it was his turn to take a spell in the crack with Newman on top.

The time passed slowly. Below, the procession of retreating troops marched past on their way to Bodo. First their colleagues in Nos. 4 and 5 Independent Companies who were to form the D1 and D2 evacuations. Later in the afternoon, the Scots Guards passed beneath with measured step, not so bright and clean as Newman remembered from that other day they passed by – a lifetime ago in Berwick-on-Tweed – but disciplined, and still the Guards.

Newman's command were now the rearguard – the last troops in the line. The outposts were manned throughout another bitter arctic 'night' and the sentries relieved at frequent intervals. The men needed no reminding to be vigilant – they were only too well aware that nothing stood between them and the enemy but barren rock and scrub.

Finally the order was shouted up from the road below – time to start their withdrawal. Other than the occasional aircraft the Germans had not shown themselves throughout the period of the rearguard. Stiff-limbed men descended the slopes to the road that followed the fjord to Bodo and the sea. It was a long trek, but to Newman it didn't seem to matter. They had done so much going back that he felt strangely relieved, even glad to be finishing this degrading experience.

The fact that they were indeed part of a beaten army was forced home anew by the sight of Bodo. The picturesque little town where they landed just a couple of weeks ago was now a smouldering, flattened ruin.

The company moved through the perimeter defences, now already manned by the South Wales Borderers. This battalion was the final rearguard and their evacuation was timetabled for D4. The ever resourceful sergeant major did find one building still intact – it had once been the home of the local mayor, now long since departed. Shelter was all important and so under this one roof Newman crammed the entire company, or what was left of it, until it came time to leave. At midnight they were to report to the jetty where, according to the plans, a destroyer was to evacuate them.

Men lay everywhere, in the rooms, the hallways and up the stairs. They lay and they listened to the most glorious piano recital. An RAMC orderly sat at a grand piano and for hours played Beethoven, Chopin, Schumann, and Rachmaninov – it was quite the most amazing performance.

At fifteen minutes to midnight all was ready for the final dash to the jetty.

Newman led the men at a trot onto the ruined jetty just as HMS *Beagle* crept around the headland. The long, sleek destroyer, with its twin raked funnels and its guns manned, was a magnificent sight. Turning in barely her own length, she eased gently alongside the shattered timbers, her main deck level with the temporary planking of the jetty. Newman responded to a wave from the bridge and the men scrambled aboard even as the destroyer maintained her way.

In a few moments the operation was complete and they headed out to sea.[1]

Ship's cocoa laced with rum, hardtack biscuits and corned beef were a godsend, and English cigarettes proved an unexpected luxury until the destroyer ran full tilt into a storm. Seasickness laid Newman's guerrillas low, much to the mirth of the sailors, but at least the weather kept the Luftwaffe at bay. Ten hours later they were unloaded at Borkenes, a few miles north of Harstaad, capital of the Lofoten Islands. Here they stayed. The men rested in barns, thumbed rides into Harstaad and scrounged kit and clothing. Newman went in search of news and orders, but found neither, just rumours. Narvik had fallen, Bodo was evacuated, and things by all accounts were not going too well with the BEF in France.

There was one item of news to which Newman reacted with mixed emotions. Lieutenant Colonel Hugh Stockwell had taken over complete command of Scissors Force from Brigadier Gubbins. Perhaps he should not have been so precipitate in his dismissal earlier of the battalion commander of the Scots Guards.

It must be acknowledged that the troops had not performed well under Gubbins's command, and his ability to exert control and influence over his units appeared on occasions to be very weak. In defence of Collin Gubbins however, he had been sent to Norway as the Army's leading exponent in guerrilla warfare. The independent companies which had been raised to act 'independently' in guerrilla roles were totally misused and abused subsequently. Through no fault of his own, Gubbins and his teachings were totally ignored, and the companies deployed as conventional infantry simply because there were no other troops available.

Auchinleck was in command. He had arrived on 7 May with orders to secure and maintain a base in northern Norway. In this short time, this product of the Indian army had reached one conclusion, namely that the British army did not compare favourably with French or German troops.

The general visited Newman in his company headquarters at breakfast time. He stayed for a mug of tea and a few cheery words before moving on, but there were no orders or guidance, and no news.

The orders did come. The company was to embark on the destroyer HMS *Echo*. Rumour had it that they were headed for Tromso, a northern port on the mainland where the King of the Norwegians was supposed to have his headquarters. But it was only a rumour, for after just a couple of hours they were transferred in mid-ocean to the ill-fated *Lancastrian*, the 20,000-ton Cunard White Star liner which very recently had been pressed into service.

The troopship was already pretty full. The Irish Guards were on board and another independent company, odds and ends of all sorts of units, RAMC, gunners and even a mobile bath unit. And there was Hugh Stockwell, who simply greeted them with the words:

'We're going home.'

Life on board ship, though crowded, was comfort supreme. This luxury cruise liner still retained her full peacetime staff of stewards and waiters. The fare was pre-war too, rich in variety and plenty.

The ships steamed round and round in large circles gathering up a good sized convoy, before later in the day forming into columns and heading for home. The *Warspite* was there along with a clutch of cruisers.

The King of Norway and his staff were rumoured to be on HMS *Devonshire*, a county class cruiser, around which a separate bevy of destroyers danced attendance.

There were other rumours too, the German navy was at sea, the battlecruisers *Gneisenau* and *Scharnhorst* were feared in the area.

The navy wasn't smiling. They were under no illusions that these latest additions to the German fleet could outgun *Warspite*, whose admittedly larger calibre main batteries had last fired against capital ships at Jutland.

It was a fast voyage and they were lucky again. On the second day a solitary German plane discovered them, swooped low to make one pass over the crowded troopship before climbing fast towards land and assistance.

Fog saved them, but not HMS *Glorious*, sailing under destroyer escort to the north. Caught unawares, her aircraft lashed to the flight deck rather than providing cover, she was hit by the 11-inch batteries of *Scharnhorst* and *Gneisenau* and sank within an hour.

Warspite and her escorting destroyers went off to chase the enemy but the *Lancastrian* steamed on towards home. The Isle of Skye was sighted and after four days the ships docked at Gourrock, the same port from which they had sailed.

A train took Newman and his men to Hamilton, just outside Glasgow, where they were billeted in the town hall and fêted like heroes. Newman felt a fraud.

All five independent companies were back in Scotland. The other five which had been raised with the intention of relieving the first group as guerrillas in Norway were close by and in a state of near mutiny. They had been embarked on ships ready to proceed to Norway when 'the campaign was cancelled'.

The companies were marched ashore where they spent time in

desultory training and guarding so-called key points against the threat of German parachutists, fifth columnists or whatever romance stirred the imagination of the staff.

For all the men of the independent companies, 'seasoned veterans' and browned-off novices alike, the one thought (other than home leave) was, 'How soon can we get back to our own units?' Battalion commanders tracked down the unit, outranked Newman, and telephoned for the release of their men. One enterprising CO even sent a couple of trucks.

It was all to no avail. Dunkirk was over, Paris had fallen, and the future didn't look bright. There would be few enough battle-hardened units available in the months ahead. Newman had his orders; volunteers or not, no men were to be returned to their old units.

The reason was clear. The independent companies had been raised to fight in a guerrilla war; perhaps this would now be the case – at home.

---

[1] D4 proved lucky too. The South Wales Borderers got away without a scratch.

PART TWO

BIRTH OF A LEGEND

CHAPTER NINE

'Uniformed Raiders'

I look to the Joint Chiefs of Staff to propose measures for a vigorous enterprising and ceaseless offensive against the whole German occupied coastline.

Churchill's memorandum to Chiefs of Staff, June 1940

In less than six weeks of active campaigning, two British expeditionary forces had been summarily expelled from the European mainland. The armies had been outfought, outgunned and outgeneraled; their defeat on foreign shores was near total and overwhelming, short of annihilation.

The field army had left virtually all its equipment and stores in Norway, Flanders and France. Over 2,000 artillery pieces alone had been lost. The returning troops in most cases probably had their personal weapons, but everything else from light machineguns to heavy artillery and tanks had to be resupplied. This was a staggering task made yet more daunting by the fact that the munitions factories were still a long way short of achieving maximum production capacity.

The scale of such a defeat can be placed into a particular and very precise context. In the two years between the evacuation from France and the summer of 1942 only four *British* divisions fought the Germans and Italians in the Western Desert. These were the 1st, 2nd and 70th Infantry Divisions and the 7th Armoured. There were in addition independent brigades, army and corps troops together with British battalions and regiments in Indian army divisions.

Apart from these formations the fighting in North Africa, Greece, East Africa, Crete and in Syria was undertaken by Imperial troops; two Indian, three Australian, one New Zealand, two African and two South African Divisions.

Despite growing numbers as mobilization took effect, the home army suffered all the defects of hasty expansion. Much of the force was immobile and lacking in equipment, and its predicament was summed up by the acid pen of General Sir Alan Brooke when he wrote: 'We still have an amateur army with an average of three pre-war officers per infantry battalion.'

Across the short sea miles of the 'moat', the English Channel, a cocky and confident occupying army stood, with France humbled, the pleasures of occupation ahead, and, who knew, perhaps the ultimate accolade – the invasion of England.

In circumstances such as these, the British could only look to their own defences, such as they were, lick their wounds, and in the short time available, learn what lessons they could, so that earlier follies would not be repeated in the coming and desperate battle. Statements such as these doubtless would have been the officially approved solution from the directing staff at the Army Staff College in Camberley.

Everybody who had a mind free to exercise expected Britain to be invaded, and defeated.

William Shirer, the American CBS correspondent who witnessed the French surrender at Compiègne, reported home that General Weygand, the 73-year-old Allied Ground Commander in Chief, gloomily predicted that the British would be overwhelmed in three weeks. Other Americans made no secret of their fears. President Roosevelt acted upon the reports of his ambassador in London. Joseph Kennedy, no friend of Britain, was defeatist and frankly sceptical of the chance for victory. The President advised that American nationals resident in Britain should leave forthwith. The wealthy and privileged in British society paid premium prices for berths on transatlantic liners and shipped their families to sanctuary.

Bullion reserves from the Bank of England were despatched to Canada for safe-keeping, and contingency plans prepared to move the members of the Royal Family into exile.

Winston Churchill did not see the threat in such sanguine terms. Throughout those crisis-ridden summer months, the Prime Minister was to goad his military committees with the same vigour and gusto that he inspired the people. Whatever his faults and failures, it is to the everlasting credit of Churchill that he did not see the failure of the BEF in France, or indeed in Norway, in the same conventional light of the received military wisdom expounded by his generals.

Thus, on 4 June, the last day of Operation Dynamo, the evacuation from Dunkirk, Winston Churchill wrote to the chiefs of staff: 'It is easy for the Germans to invade us . . . why should it be . . . impossible for us to do anything of the same kind to them?'

Indeed the Prime Minister's remarks were out of date. The first raid had already occurred.

On Sunday 2 June, three officers from MI-R, the intelligence and raiding section of the War Office which had raised the independent companies, came ashore in France from a naval trawler. They landed south of Boulogne and made their way to Harfleur where they fired their intended objective, storage tanks containing some 200,000 tons of fuel oil. These intrepid raiders spent a week in France and eluded pursuit despite the hue and cry that their attack provoked. On 10 June they stole a small boat and rowed 13 miles out into the Channel to rendezvous with their trawler. Not only did they return home completely unscathed but they also brought back a lonely straggler from the BEF. By any measure this was arguably one of the most successful operations in the annals of small-scale raiding.

Even whilst these raiders were performing such heroic feats, Winston Churchill's imaginative if not fertile mind sought other means to take the fight to the enemy across the Channel. On Monday 3 June he had asked his military adviser whether it would be feasible to create raiding units from a contingent of the first Australian troops that were about to arrive in Britain. Churchill suggested that these troops should be reorganized into 'special detachments' each of 250 men: equipped with grenades, trench mortars, tommy guns, armoured vehicles and the like, capable of acting against an attack on this country, but also capable of landing on the friendly coasts now held by the enemy.

Other schemes were positively harebrained. Major General Hastings Ismay, chief of staff to the War Cabinet, had better things to occupy his time in such anxious days, than answering memos from his Prime Minister which proposed amongst other things that: 'enterprises must be prepared, with specially trained troops of the hunter class, who can develop a reign of terror down these coasts, first of all on the "Butcher and bolt" policy, but later on, perhaps as soon as we are organized, we should surprise Calais or Boulogne, kill and capture the Hun garrison and hold the place until all preparations to rescue it by siege or heavy storm have been made, and then away.'

On 6 June the chiefs of staff considered the Prime Minister's ideas and orders that plans were to be drawn up for the creation of a force of some 5,000 men divided into 'striking companies' and formed from volunteers.

Churchill's early enthusiasm for raiding operations, particularly in the summer of 1940 when such ideas flew in the face of conventional military wisdom, is beyond question. But perhaps there was another consideration that provided motive enough for these actions. It was the failure of Gallipoli in 1915 that had put such a blight on Churchill's political career. These memories, even when the national interest is taken into account, must have been a major consideration for so consummate a politician as Churchill. The Prime Minister might well have considered raiding as an answer to at least part of Britain's position; it is also clear that he had little confidence in the generation of senior generals then at the helm to conduct such operations. Indeed he had voiced his fears as early as 3 June in a minute sent to the chiefs of staff which began: 'The completely defensive habit of mind, which has ruined the French, must not be allowed to ruin our initiative.'

Although the Prime Minister was to bombard his military advisers and commanders with a barrage of ideas, sensible, mundane, bizarre and occasionally brilliant, there was one which dominated those early years. It was in Churchill's opinion essential: 'To get out of our minds the idea that the Channel ports and all the country between them and behind them are enemy territory.'

There were others too who pondered Britain's military predicament and how best to carry the fight to the enemy. Innovation and new ideas did still come from the army, that very service which had received the greatest drubbing of all in the war to date, and was still influenced to a marked degree by a hidebound and conservative-minded military bureaucracy.

The establishment apart, there were a number of influences at work which fostered the spirit of military enterprise. There were leading personalities, men like Sir Alan Brooke who had commanded the Second Corps in France with such deft skill, and who now was the newly appointed Commander-in-Chief, Home Forces. Brooke was directly and literally responsible for the army's defence of the realm. Although an 'establishment' figure, Brooke was ruthless, quick-witted, utterly dominant, and now embarked upon a wartime career which would take him to the pinnacles of military power and prestige, yet deny him the opportunity of exercising high command on the field of battle: that was to fall to the Americans, to General Eisenhower. In the course of the war perhaps one of Brooke's most important roles was in curbing and controlling the worst excesses of his Prime Minister. Brooke too was an innovator, and he too had no intention of leaving the initiative with the Germans. The need, he believed, was to attack, to hit hard and to hit often, to raid the enemy in his camp.

In this Brooke was supported to some degree by Sir John Dill, his superior officer. Field Marshal Sir John Dill was about to take up the appointment of Chief of the Imperial General Staff, having already been passed over once before for this coveted post. Dill belonged to that cadre of senior generals who were the most unfortunate in the war. It was their lot to carry the blame for the disasters, while not being responsible for the conditions, namely the peacetime years of mismanagement and neglect which caused them. Patient, courteous, painstakingly thorough, and eventually too cautious by half for Churchill (he was succeeded as CIGS by Brooke), Dill opposed premature operations which would waste resources better conserved for action later on. At this time, early June 1940, Dill was Vice-Chief of the Imperial General Staff, and in such a capacity responded to the memos which came from the Prime Minister. Dill floated the idea of a new mode of offensive operations amongst his personal staff and close advisers.

Another factor also exerted an influence over events at this time: inter-service rivalry. The army, at least in the eyes of the other two services, was discredited. As a result of military failure on the continent, Britain's strategic predicament now left the navy and the air force with the primary roles of defending the homeland. It could not have been lost on the senior generals that unless the War Office was very careful, the army could well end up with a back-seat role.

One officer in particular is credited with the gem of an idea which was to lead in a very short period of time to the emergence of the commandos.

Lieutenant Colonel Dudley Clarke, a career officer and Royal Engineer was at the very centre of things. He was on the Central Staff and had the key appointment as Military Assistant (MA) to Sir John Dill. A South African by birth, Clarke was a dedicated soldier who took a genuine interest in the history of his profession. He had been raised on the exploits of the Boer commandos, and as an impressionable young schoolboy had read of the experience of Denys Reitz, one of the most successful of their guerrilla leaders. Later his own military education at the Royal Military Academy Woolwich had concentrated on the Spanish Peninsular War, in which he had made a special study of the guerrilla campaigns. Subsequently in his military service Clarke served as a staff offficer in Palestine and was there in 1936 during the Arab Insurrection. What impressed him most about Palestine was the ability of small groups of ill-disciplined and poorly armed guerrillas to tie down two divisions' worth of British troops and colonial police.

Clarke responded to Dill's initiative by drawing on his own background and experience; one steeped in guerrilla warfare, historical and contemporary. In Spain and South Africa, there was a common theme. The main armies had lost out strategically but local forces retained the tactical initiative. The Boer had the horse, the Spaniard the mountains. Britain had the sea to give her raiders the mobility which would help to neutralize the strategic assets of the enemy.

Late on that Tuesday evening in June, when all the troops which could be lifted off the beaches about Dunkirk had been removed, Dudley Clarke sat in the quiet of his London flat and set his thoughts down on paper. The following day he discussed his ideas with Sir John Dill.

The office and secretariat of the Imperial General Staff was filled with some of the brightest officers in the army. It was a wise general who listened to the views and opinions of such subordinates.

It was the custom of Sir John Dill at the end of what were now crisis-ridden days to gather two or three such officers to his office, where over a whisky they would discuss affairs – even the most weighty matters – in a less formal atmosphere. Clarke was part of that group on Wednesday 5 June. The Prime Minister's memo on raiding forces was the topic of conversation. Dudley Clarke reached for his notes and quietly expounded his ideas.

The field marshal asked Clarke to submit a full paper the following morning which he could place before the chiefs of staff for discussion.

It is difficult to believe that Clarke's thesis found complete favour with the field marshal. As one of the army's senior serving officers, he was hardly about to preside over the creation of raiding bands of irregulars and guerrillas, albeit in uniform. Such formations would have been anathema to his training and experience. Nevertheless Clarke had an answer to Churchill's memo and the case was well argued. Even so, this cautious and conservative field marshal spelt out the constraints and limits to Clarke. No existing and formed military unit would be diverted to the raiding role, and there had to be the minimum of inroads into the precious cache of weapons.

The commando concept was a compromise between Clarke's brilliance and Dill's practical constraints.

In the War Office things moved surprisingly quickly. On the morning of Thursday 6 June, Field Marshal Dill presented Clarke's paper first to the chiefs of staff and then straight to the War Cabinet. By the early afternoon approval had been given and Dudley Clarke found himself posted out of the secretariat of the General Staff. He was to head a brand new section which was to organize 'uniformed raids'. It was called MO-9 and came under the secretariat of Military Operations.

The appointment was with immediate effect as was Clarke's promotion to a full colonel. So the military pyramid stirred and the personnel department (Officers' Postings) of the adjutant general's office sought a replacement Military Assistant to the Vice-Chief of the General Staff.

These were heady days, and Dudley Clarke in the CIGS secretariat was at the very centre of the national defence effort. His was an appointment much sought after, awarded only to the best and to the brightest. It was a brave decision for a career officer to leave such a 'plum posting' and join a new, untried and thus obscure undertaking.

All of this of course assumes that Clarke had any choice in the matter. Perhaps he was to pay the price, not for impetuosity or presumption, but rather for proposing a course of action which, privately, appalled his chief and the military establishment.

The 'military management' did not place all their eggs in Clarke's basket. The decision taken that same day to create the 'striking companies' was for a force completely separate from Clarke's, and completely within the orbit of military organization and structure. At least for the time being. The result was a degree of confusion, two formations with the express purpose of raiding the enemy, being created at the same time.

At the end of that frantic day, Clarke took leave of his chief. The field marshal left his subordinate in no doubt that both he and his scheme were very much on trial. 'The bottom line' was proof that the concept was viable. Dill instructed Clarke to launch a raid on the enemy within the shortest possible time, and with the greatest degree of success.

Clarke could have been under few illusions as he strolled through the summer evening back to the seclusion and privacy of his apartment. Was his career in shreds? He might now be a full colonel, with red tabs and hat of the General Staff, but in less than 24 hours he had moved from one of the most attractive career appointments for any regular officer, into at best an uncertain world.

CHAPTER TEN

New People – New Ideas

'It is easy for the Germans to invade us . . . why should it be impossible for us to do anything of the same kind to them?'

Churchill: Memorandum to Chiefs of Staff June 1940

On Thursday morning, 6 June, Dudley Clarke reported to his new boss at the War Office. This was Brigadier Otto Lund who was deputy director of Military Operations (MO). Lund arranged for Clarke's fledgling MO 9 to occupy three rooms next to his own suite at the War Office. Together the two discussed how Clarke could best achieve the results demanded of him by his erstwhile chief and stay within the constraints which had been laid down so rigidly during his final interview.

Clarke knew that the key consideration to guerrilla warfare is tactical mobility. For the Boers at the turn of the century, it was their shaggy ponies which could outpace regular cavalry thoroughbreds, and their intimate knowledge of the veldt which placed the British officers (who even in those days were notoriously poor map readers) at a crippling disadvantage.

In the summer of 1940, Britain was strategically on the defensive. The island was a refuge and a fortress, but it was also fast becoming a prison surrounded by a moat. So the immediate requirement for Clarke was a *guerrilla navy* to support his *guerrilla army*.

Brigadier Lund made an appointment for Clarke at the Admiralty. It was arranged for him to meet the assistant chief of the Naval Staff. In recent months the Royal Navy had paid a high price in men and ships for its rescue of the army's expeditionary forces. Clarke must have approached that interview with considerable trepidation and apprehension.

In the event he met with a surprising reception. Instead of being shown the door, the admiral fairly bounced out of his chair in enthusiasm.

'What!' he exclaimed in response to Clarke's request for ships. 'The army wants to get back to the fight already! That's the best news I've heard for days. For that you can have anything you like to ask from the navy.'

Clarke asked for a pirate. The admiral gave him Captain Garnon Williams RN. He was a retired regular naval officer recalled to service. Garnon Williams would be made available after he had completed his present assignment to block Zeebrugge.

It was to the War Office that Clarke returned to find the manpower for his raiders. Some have argued since that he should have stayed in the Admiralty for a seaborne raiding force which logically pointed to the Royal Marines. However, amphibious operations in 1940 were practically non-existent. True the navy had been responsible for the Inter-Service Training and Development Centre (ISTDC), which had been created years back to foster amphibious warfare skills. Starved of funds over the years, regarded as a 'backwater' by all services and to be avoided like the plague by career-minded officers, all it had managed to produce was a couple of indifferent landing craft.

The Royal Marines did have a landing force. This was called the Mobile Naval Base Defence Organisation and was primarily concerned with the *defence* of harbour installations.

There were also four battalions of Royal Marine light infantry which were technically available. These had not been committed to battle in either the Norwegian or Low Countries campaigns. Instead they had spent the war to date training and compensating for the interwar years of neglect, held in readiness – should the Germans invade the Irish Republic! In any case, as a formed body of troops which appeared in the battle order, they were severely off-limits to Clarke – even if Dill could have influenced the Senior Service to allow one of his number to poach them.

Clarke travelled to Scotland to find his volunteers. On Friday 7 June he caught the train northwards to seek out the independent companies. They were the only formed body available because they were *ad hoc* formations, and not on the army order of battle. At the time, five languished in Scotland in a semi-mutinous state awaiting redeployment, disbandment or whatever. The other five had already been transferred to the Scilly Isles and Cornwall in case the Germans continued on from the Channel Islands.

Clarke toured the independent companies which he found stationed in and around Glasgow where they spent their days on tedious guard duties. The men watched vulnerable points such as power stations, bridges and the gas works against the threat of German parachutists, saboteurs and the fifth column. It was not lost on Clarke that his first recruits were guarding the sort of targets which he intended they should train to destroy.

On the day the Germans and the beaten, deserted Norwegians signed an armistice in Oslo, Clarke recruited the first officers to his new formations. They were both men who subsequently were to build formidable reputations raiding Norway. One was Major Rice, a Royal Suffolk, who had served with Clarke in the Transjordan Frontier Force a decade before. The other was Ronnie Tod, a major in the Argylls, who was destined to become one of the commando legends.

Clarke instructed them each to raise a hundred volunteers from the independent companies and then to travel south without delay. Tod was given overall command of the new force which for the present was called No. 11 Independent Company. The unit was to train for a raid on the coast of France.

On Monday 10 June Clarke was back in his office in London. Sir John Dill had been appointed to succeed Ironside as chief of the Imperial General Staff. He had taken Clarke's successor with him as his personal staff officer or military assistant, but it was too late for regrets. Italy had also declared war on Britain and France, although that was hardly worth a second thought.

Garnon Williams was in post and brimming with ideas. They agreed that the new force should be based on the Hamble River, and it was there that Garnon Williams set about the formidable task of gathering together suitable small craft for the raiders. Once again the paucity of pre-war policies came home to roost, for there were no craft suitable.

The best the navy could find were RAF crash boats. These were fast motor-boats intended to rescue air crew downed at sea, and there were a few spare at the time, on condition the navy provided the crew.

These were noisy boats, lightly armoured with meagre troop-carrying capacity and even less in the way of defensive armament – a couple of machineguns at most. With the high freeboard and frail hulls, the last thing they were intended for was stealth. Nothing less suited to raiding operations could be imagined, but then Dudley

Clarke and his embryonic and still untried organization were very low on the national order of priority.

Undaunted by such difficulties, Garnon Williams threw all his energies and enthusiasm behind the enterprise. By 15 June he had gathered by means fair and foul 20 officers and 200 ratings to provide Clarke's guerrillas with their seaborne mobility. He had established his headquarters in the Admiralty yacht *Melisande* around which huddled the flotilla. Besides the RAF craft he also acquired a gaggle of small vessels, mostly private steam yachts used at Dunkirk and still awaiting collection 'by their rightful owners'.

Meanwhile, Section MO9 was beginning to take shape and to function. Doubtless it benefited from Lund's close tutelage but Clarke found in those early days that all three services were more than anxious to help.

Staff were recruited to the cause. Otto Lund had lifted a Royal Engineers captain called Thompson out of the Norwegian section of the War Office, they were pretty spare with time on their hands now their 'patch' had succumbed. Thompson became the staff captain and administered the section.

Other appointments were rather more bizarre. Within a week or so, Section MO9 functioned around a triumvirate of females who joined as 'unestablished (and presumably unpaid?) volunteers'. Their appointed leader was Constanta, daughter of the one time British ambassador to Berlin, Sir Horace Rumbold. It was her responsibility to ensure absolute secrecy and strict confidentiality, never an easy task amongst the military, and never more vital than in the case of raiding operations.

Constanta was a well-known London socialite, and she used this to good effect to create a most elaborate cover. The capital, full of refugees from a dozen nations and more, was gripped by the spy scare and the threat of German parachutists masquerading as nuns. Constanta was also a charity worker, and frequently photographed in the society pages in conjunction with one good cause or another.

Charity was used as the cover for section MO9 activities. Officers attended conferences on projected raids, dressed in civilian clothes, at Sir Horace's residence in Grosvenor Crescent, where they would be welcomed by the butler as members of a charity committee. It may not have been very efficient, since it is quite easy to spot an army officer even in his civilian clothes. It was overly dramatic, but it fitted the conspiratorial mood of the time.

'Buster' Harding, a distant relative of the brigadier's, was a formidable but kindly lady who dispensed tea and sympathy in the organization. It was her task to collect for safe keeping all the men's personal effects, such as letters from home etc., before they embarked on a raid. Last minute messages home were also entrusted to her care. Invariably, too, Buster was there on the quayside to greet them on their return, dispensing hot tea and quietly returning those letters which were now a source of embarrassment.

Finally there was Joan Bright, who came into MO9 from the murky world of Intelligence. She ran the clerical side with super efficiency and was clearly under-employed. Late in the war Joan Bright joined the Prime Minister's personal staff, and remained with him throughout. These three ladies, together with their secretaries, typists and drivers, were to be the first all-female staff to be seen at the War Office.

There were others too who joined in those early days. A jolly, rotund captain called Hailsham shared an office with a liaison officer from the Rifle Brigade. His name was David Niven.

In pre-war days, Niven had been a gentleman cadet at the Royal Military College Sandhurst and commissioned into the Highland Light Infantry. When he changed such an august regiment for Hollywood and stardom, it was more than the establishment could stomach. Neither did his infectious humour and wickedly brilliant talent in practical jokes do much to heal the rifts in Whitehall.

According to David Niven, volunteers usually fell into two groups. There were the generally courageous, itching to get at the throat of the enemy, and there were the rest, who would volunteer for anything in order to escape from the boredom of what they were doing at the time.

The boredom of garrison duty with the 2nd Battalion The Rifle Brigade at Tidworth (his old regiment would not have him back) was too much for Niven. On the War Office grape vine he heard about Dudley Clarke and the intention to raise a secret new 'élite force'. The value of appointing someone with Niven's 'glamour' to the new force was not lost on Dudley Clarke, and so Niven found himself acting as a liaison officer between MO9 and the new raiding forces.

It was David Niven who would introduce a man who was destined to become one of the great legends in the commando world. His new uncle by marriage was Robert Laycock, then a languishing captain in the Royal Horse Guards who had just received a posting to India. He was to join the staff of an Indian army infantry division as gas officer.

Niven took his uncle to meet Dudley Clarke, and Laycock quickly found himself promoted to Lieutenant Colonel and ear-marked to raise and form one of the new commandos.

Dudley Clarke, meanwhile, was to enjoy the unfettered control of his empire and the patronage of Brigadier Lund for just another week.

Churchill in his capacity as Prime Minister, Wartime Minister of Defence and political leader of a coalition government of national unity, had concentrated enormous power in his office. He could, and all too frequently did, intervene directly in the military conduct of the war, whether it was the appointment or dismissal of a senior officer, a new policy or ground strategy.

On Wednesday 12 June, Churchill decided to take a new initiative on raiding. The days of passive resistance were over and active defence was now to be the cry. A very senior officer was to be chosen to take charge of all raiding operations and to lead a combined staff from all the services. This intervention and new direction was the origin of a series of developments which led directly, through raiding, to combined operations and amphibious attacks like Dieppe, and to the seaborne invasion of Normandy which, four years later almost to the day, was to mark the beginning of Hitler's downfall.

Captain Garnon Williams broke the startling news to Clarke that the Prime Minister was about to appoint a senior officer to assume command.

CHAPTER ELEVEN

What's in a Name?

'If guerrilla warfare is co-ordinated and also related to main operations it should, in favourable circumstances, cause such a diversion of enemy strength as eventually to present decisive opportunities to the main forces.'

MI(R) War Office 1939

The Prime Minister at this time envisaged two types of raiding operations. There were to be the more conventional or regular 'type' of operations on the model of Zeebrugge twenty years and more before – large scale attacks from the sea which involved regular formations of troops, albeit specially trained in the particular skills of amphibious warfare. These were to be spearheaded by the 'striking companies'.

The second was the unconventional or irregular style of raid on a very much smaller scale along the lines which had been proposed by Dudley Clarke.

So even in these early days, there was a major distinction drawn between combined operations by specially trained but conventionally organized formations (whose intention was to stay ashore, advertise their presence, and even hold ground, if only for a short time), and the hit-and-run raids by Clarke's commandos. But this strategy had one major flaw. The logic was that once conventional forces had received amphibious training they could undertake the small scale raids as well. Clarke's commandos were unnecessary. They need never have come into existence, and this argument was not lost on a number of senior officers at the time.

Another problem was that originally the Prime Minister saw the raiding policy occurring within a particular context. True the Germans had captured the Channel ports, but, in a number of his minutes and memos to the chiefs of staff, the assumption was that the French would continue to resist. On the day that Dudley Clarke was appointed to MO9 Churchill had minuted the following to General Ismay:

> Tanks and Armoured Fighting Vehicles must be made in flat-bottomed boats, out of which they can crawl ashore, do a deep raid inland, cutting a vital communication, and then back, leaving a trail of German corpses behind them. It is probable that when the best troops go on to the attack of Paris only the ordinary German troops of the line will be left. The lives of these must be made an intense torment.

A week later Churchill was planning a new structure and organization, and 24 hours afterwards Paris was declared an open city. There is no evidence to suggest that the drastic change in the strategic picture exerted any real influence over the new policy directives.

Although the Prime Minister saw offensive action as two distinct operations, he believed they could be more effectively handled if they were placed under a single command.

The first choice for the post of commander Offensive Operations was Major General J. F. Evetts, at the time in command on the North-West Frontier of India where he was pacifying the Pathans. Evetts was 48 years of age, and his military career had included a number of tours of duty as a staff liaison officer with both the navy and the RAF. Evetts had energy, drive and, for the general officer rank of the day, comparative youth on his side; but the North-West Frontier was a very long way away, and with Italy in the war and France collapsing they could not afford to wait for him to return.

Lieutenant General Sir Allan Bourne, an aesthetic, thin and rather scholarly officer, was the second choice. At the time he was Adjutant General of the Royal Marines, and but for the outbreak of war would probably have been looking forward to his retirement, having reached the top of his profession.

Bourne's appointment changed the whole nature of raiding, even before it had begun. He had been appointed commander of Raiding Operations and advisor to the chief of staff on combined operations. Hitherto, the three services had looked upon Dudley Clarke's initiative with a sort of paternal indulgence. It was offensively minded which pleased the Prime Minister, sufficiently small scale and staffed by amateurs so as to be no threat to their own establishments.

The appointment of a 'three star' general lifted raiding into a brand new level which required conferences rather than discussions, and positional papers to be prepared rather than informal minutes circulated later.

Bourne too had unfettered access to the chiefs through his appointment as adviser on combined operations, and thus to the very core of the military decision-making body. The strange feature too was that Bourne remained Adjutant General Royal Marines, which gave him a prestigious and established position from which to address the needs of his new appointment.

As commander of Raiding Operations, Bourne's remit covered Norway, Holland, Belgium and France. In this role too he was answerable directly to the chiefs of staff. The troops at his disposal were the Royal Marine Light Infantry Brigade (which had just about completed its training) the new striking companies which were likely to number some 5,000 men, and the residual elements of the independent companies.

To have such forces dedicated to raiding at a time when the nation stood in mortal peril and under imminent threat of invasion, struck many officers as the height of folly.

Not since the American War of Independence had Britain faced so dangerous a strategic situation, so isolated and so ill-prepared. After Dunkirk, there were only 15 formed divisions available for home defence, including one armoured and one Canadian division; but much of the force was immobile and lacking in equipment.

A minor, but pressing problem at the time was what on earth to call the raiding forces. From the first Dudley Clarke had called his raiders 'commandos'. Nobody had questioned this and so the name stuck. Then the bureaucrats intervened and suggested that 'commandos', having been used by the enemy, was a term which was entirely inappropriate for British forces. For a little while such arguments held sway, and the new formations were referred to as special service troops, and this with a naive disregard for Hitler's own Schutzstaffel (SS). It would be some weeks before Sir John Dill, as chief of the Imperial General Staff, intervened to give the word 'commando' his blessing.

For his part, the Prime Minister had no intention of treading softly where national sensitivities were involved. He was firmly wedded to the conviction that there were a number of aspects of the German army which were well worth closer examination and even emulation.

On 18 June, celebrated as Waterloo Day at home, and with the French government under Pétain formally requesting armistice terms from Germany and Italy, Churchill sent a memorandum to Ismay in which he commended the German 'storm troopers'.

The Prime Minister proposed that his generals could do far worse than to copy the foe, and called for the creation of a force of 20,000 storm troopers. Churchill called these new élite troops 'Leopards', which would be 'drawn from existing units, ready to spring at the throat of any landings or descents'.

General Paget, one of the very few senior officers to acquit himself with any distinction in Norway, and now chief of staff Home Forces, vehemently opposed the idea of British storm troopers. In their place he proposed the creation of special 'tank-hunting platoons', the retention of the independent companies and 'special irregular units'. The latter Paget suggested could be created from the large numbers of young Americans who had arrived in Britain to volunteer for military service.

Precisely what the Prime Minister was seeking to achieve at this time is difficult to ascertain and more than one observer of the period cast doubt on his motives.

'Winston is goading the C in C Home Forces (Ironside) who seems to lack imagination and is busy forming special anti-tank units of mobile forces.' So stated John Colville[1] in his diary on 20 June.

Perhaps this was a harsh judgement. Churchill was not a cool and patient strategist, but a man of powerful emotions. If a serious invasion of western Europe might be impossible for years, then at least there could be raids and landings of the kind familiar for centuries. These in turn could only be launched by an efficiently organized and relevant army. Churchill earnestly desired to remedy the obvious flaws in the army. Just a few days previously he had addressed a long memorandum on the subject to Anthony Eden, Secretary of State for War.

'There is a great opportunity now for picking leaders; not only amongst those who have had the opportunity of meeting the enemy, but also those who have prepared themselves so to do.'

Churchill was looking for men of 'force and intelligence and personality', who in times of peace would have risen quickly to the top of their chosen professions. It was men such as these that the Prime Minister advocated should be promoted rapidly in the new army and men such as these who should be encouraged to volunteer into the 'special forces'.

'We want live wires not conventional types,' concluded Churchill. 'Men in their twenties with the right qualities should be promoted to the command of the new battalions.'

The spate of proposals for the creation of special élite units of volunteers was now meeting an even more concerted voice of opposition from the army leadership. They feared it would be only natural that the most adventurous among the young soldiers would volunteer, and that the best would be accepted, leaving the residue of indifferent quality to soldier in line battalions.

Others expressed the view that all troops could and should be trained for raiding, and some went further to raise their own specialists.

General Allan Brooke, although offensively minded, never approved of the special forces policy from the very outset. He considered it was a dangerous drain on the quality of an infantry battalion, and that it deprived conventional divisions of the challenge of maintaining and training their own raiding forces.

Churchill, however, was adamant. Considerations of personality apart, in constitutional terms Parliament, by default, had allowed the Prime Minister to assume almost dictatorial powers. The objections of the generals were brushed aside, and before the month was out nine special Leopard groups had been established and six more were in the course of formation. These were in addition to the 'striking companies', who were to number 5,000 men in total and the residual independent companies. Only the latter two organisations fell under the remit of General Bourne, who could also lay claim to the Royal Marine battalions.

High politics apart, General Bourne sought to come to terms with his new role. Initially at least it was not looked upon with favour by either Colonel Dudley Clarke or Captain Garnon Williams RN. Whilst it was heartening to see his appointment as evidence of the importance placed by the government on raiding policy, there was little else to recommend it in their view. The very weight of the new organization for combined operations threatened to swamp them, at a time when raiding forces themselves still numbered no more than 200 men and a few redundant RAF crash boats and yachts.

Clarke undoubtedly would have preferred the first few raids to have been quiet affairs, while they ironed out their mistakes and earned the sympathies of the Admiralty and War Office as well-meaning amateurs.

To his credit, General Bourne did much to defuse what could have been a difficult relationship. In his first meeting with Clarke, this quietly spoken and sympathetic officer showed every understanding of Clarke's views. He had no intention of interfering in the raid planned for No. 11 Independent Company. Bourne emphasized that he believed his most valuable contribution would be to secure from the three services the best possible facilities. In addition he would concentrate on his other role as adviser on combined operations, and by these means help promote the commando concept.

As adviser to the chiefs of staff, General Bourne took two establishments under command. The first was the Combined Operations Training Development Centre, where special ships and landing craft were being prepared, converted and evaluated. The second was the Irregular Warfare School, started in May 1940 by MI(R) at Inverailort. To these he added a number of small boat bases around the coast and run by his naval staff. The first were at Warsash, Brightlingsea and Falmouth.

A former holiday camp on Hayling Island, once popular with London's 'lower middle class', was taken over to train sailors who were going to man the boats for combined operations. It took some months to persuade sailors deliberately to run their boats aground. Bourne had the camp commissioned as HMS *Northney*. Unfortunately it had only ever been a small and rather primitive holiday camp, and could only provide 18 lavatories. Until this problem could be remedied, Captain Garnon Williams's side of the operation and the expansion of the naval arm was constrained by the number of toilets on Hayling Island.

Bourne set off to tour these new establishments and to decide on a permanent home for his combined operations staff; with the exception of a small liaison team at the Admiralty in London, he wanted to establish his main base near the sea.

Dudley Clarke hurried over to the Isle of Wight where Ronnie Tod had settled No. 11 Independent Company into the first *de facto* commandos. The date for the first raid was fast approaching.

---

[1] Seconded from the Foreign Office to 10 Downing Street as one of Churchill's 'bright young men'.

CHAPTER TWELVE

'To Set the Coast Ablaze?'

Oliver Cromwell's system of major generals had lingered into the twentieth century, albeit in a modified form. Various military reforms and enactments had seen the United Kingdom divided into large geographical commands (Western Command with its headquarters at Chester, Northern Command with its headquarters at York, Southern Command at Aldershot etc.) under lieutenant generals.

A signal was despatched to all these military commands on 20 June, instructing them to collect the names of those officers who possessed certain qualifications and were prepared to volunteer for 'special service' of an undefined 'hazardous nature'.

Officer volunteers had to be fully trained soldiers with the following qualities – a high standard of physical fitness, ability to swim and immunity from sea and air sickness.

A commando or 'striking company' comprised 500 officers and men with a small command element, and there were to be ten such units spread throughout the military commands.

The system of selecting the volunteers worked very simply. A few officers under the age of 40 were to be nominated by the commanding generals as likely commando leaders. From these, the final selections were to be made after candidates had been interviewed by Bourne, Dudley Clarke and their team at the War Office. Once chosen, the commando leader, now given the temporary or acting rank of lieutenant colonel, was to return to his own command headquarters to select ten troop leaders from the list of officer volunteers.

From the outset it was intended to be a commando principle that an officer would personally select the men he was to lead into battle. Thus the troop leader would first select two junior officers to act as section commanders. Together the three officers would then choose the 47 non-commissioned officers and other ranks which comprised a troop. The soldier volunteers were to be weeded out from those who displayed the same physical fitness and immunity from sickness, but also were men chosen for their intelligence and self reliance which would fit them to carry out on their own initiative any kind of unusual and dangerous task.

The final step was the assembly of the commando with its ten troops at its new base, a seaside town within the boundaries of the military command. Scotland, Northern Ireland and Wales were to have their own commandos selected from their locally recruited territorial army divisions.

Having set the wheels in motion for the creation of the striking force, Dudley Clarke devoted his full attention to the first raid on Axis Europe to be undertaken by the commandos.

Within the short period available, Tod had worked his men hard. Physical fitness and stamina had been relatively easy although far from painless. The real problems had arisen over tactics, and therefore training and equipment. In 1940, the British army had lost the art of amphibious warfare, and Tod was about to pay the price for the years of neglect. Everything had been a matter of feeling in the dark, educated guesswork and improvization. Everybody knew that flat-bottomed landing craft were needed, but if there were none in existence, then one could only improvize with small rowing boats and rubber dinghies, in order to get the men ashore from the crash boats.

On Saturday 22 June France surrendered. The ultimate humiliation was enacted in the identical railway carriage (brought from a Paris museum for this purpose), and on the identical spot in the Forest of Compiègne, where the Allied representatives had met the German plenipotentiaries to hand them the armistice terms in November 1918. At 2.45 pm that Saturday afternoon, Hitler entered the railway carriage and occupied Marshal Foch's chair.

Less than 24 hours later, Lieutenant Colonel Ronnie Tod with 19 officers and 96 other ranks set out for the first raid on the coast of France. Operation Collar, as it was called, was under way.

The raiding force was carried in one 18-knot steam yacht called the *Jamarna* and seven RAF crash tenders. Six of the crash boats had naval crews and the seventh, for some strange reason although commanded by an RNVR Sub Lieutenant, had a civilian crew. To overcome the noise problem, it was arranged for RAF bombers to buzz the coast of France and thus drown the noise of the approach. Presumably it was not considered that such a tactic would arouse the enemy, who in turn might take time off from anti-aircraft duties to look out to sea.

The force sailed from Ramsgate, Dover and Folkestone in the hope that their departure in such penny packets would not arouse suspicion as to their true intentions, and then rendezvoused in mid Channel. They were due to land on the coast at midnight.

The intention was to hit the beaches at four different points along a 20-mile stretch of coast above Boulogne. The beaches identified as the targets for the raiders had all been thoroughly checked. Commander Milner-Gibson had crossed over to France on nine occasions and conducted a solo reconnaissance of the likely landing sites. The raiders were to move inland, seek out 'intelligence' in the form of prisoners, do what damage they could and re-embark at 0130, before rendezvousing once again mid-channel for the voyage home. Tod distributed among his raiders 20 Thompson submachine-guns. This was a heavy and cumbersome weapon, but it did fire a 45-calibre slug at the rate of 1500 rounds a minute with sufficient force and punch to tear off an arm rather than cause a flesh wound. Up to 40 metres it was lethal, thereafter the slugs could go anywhere.

The Thompson or tommy gun had been immortalized by Al Capone and the Chicago racketeers of the Prohibition Years. Its use by Tod's raiders was entirely in keeping with their image of themselves. The fact that more were not deployed was down to availability. Tod's allocation represented precisely 50 per cent of the entire national stockpile at the time.

Commander Milner-Gibson sailed with the raiding party to act as master navigator and to lead the main party which Tod commanded to its landing beach. This was the night that Milner-Gibson's compass proved to be faulty, and instead he navigated them close to the main harbour entrance at Boulogne before he realised his mistake. This put them even further behind schedule, and they were already running late; for the RAF, instead of escorting the flotilla, had buzzed the ships in mid-Channel, and proved to be a thorough menace until identification was verified. Delays and mistakes resulted in less time being available for the raids ashore.

Of the four landings, only one group could lay claim to any success, and even that was qualified. The party were put ashore some 500 yards south of Plage de Merlimont, near to Le Touquet. A little way inland, they came upon a heavily wired and fortified house standing in its own grounds. There were some German staff cars parked outside and the sound of voices could be heard from the well-lit windows on the ground floor.

The patrol commander sent a couple of men up to make a reconnaissance of the area while he studied the house. The scouts reported that there were two sentries down at the entrance to the driveway, but no-one else outside the building. The amount of noise from within however suggested there might be more enemy than the 18 raiders could handle.

Plans were made, orders given and the group moved out to the attack.

The young officer in charge deployed four men behind a low wall to provide covering fire should the need arise. Another four were sent to deal with the sentries. In their enthusiasm they forgot all about the instructions for prisoners, and the enemy were rather messily but very effectively dispatched into their Führer's 'Valhalla'.

The main party launched into their attack on the house. The intention was to cause as much mayhem and damage as possible and then beat a hasty retreat. Grenades were hurled in through the windows, and the building laced with tommy gunfire, the transport in the yard was shot up, and, at the lieutenant's signal, the party fell back.

The raiders had suffered no casualties and gleefully set off for the beach and their boat. Screams and cries of pain echoed in their ears from the shattered building and they were well pleased with their night's work. The two dead sentries were collected and the officer had his men carry them to the beach; they did not have any prisoners, but perhaps the 'intelligence people' at home might learn something useful from the bodies.

The only problem was that the crash boat was very crowded and the bodies were particularly messy. The lieutenant agreed that the bodies could be towed on a rope. At some stage during the night the bodies disappeared, and nobody, in their anxiety to get away from the beach, had thought to search the dead beforehand for papers or documents.

It later transpired, via Free French sources, that the building they attacked and destroyed was not a Wehrmacht headquarters. It was a dance hall, and the grenades fell among French people who were attending a party with their new conquerors. The first raid did result in casualties being inflicted on the enemy; soldiers and collaborators paid the same price.

Lieutenant Colonel Tod landed with the main party that night. The two boats which carried this group became separated and the raiders were dispersed. Nobody was quite sure where they were.

Colonel Dudley Clarke was with Tod. He had come along for the ride but was under strict instructions not to go ashore.

Tod was convinced that he had landed just south of Hardelot, and, while Clarke remained behind to guard the boat, set off inland with his party. He was back within the hour having had neither sight nor sound of the enemy. While his men, with true textbook tactics, took up a defensive perimeter around the beach, Tod and Clarke discussed what they should do next.

Precautions not withstanding, the raiders were surprised by a German patrol which suddenly appeared along the path running parallel to the beach. The Germans recovered first, went to ground and promptly opened fire. The raiders returned the fire but with no great effect. Tod had one of the tommy guns but the magazine fell off.

There was little the raiders could do other than get away to sea as quickly as possible. With considerable skill and composure, Tod disengaged and withdrew his small force under still quite effective enemy fire. Their boat was struck repeatedly by small arms, and the group suffered the only British casualty of the operation. Colonel Dudley Clarke lost an ear lobe to an enemy ricochet. With the rising tide, the last group off the shore were forced to wade shoulder deep to the boat. Tod was in this party, and it did little to improve his temper since he was rather short.

The second boat in Tod's party had a very boring time. The troops had disembarked further to the south, wandered around inland, and, having encountered neither the enemy, nor the French, returned to their boat and made for the rendezvous.

The other two main landings experienced a similar fate. The RAF had buzzed the coast with the predictable result that there was plenty of enemy activity – search lights scorched the heavens and then swung their beams to probe out to sea. Very lights and signal flares shot skywards at irregular intervals. One party capsized its dinghy and returned to the crash boat. The motor yacht *Jamarna* nearly rammed a German flying boat. The yacht was moving in slowly towards the shore to land its raiders, when the flying boat suddenly appeared out of the gloom on idling engines, until it had cleared the shallow water when it opened up to full power and took off, seemingly unaware of its narrow escape. The army officer in charge of the raiders on the *Jamarna* now concluded the enemy must be thoroughly alerted to their presence, called off his part of the operation and the yacht returned to Dover.

The men who took part in Operation Collar received a very mixed reception upon their return home. The crew and raiders of one of the boats which made for Folkestone had taken their youthful skipper's instructions to 'splice the mainbrace', rather too liberally. The harbour picket boat mistook them for drunken deserters and kept them at bay until their true identity was confirmed.

By contrast the boats which sailed with Tod into Dover were given a heroes' welcome. General Bourne saw to that. Ships at the quayside sounded their sirens, sailors manned the rails and cheered the raiders ashore. Bourne had organized the newspapers and held an impromptu press conference on the quayside in which he proclaimed the unqualified success of the operation. The next day *The Times* gave the raid banner headlines and fulsome praise:

BRITISH RAIDERS LAND ON ENEMY COAST!
SUCCESSFUL RECONNAISSANCE.
In co-operation with the Royal Air Force, naval and military raiders yesterday carried out a successful reconnaissance of the enemy coastline. Landings were effected at a number of points and contact made with German troops. Casualties were inflicted and some enemy dead fell into our hands. Much useful information was obtained. Our forces suffered no casualties.

Political reactions were less forthcoming. The Cabinet was furious. The first they knew about the raid was when they read about it in the newspapers.

On the credit side, however, Tod had proved that raids on the enemy coast were possible. The fact that this one had occurred at all, and so soon after Dunkirk, was something of a miracle in itself.

The Prime Minister was not impressed. Perhaps his enthusiasm for special forces was already being tempered by the need to cater for more urgent priorities. Even so, his final judgement on Tod's after action report was less than charitable when he penned at the bottom of the page that it was: 'unworthy of the British Empire to send over a few cut-throats.'

Churchill's verdict was coloured by the fact that he had just about completed a series of visits to the 'storm trooper battalions'. The difference between the concept and reality was sufficiently stark for the Prime Minister to have an uncluttered impression of their limitations. The units had to be created from existing formations and they were poor. Storm troopers whose company commanders and senior NCOs were well into their forties and proudly displayed World War One campaign medals were hardly what the Prime Minister had in mind as the lightning-fast formations to counter invasion or take the fight to the enemy massed across 'the moat'.

So for the meantime, it all seemed to rest with Department MO9 where there was no shortage of ideas for future raids. By the time that Tod had completed the first operation there were half a dozen schemes wafting between the various 'in-trays' of Niven, Hailsham and other fertile minds.

For the most part the operations suggested varied from the impractical to the bizarre. Operation Comet proposed cutting the rail link between Sweden and Narvik to deny the Germans access to their precious iron ore in the winter months. Why this horny old chestnut had not been undertaken when a month or so before the British and French had actually occupied Narvik was a question which nobody seemed to ask.

Operation Colorado had ambitious objectives. It proposed nothing less than the seizure of Denmark. Quite what purpose this would serve, leaving aside questions of feasibility, is obscure.

There were other operations which MO9 saw simply as the translation into action of Churchill's directions and memoranda. Thus, Operation Attaboy planned to seize the Belgian town of Knocke which housed a major German headquarters, or so it was believed. The intention was to cause as much damage as possible, catch the enemy off guard and taunt or provoke him into a battle. One would have thought that the last thing a rampant and victorious Wehrmacht needed at this stage was provocation.

Besides these, and many more schemes, MO9 was also planning a second and more immediate raid against enemy-held territory. The intention was to hit the German garrisons on the Channel Islands.

After the evacuation of British troops from France, the chiefs of staff had advised the Prime Minister that the Channel Islands should be abandoned militarily. At first Churchill opposed their recommendation, feeling that, with the proper use of the Royal Navy, an invasion of the islands could be prevented. 'It was repugnant now,' he said, 'to abandon British territory which had been in the possession of the Crown since the Norman Conquest.'

For once the chiefs of staff refused to be swayed, pointing out that naval power without air cover was vulnerable and air cover needed airfields which in turn could be defended. The resources were not available and the Prime Minister was first to accept the logic of the arguments.

Within a week, the islands had been demilitarized, some notables and young men of military age evacuated, and the population left to its fate.

On 28 June the Germans officially occupied the Channel Islands, the only British territory to fall under their control in the war.

The commando raid was Churchill's idea. Having learned on 2 July that several hundred German troops had landed in the Channel

Islands, he sent a minute to the chiefs of staff suggesting that: 'plans should be studied to land secretly by night on the Islands to kill or capture the invaders'. Such a raid, he concluded, 'is exactly one of the exploits for which the Commandos would be suited.'

Operation Ambassador was planned for Sunday 14 July, Bastille Day. A hundred men drawn from the newly raised No. 3 Commando and Tod's No. 11 Independent Company, under the command of Lieutenant Colonel Dunford Slater, were to attack the German garrison on Guernsey.

As with Operation Collar the men trained furiously, improvized and tried to make do with the resources that were available.

The raid was mounted from the Royal Navy College at Dartmouth. The men assembled in the gymnasium where the young cadets and midshipmen helped load the magazines of the tommy guns and bren light machineguns. Two ancient S-Class destroyers, *Scimitar* and *Saladin*, stood by in the estuary of the Dart. They carried the raiders and towed a motley collection of motor boats, whalers and a couple of RAF crash boats. The small boats were towed across to save on fuel, and the raiders transferred into them for the actual assault. Operation Ambassador was a disaster. One group made it ashore to Guernsey only to find the barracks empty and no sign of the enemy. There was a heavy swell running and some of the boats capsized while others failed to find a suitable beach on which to land. Men lost their weapons overboard and when it came to re-embark those who had made it ashore, three were too exhausted to swim out to their boat. They were left behind.

One group mistakenly landed on the Isle of Sark where they found no Germans, but had a drink with the locals in the pub before heading for home.

So ended the last raid to be launched against the enemy in Occupied Europe that year. Churchill was furious with the failure of Operation Ambassador, a 'fiasco' as he called it, and promised swingeing changes. Even the optimistic Bourne could find little to present to the press while the phlegmatic and unruffled Dunford Slater described it as an 'amateur affair'.

But the greatest service that operations like Collar and Ambassador did perform was to ensure that some of the harebrained schemes discussed earlier never saw the light of day.

CHAPTER THIRTEEN

The New Volunteers

Captain Jack Churchill was evacuated from Dunkirk on 1 June along with the remnants of his battalion. He had fought in the rearguard through Belgium before thankfully passing through the defence perimeter along the Yser Canal and onto the beach. In those last hectic days of fighting, when it appeared the German onslaught would overwhelm 'the thin red line', Churchill had been in the forefront of the battle and his actions had resulted in an immediate citation for the Military Cross.

He came home in the Halcyon-class minesweeper, HMS *Leda*. The ship made a night crossing and was under constant attack and frequently singled out by the Stukas for a target. Despite the screaming divebombers, the rattle of the ship's pitifully inadequate anti-aircraft defence, and the crump of the bombs, Churchill slept, in the ship's tiny wardroom, along with twenty other men all oblivious to the battle and exhausted beyond caring.

The ship survived and docked at Margate. The weary troops piled onto the quayside to be greeted by women with doorstep sandwiches and mugs of hot tea. Churchill gathered his few possessions and moved towards the rail. His battledress was torn and stained, but the French cavalry buttons were still resplendent. He looked up to the wing of the bridge and caught the bleary eye of the ship's captain, an equally weary lieutenant commander.

It was at times like these that Churchill, although a rebel, remembered his Sandhurst training and the common courtesy befitting an officer and a gentleman.

He threw the skipper a smart salute and said, 'Thank you very much for bringing us across. It's very kind of you to give me a lift over.'

'Thank you for thanking us,' replied the captain returning the salute. 'You're the first one who has.'

It was dawn. The day promised to be fair and warm, and he was home; that was enough.

Churchill boarded the train, already crowded with troops, and they headed westwards across the flood plain that parallels the Thames Estuary. Into London via the East End and the City, and beyond to the outer suburbs by way of one of the few lines that avoids the great railway terminals.

Churchill recognized the route, reached into his small pack and hastily scribbled on a postcard:

> This is from Jack. I've just got back from Dunkirk and I am now on my way to Camp, I think at Oswestry.

The next station down the line was Gerrards Cross, where his family lived at the time. He addressed the card and added his parents' telephone number for luck. As the train moved slowly through a station packed with commuters, Churchill leaned out and thrust the card into the hand of a bowler-hatted 'City gent', who stared back in wide-eyed amazement.

'Please post it!' yelled Churchill.

The man immediately rushed to the station master's office and called the family. At least one of the Churchills' soldier sons was safely home from France.

The battlion reformed at the barracks in Lincoln where, along with other units of the Second Infantry Division, it was to defend the east coast. Churchill took a few days' leave and then hung about waiting for the new equipment and drafts to arrive from the depot.

On Tuesday 18 June, Waterloo Day, together with the other immediate awards for the British expeditionary force, Churchill was invested with his Military Cross. After the ceremony at Buckingham Palace he had a day in London with his wife and parents before returning to Lincoln and garrison duty.

Churchill was bored with battalion life. It was as bad as anything he could remember in the days of the Phoney War. Few officers had survived the retreat. There were many new faces around, and he found himself frozen out as an unwanted minority tainted with the stigma of defeat. He had another run-in with officialdom when a visiting brigadier congratulated him on his MC with one breath and then immediately rebuked him for wearing non-regulation buttons on his battledress.

'They were good enough for His Majesty,' responded Churchill.

So in rebellious mood yet again, Churchill read the War Office directive calling for volunteers for a new special force.

The directive listed a series of instructions which the volunteers had to follow. One that appeared particularly intriguing was that they had to be in possession of civilian clothes. This was the subject of much comment and speculation.

The view of Churchill and his contemporaries was that a special force was to be infiltrated into the neutral Republic of Eire wearing plain or civilian clothes. If the Germans were then to land at Cork or somewhere, this special force would quickly gather, leap out of their civilian clothes, put on battledress and surprise them. It presumably would have surprised the Irish too, but the theory gained credence through a large segment of the British officer corps. In a very short time, it acquired the force of a received idea. The result was that a lot of officers did not want to become entangled in Irish problems again. Memories of the 'Troubles' still lingered.

In the quaint English way of doing things, Lincoln fell within the geographical boundary of Northern Command. Headquarters were at York where the commando was to be raised.

Irish troubles or not, Churchill was determined to have a try at the special force. He tried to persuade a fellow captain called Nobby Clarke to come with him; but he had just been given command of a company and the promise of promotion to major. Churchill was thus the sole representative of the Manchesters to travel to York for an interview. Anything had to be better than garrison duty with a regular battalion now full of territorials and reservists, exercising in the Lincolnshire Wolds.

He decided to travel up the day before and booked a room at the White Swan for a couple of nights. This famous old coaching inn in Piccadilly was just a short stroll from the Shambles (from Old English *Shamel*, meaning slaughterhouse) where ancient timber-framed houses lean towards one another.

After dinner Churchill strolled the cobbled streets and lanes, presided over by the dominating magnificence of York Minister. In the cool of the summer evening, the war seemed very far away.

The camp cinema at command headquarters had been set aside for the special force, and it was there that Churchill duly reported the next morning. The dim and gloomy hall stank of stale tobacco and humanity. The poster outside advertised last night's film, Jeanette MacDonald in *Broadway Serenade*.

There were more than a hundred officers waiting, and Churchill was welcomed by many a familiar face and friend from France. Almost every officer there was a veteran of the campaign.

They were addressed by Lieutenant Colonel Pat Wood, Royal

Tank Regiment, who had already been selected by Northern Command and the War Office to lead the commando.

'This is going to be a raiding force. I can't tell you anything about it and it will be pretty damn dicey. You must be able to swim because we will be going to raid God knows where.'

There was absolute silence in the hall as Pat Wood continued.

'Now if you can drive a car, if you can ride a horse, ride a motorcycle or anything else of that sort it is going to help; because we will be raiding parties . . . If we can pinch any cars or anything to get us to a place, we will do so. The more ability you have in that sort of way the better.'

Wood paused for a moment, looked down at his audience from the wooden stage, and then pointed to an officer in the front row.

'Do you want to join?'

The hapless individual was a young captain from a fashionable cavalry regiment who, Churchill knew, had had two armoured cars shot out from under him during the retreat.

'Well it seems interesting, Sir.'

'Right, good man,' retorted Wood who clearly took this as an affirmative. 'Write down the name of everybody who wants to join, and I will talk to each and every one of you before we finish today. 'Now I'll be talking to you for about three or four minutes. Tell me anything. I want you to tell me if you have any claims to fame and why you want to join this raiding force.'

The cavalry captain groped for a paper and pencil only to be rescued by the garrison RSM who had hovered near to the stage throughout, and now handed him some paper mounted on a stiff board, and a pencil.

Pat Wood moved to the very edge of the stage, hands on hips and legs braced apart.

'The rest of you, if you don't want to get involved in this thing, you can f--k off back to your units! 'Nobody knows that you have come here and you can go back and shoot your cannons or bren-guns or whatever you do.'

A large minority of the assembled officers moved quickly, even furtively towards the exits, but the majority gathered around the name taker.

Churchill sat in his seat and waited for the crush to subside. 'Not quite Henry V at Agincourt', he thought, 'but it will do for me. I'm staying.'

Pat Wood set up shop in the projection room and Churchill waited patiently for his turn to be interviewed.

Most of the officers left the cinema after their session in the projection room, but a trickle returned to the auditorium and sat apart from those who were still waiting. Churchill guessed these were the successful ones. He was rather amused to see the group included the young cavalry captain. He suspected that it had been a put up job.

'What claim to fame do you have?' queried Wood.

'I just got an MC three days ago,' replied Churchill, realising that he had forgotten to sew the distinctive purple and white ribbon onto his battledress. He was loath to mention the medal, but it was the best testimonial he had, and there were an awful lot of officers still waiting to volunteer.

Wood thought for a moment, and then questioned Churchill some more about his past. The Fifth Battalion Scots Guards together with his pre-war days as a film extra and stuntman seemed as important as his repugnance for conventional soldiering.

'Right,' said Pat Wood. 'You will be my second-in-command; and you had better be promoted to major since that goes with the job.'

By the end of the day, Wood had selected his ten troop captains, and a number of subalterns were also offered appointments. He gathered the successful candidates together and introduced Churchill to them. They were a superb bunch, battle-hardened soldiers united by a common desire to kill Germans. They came from a mix of battalions and regiments, but prominent among them were a trio of Dorsets, one of whom had won the Military Cross. Bray was a captain, and Chips Heron and Peebles subalterns.

Pat Wood had a pokey little room in the Headquarters Mess; the others were dotted in pubs and hotels across the city.

'Now after dinner, say about ten o'clock tonight, we will meet in the lounge of the White Swan, and I will give you more information. I then propose to send you back to your regiments to recruit the rest of your troops.'

Churchill had suggested the White Swan as a suitable place to meet and he hurried away to prevail upon the hotel manager to allow him to reserve the lounge for the evening. A queue was already forming outside the main entrance to the cinema as Churchill bounded down the steps.

Soldiers, young and older ones waited patiently for the first house, in much the same way as they had waited in those long lines which had stretched from the beaches out into the sea off Dunkirk. These however were happy men. Although in uniform they were off duty, caps and berets pushed to the back of the head, the inevitable Woodbines dangling from their lower lips. The lucky ones had pretty girls in uniforms on their arms and were the envy of their mates.

Some gave an ironic cheer as Churchill bounded down the steps. It was ten minutes before the main feature was due to start, Lon Chaney Jnr and Claude Rains in *The Wolf Man*. The RSM who had accompanied him to the door stared the malcontents into silence, and hurried back inside to tactfully remind Colonel Wood that, unless he was careful, he was about to become the most unpopular officer in York.

They talked long into the night. Wood explained that the raiding force was to be a new type of military formation. General Wavell had caused more than a ripple of outrage among the peacetime military establishment when he once described his ideal infanteer as a mixture of cat burglar, poacher and gunman.

They were now to look for a man who not only had Wavell's qualities, but who combined the dash of an Elizabethan pirate, the cunning of a Chicago gangster, and the guile of a frontier tribesman, with the professional efficiency and the standard discipline of the best regular soldier.

Wood asked his officers to look in particular for the independent-minded man, who could and would survive on his own if the need arose. This quality of independence, rather than the traditional emphasis on the team spirit, marked a radical departure in military thinking. It was also reflected in the structure and organization of the commandos. There was to be no administration to support the troops, nothing that could sap their self-reliance.

On a raiding operation, a commando soldier would have to fend for himself, find food, transport and shelter. Thus it seemed only sensible to begin as they meant to continue.

There were to be no barracks, no cooks and no rations. The officers were aghast. All commandos, officers and men alike were to be thrown entirely on their own resources. Accommodation would come in the form of 'digs' in the local town where they were to be stationed. An officer would receive a daily allowance of 13 shillings and 4 pence (or 68p), and a soldier half that amount from the War Office. This was to cover bed and lodging, breakfast, packed lunch and evening meal.

There was to be no unit transport. The commando would have to use his own resources to get from A to B and by whatever means, provided that it was reasonably legal. The choice was left to the unit. If for example they were to attend an exercise, use the live firing ranges or whatever, they could march as a unit, thumb a lift or use public transport.

Once Wood had taken his new officers through the new organiz-ation, the discussion turned to the question of location. Where were they to base the new commando? 'Now we want to get somewhere on the coast,' Wood said. 'Anybody know of a good seaside town in the divisional area?'

A number of suggestions were thrown about in the discussion before they settled on Bridlington. It was a totally novel experience to have such a freedom of choice, and who would have believed that a new force could be raised in such a fashion where the officers could select where they were to stay?

'Right Jack,' said Wood. 'You get yourself to Bridlington and see all the right people. The commando will form in two weeks.'

'I'll go down first thing tomorrow and see the mayor, head of the WVS (Women's Voluntary Service) and the local police. Anybody else you can recommend?' asked Churchill. Somebody suggested the town clerk since he would have a list of all the houses in the town which had spare accommodation.

The next morning Churchill left for Bridlington. He had thought to book some transport but then, remembering Pat Wood's advice, decided instead to take the bus. It was as well to get into the new habits demanded of a commando from the beginning.

CHAPTER FOURTEEN

In Defence of the Realm

Bridlington lies some 40 miles east of York. It is a small seaside town, with a superb beach which is the hallmark of the Northumbrian coastline. Flamborough Head, whose chalk nose was the scene of many a successful Viking landing, protects the town from the worst of the cold North Sea and the bitter winds from the east; and the little harbour provided a refuge for the fishing boats that would sail as far as the Dogger Bank in more peaceful days.

The local bus took almost three hours to reach its destination, making frequent detours off the main A166 to call in at the little villages, whose churches soar behind farmworkers' red brick houses and the surrounding fields. Churchill sat back and enjoyed the journey, the unmistakable northerness of his fellow travellers, and the stark beauty of the Yorkshire Wolds. The bus stopped at Stamford Bridge, where Harold, last of the Saxon kings, defeated one rampaging army, before hurrying south to Hastings and death at the hands of the Norman invader. A signpost pointed to the battle site, and Churchill, a keen military historian, could not help but link those times with the new threat of invasion. Perhaps there would be a second Stamford Bridge where his commandos would fight and die?

Bridlington had been earmarked to accept evacuees from the industrial centres. The town clerk had already fulfilled his legal obligations under the war regulations and produced a list of houses which had spare rooms. The guest-houses which lined the roads to the beaches had already been listed and graded. The old town about a mile inland had some substantial private houses and these too were on the list.

Churchill visited a number of those listed and found no difficulty in persuading the ladies to billet soldiers. At a time when the average weekly wage for a skilled craftsman was £4 a week, the thought of a soldier or two, each at six shillings and eight pence a day, or an officer at double the price was most attractive. Another advantage would of course be that the house could no longer be listed for evacuees.

Over the succeeding weeks hundreds more would follow Churchill's path and volunteer for the special forces. However it was not the same for all officers.

Lieutenant Anthony Deane-Drummond, a 23-year-old officer in the Royal Signals was volunteered.

In 1940, he was signals officer to Brigadier Ambrose-Pratt, who commanded the four regiments of artillery which supported the First Army Corps. The gunners had had to abandon all their equipment, guns, limbers and tractors, not to mention their second line transport in France.

The losses in guns left behind in the evacuation of the BEF was enormous, but in retrospect mostly beneficial, since it provided the incentive to put more modern designs into production rather than continue to make do with the older weapons. Only in the instance of the anti-tank guns did Dunkirk have a detrimental effect. Six hundred were abandoned and now with an invasion perhaps imminent, anti-tank guns were high on the list of priorities. Next came the needs of anti-aircraft defence, while the medium and heavy guns of corps artillery were way down the list.

It was going to take a long time to resupply the destitute regiments and to swell the thinned ranks with fresh replacements of soldiers.

Deane-Drummond saw the War Office directive calling for officer volunteers to join a special force. A regular officer in pre-war days, he had been keen on gliding and flying and on one occasion tried a parachute jump (which he did not like) for the fun of things.

There was little for him to do and no sign of the replacement equipment. Like many young officers at the time, Deane-Drummond felt 'surplus to requirements', and if his country was about to be invaded, then he had no intention of standing on the sidelines as an observer. Boredom, frustration, impatience and patriotism were the motives which drove him to become an irregular part of the defence of the realm. He wrote to the brigadier and asked his permission to join the new force.

Ambrose-Pratt sent for his signals officer.

'I'm not going to have my officers volunteer for commandos or special forces. I will select them.'

Brigadier Ambrose-Pratt was an eccentric officer who did not believe in volunteers, since enthusiasm did not account for suitability or aptitude. However, he considered Lieutenant Deane-Drummond to be one of the best young officers on his staff, and so selected him to volunteer for the special forces.

On 22 June 1940, the Prime Minister sent a memo to General Ismay, his chief of staff:

> We ought to have a corps of at least five thousand parachute troops. Advantage must be taken of the summer to train these forces, who can nonetheless play their part meanwhile as shock troops in home defence. Pray let me have a note from the War Office on this subject.

Two days later Major John Rock, Royal Engineers, was summoned to the War Office to be told that he would be given the task of establishing a parachutists' training school. Although the German army and the Soviet Red Army both had significant formations of parachutists, Britain had not even contemplated such an option at all seriously. Indeed in the 1930s, when German and Soviet intentions had been brought to the notice of the War Office, the concept was 'laughed out of court'. After all a parachutist in descent would be vulnerable to anti-aircraft and small arms fire directed from the ground, and it was quite beyond the capacity of transport aircraft to drop men in sufficient quantities to overwhelm the defences. Such criticism seemed to be validated by bizarre Soviet experiments, where parachutists clung to the upper wing surface of a bomber and then 'dropped off' at the given moment. Even in the summer of 1940 parachutes, although issued to RAF flight crews, were very much a last resort measure, and there were no instructors in uniform.

Major John Rock did not volunteer for the special force, but he was promoted to lieutenant colonel, which was a reasonable compensation. The reason why he was chosen to lead the new organization was because of his interests, during peacetime years, in gliding. With his rank and seniority in the army, that was about as close as the War Office could come to producing a specialist or expert.

The new organization was based at RAF Ringway, an airfield some ten miles south of Manchester. It was designated the Central Landing School, and everybody involved was sworn to secrecy. The immediate area and especially the public houses in and around the neighbouring market town of Knutsford swarmed with plain clothes security men, who vainly tried to 'blend in with the local scene'. Their presence in such large numbers simply served to draw attention to Ringway.

Early in July, the men of No. 2 Special Service Company, under Lieutenant Colonel Jackson, were sent to Ringway and the most suitable candidates selected for parachute training. This was the very beginning of the Parachute Regiment, the Glider Pilot Regiment and the Airborne Army which was to spearhead the combined operation into Normandy less than four years later.

Lieutenant Deane-Drummond had barely joined No. 2 Commando as a section officer before he found himself on the selection course for Ringway. When they learned that he had actually parachuted, if only as a sport, his welcome was assured.

There were others too who were destined to become part of the special forces although they took yet another route.

Major Charles Newman, late of the Essex Regiment, sat with the simmering rump of his independent company in Glasgow. He sort of drifted into the commandos.

After a couple of weeks of inactivity, Newman was called in by Hugh Stockwell who nominally at least was still in command of the 'Norwegian contingent'. There was to be a future for the independent companies. Meanwhile Newman was to sort out the men in his own company. Those who would 're-volunteer' could stay on, the remainder would be returned to their units.

It wasn't the easiest of tasks to address the assembled men. They had every right to feel bitter and aggrieved at their past treatment, and by the same token he could not tell them what would be in store if they chose to stay with him. He didn't know himself.

After a pep talk to the assembled company, and some quiet words on an individual basis to those he wanted Newman found he had 150 men who volunteered to stay with him for an uncertain future. The remainder were quickly returned to their battalions before the volunteers could change their minds.

The company was relieved of its guarding duties (and looking for German parachutists disguised as nuns), and underwent a vigorous training programme in physical fitness. Then they were away. Trucks took them up to the west coast of Scotland to Inverailort Castle, home of the Irregular Warfare School, where they found Hugh Stockwell in command.

This wild Highland country, ancestral domain of the clan MacDonald, where Bonnie Prince Charlie had first raised his banner in 1745, was to become part of the training ground of the special forces for much of the Second World War. Newman's company was lodged under canvas in the Castle grounds surrounded by the most glorious country – plenty of mountains, and the sea in which to bathe and to practise the new techniques of raiding.

Stockwell outlined the programme to Charles Newman and his officers. The company was to be brought back up to strength with new volunteers from their own division and then the training would begin for their new role.

'Raids on the enemy coast', was the order of the day. The new ways of war which had been developed and then proven with such devastating success by the Germans required equally new and different means of counter. This involved tip-and-run raids anywhere on the German-held coastline, from Narvik to Bayonne. This was where the opportunity lay, for the enemy could not deploy forces to defend at every point.

In their purest form, such raids were to represent a form of 'psychological warfare', both creating a sense of tension and uncertainty in enemy garrisons across the water, and providing confidence and battle experience for British soldiers. The nation at large too would draw strength and comfort from the broadcast news of their success.

Hugh Stockwell lived up to his promise of ensuring that Newman's company would be superbly prepared for what lay ahead. Stress was laid on night operations.

Their physical fitness was that of the trained athlete. This in turn meant long endurance marches and cliff scaling, as well as swimming rivers in full kit and often under fire. Endurance meant withstanding the extremes of heat and cold and fatigue. The men worked in pairs in what the Americans were later to call the 'buddy' principle, but which was in reality one of the oldest principles of warfare. The emphasis centred on initiative. In the special forces the men had to think for themselves, the army no longer did their thinking for them. Thus, a not uncommon practice for Newman, his officers and men, was to come off an exercise mid-afternoon, only to be told by Stockwell or his instructors, that the next parade would be at 5.30 the following morning.

They would then be given a map reference to a spot some 60 miles away, usually way inland up some inaccessible glen. It was up to each pair how they made the rendezvous and woe betide those who were even a minute late.

Failure meant the threat of being dismissed and sent back to their parent unit. This was known as 'RTU' (returned to unit), and became the ultimate sanction and standard form of punishment in the special forces. Introduced by Dudley Clarke, it was to remain a potent weapon in the hands of special force officers throughout the war.

Most of all, the training emphasized killing. The raiders had to strike fear into the very heart of the enemy. Even in these early days, Stockwell had applied his own ingenuity and initiative, and his instructors had gathered an awesome array of weapons and fire power. Most were the short range submachineguns, since the raiders would hope to get in close before moving into the assault.

Fire-arms, even at close range, kill at a distance; and perhaps there is some comfort in that for those of a gentle disposition. But other forms of killing were taught.

The virtuosos at Inverailort were two formidable Shanghai police-men, Mr Sykes and Mr Fairbairn. It is thought by some that these gentlemen first introduced the commando knife, although others would challenge this claim. What is not in doubt is that Mr Sykes and Mr Fairbairn made a lasting impression on a whole generation of young men who probably already considered themselves tough-ened to war after the rigours of basic training. At the hands of the Shanghai police duo they learned a dozen and more different ways of killing without making a noise. Knifing, garrotting, neck snapping and gouging were all elevated to the syllabus of thuggery.

The training also included seamanship, boatwork and landings; these were achieved with the help of some old herring boats from Mallaig. There was a softer side too: the men would have their lines out as the boats nosed into Loch Nam Uamh, spinning for mackerel and breakfast. Then they would land on some island, invariably on a rock ledge with a near impossible cliff to climb, and only the chuckles of the departing sailors to taunt them.

David Niven was at Inverailort at this time. He had been sent there by Dudley Clarke to learn the ropes. By his own admission Niven volunteered out of boredom. Here at Inverailort he worked alongside those who were genuinely courageous. Bill Stirling, Brian Mayfield and the Everest climber, Jim Gavin, all attended in the first months. David Stirling, Mike Calvert, Lord Lovat and Freddie Chapman, the men who were to lay the foundations upon which today's élite 22 Special Air Service Regiment is based, were all graduates of the Irregular Warfare School.

General Bourne came to the centre. He warned Newman that his company would soon be required to undertake a raid on the French coast; and then stayed to see the men training.

There was an exercise planned that night. It was to take the form of a silent landing at midnight in a secluded bay in Loch Nam Uamh. Newman sat with General Bourne in the staff car which had been parked on a track just above the bay. It all went exceed-

The Prime Minister, in characteristic pose with the Tommy Gun, a weapon favoured by the early formations of his 'Private Armies'.

Commando officers pose with their Naval colleagues for the War Correspondent. It was a Combined Operation after all.

In August 1941, the Commandos exercised before the King at Scapa Flow. The early infantry assault craft were not at all easy to leave in a hurry. This was classed as a 'dry shod landing'.

King George VI is greeted by Admiral of the Fleet, Sir Roger Keyes. The King had travelled north to observe the Commandos on exercise at Scapa Flow.

The early version of the Higgins boat, though a primitive affair, served its purpose. This exercise before the King at Scapa Flow went wrong from the outset and helped to seal the fate of Admiral Keyes.

Commandos, having landed from their assault craft, are mustered in an orderly fashion and await fresh instructions. It was to take the bitter experience of Dieppe to convince authorities that the landing beach was the least healthy place to linger.

Casualty evacuation was no easy thing at Sör Vaagso especially when German
snipers controlled the high ground.

Before the Commandos withdrew from Sör Vaagso, everything of value was put to
the torch.

Lt General Sir Alan Brooke was appointed Commander in Chief of the Home Forces after the evacuation of the BEF from Dunkirk. From this appointment, he implaccably opposed the creation of special forces such as the Commandos, and constantly challenged the actions of Admiral Sir Roger Keyes.

Major Frost and his paratroopers prepare to board the Whitley Bombers for the highly successful Bruneval Raid.

The second raid on the Lofotens ended with the complete destruction of the local industry at Stamsund.

The Lancastria, pressed into service as a troop ship, was instrumental in the evacuation of the Independent Companies from Norway. On 17 June 1940, she was sunk by German dive bombers off St Nazaire.

The landing at Spitzbergen was a gentle affair. It was just as well, considering that the only craft available to take the men ashore were the ship's lifeboats.

Lord Louis Mountbatten inspects members of 3 Commando on board their assault ship and immediately prior to their departure for the Vaagso raid. Behind stands Lt Col John Dunford Slater and Major Jack Churchill, battledress resplendent with French army silver buttons.

Anthony Dean-Drummond. A photograph taken after the war whilst on the staff of the Royal Military Academy, Sandhurst.

The Vaagso raid occurred before the introduction of the Green Beret, and so Commandos wore their Regimental headdress, out of operations. In this photograph representatives from five Scottish Regiments are in evidence together with the Royal Tanks and the Royal Engineers.

Major Jack Churchill, claymore at the ready, leads his troops ashore during an exercise in Scotland, 1941.

Bridlington July 1940. Major Jack Churchill, second in command of the newly raised 5 Commando.

Major Jack Churchill removes a shell fragment from the barrel of one of the captured 75mm guns at Maaloy. The gun, much the worse for wear after the naval bombardment, was captured in France and then brought to Norway, where it was mounted on a rotating platform in its new anti-shipping role.

ingly well and the general complimented Newman on a remarkably silent operation. He hadn't seen or heard a thing. Newman stepped out of the car, saluted the general and then hurried off down the track to join up with his men. The general drove away in a shower of gravel for the castle and then back to London.

It took Newman a little while to find his company, which certainly wasn't anywhere near where it was supposed to be. Increasingly angry and exasperated, he came upon an equally concerned Hopkirk who had been sent to find him. Apparently the trawler had landed him in the wrong cove 400 yards away from the target. No wonder General Bourne hadn't heard a thing!

At an hour's notice the company was ordered south to Ryde on the Isle of Wight. It was a mad scramble but the men were soon aboard the trucks which drove them the short distance to the railway station. There was to be no initiative test on this journey, the company were to be taken south care of army transport authorities. A special three-coach train waited to take them down the branch line to the main station at Fort William. From there they were shunted onto a southbound express to London and on to Southampton. Forty-eight hours later, they marched through Ryde and into the grounds of a large, empty house on the edge of town. This was to be their temporary home while they prepared for the raid. Close by was No. 8 Independent Company which was commanded by Major Priddie.

The large drawing-room on the ground floor was set aside as an operations room. Here Newman and Priddie were briefed on a joint operation. Staff from MO9 came down from London and helped prepare the raid. Dudley Clarke was much in evidence and Bourne attended on a couple of occasions. Newman and Priddie were given maps and photographs of a place which they were ordered not to recognize, the names had been cut out or inked over on the map. It was unmistakably Cape Gris Nez. There were five cement-gun implacements being constructed on the point. The orders were to go and destroy them.

Commander Sir Jeffrey Congreave joined them to lead the naval force. He brought with him a collection of motor yachts and the inevitable RAF crash boats which Garnon Williams had released from his collection on the Hamble River. While the more senior officers prepared and planned for this, their first raid, the men trained hard and practised landings at night.

It had been decided that Priddie and No. 8 Independent Company were to storm the position and destroy the implacements. Newman's task was to head inland and seal off the cape from

German interference while Priddie completed the demolition, then to act as rearguard as the others re-embarked on the boats.

Just 24 hours before the raid, information in the form of aerial photographs revealed that the German garrison at Cape Gris Nez had been heavily reinforced and formidable defences prepared. Coincidence, or did they have wind of something? Newman was furious, convinced that there had been too much loose talk. He had been appalled at the lack of care shown by the 'London crowd'.

Inquests were futile. The raid was cancelled.

The staff from MO9 packed up and left. The independent companies were forgotten. There were no orders, instructions or communications of any sort from London. The men were left to their own devices at the seaside in the middle of a hot and glorious summer.

Newman saw to it that his men made the most of this unexpected development. He knew that the war would soon catch them up, so in the meantime there were sports, swimming and sunbathing parades. They held cricket matches, while in the skies above young men in fighter aircraft fought their deadly duels.

The officers would gather at the end of the 'working day' on the roof of the Starboard Club – the local yacht club, which they had adopted. From the balcony they could look across the Solent, sip their gin fizzes and watch the Luftwaffe pound the hell out of Portsmouth.

PART THREE

KEYES AT THE HELM

CHAPTER FIFTEEN

In Caesar's Steps – Invasion Scares, Alarms and Excursions

'Since England, in spite of her hopeless military situation, shows no sign of being ready to come to an understanding, I have decided to prepare a landing operation against England, and if necessary carry it out. The aim of the operation will be to eliminate the English homeland as a base for the persecution of the War against Germany and, if necessary, to occupy it completely.'

Adolf Hitler, Directive No. 16

On 16 July 1940, Adolf Hitler issued Directive No. 16 for the invasion of Britain. It was codenamed operation *Seelowe* (Sealion). Although France had collapsed, the German army was in no way prepared for such an undertaking. The Army High Command OKH (*Oberkommando des Heeres*) had not even contemplated the invasion of Britain, let alone studied such an operation. The Wehrmacht had been given no training for seaborne and landing operations, and nothing had been done to build landing craft for the purpose.

A tumbling spiral of events through that hot midsummer, which had begun earlier with the resoundingly successful Blitzkrig in the west and had culminated in the defeat of France, had caught everyone unawares, and unprepared.

In Berlin, plans were hurriedly drawn up and the regiments re-equipped for a new battle. Forty-one Wehrmacht divisions were committed to the beaches on a front which stretched from Ramsgate to Lyme Regis.

Führer Directive No. 16 ordered that all preparations were to be completed by mid-August.

Hurried, if not frenzied, efforts were made to collect together all the available shipping. Barges from Germany and the Low Countries were concentrated in the Channel ports, while the assault divisions received some basic training in embarking and disembarking. In the meantime, the Luftwaffe sought to ensure the RAF was made 'morally and physically' incapable of attacking the invasion force.

Everything that summer depended on Britain's first line of defence, a few hundred fighters of the RAF. The respective high commands were equally aware of that single all-controlling fact: before the armada could leave the shelter of the French coast, the Luftwaffe had to win command of the daytime skies over southern England. If the air force could hold the line through to September then the Germans dare not invade in 1940. For the panzers, the guns, the infantry and their landing barges packed into the Channel ports were useless so long as sufficient Spitfires and Hurricanes, and the pilots to fly them, survived.

From the moment in July, when Operation Sealion was accepted by Winston Churchill and the War Cabinet as imminent, all the nation's efforts were devoted to defence. The local defence volunteers, or 'Home Guard' as Churchill dubbed them, a force which had been first raised in May 1940, swelled its ranks and drilled with anything that came to hand; broomsticks, pikes and shotguns abounded. Private and commercial vehicles were hastily adapted as platoon vehicles in garages and blacksmiths. Heavy stakes were driven into flat or open terrain especially around the coast to thwart airborne landings. Tank traps of dubious value appeared under railway bridges and in narrow defiles. Brick and concrete pillboxes, able to withstand small arms fire on a good day but little else, and wrongly sited on skylines and other conspicuous points, sprouted the length and breadth of the country.

The imminence of invasion brought into even sharper relief the temporary nakedness of the British army. The War Office viewed the prospect of some 5,000 soldiers in the new commandos being removed physically from their control, at the very moment when every man might be needed for the defence of England, with dismay and great alarm.

Against a mounting barrage of criticism and opposition, General Bourne used his ample reserves of tact and skilled diplomacy to head off internecine conflict. He could not alter the fact that the troops under his command were answerable only to the three chiefs of staff and the Prime Minister; neither could he halt the process of raising the new special forces – even assuming he had wanted to. What he did offer, however, was an honourable compromise to an embarrassing impasse. General Bourne gave an undertaking that not a man or boat would be diverted from the vital task of repelling the invaders. As soon as the commandos were formed and trained, they with their naval complement would be distributed to the seaside resorts, where along with the independent companies, they would be available to the local commanders in an emergency as reserves.

In the meantime, the special forces would be taken for raiding operations of a few hours' duration. The intention was to force the enemy to disperse their strength and disrupt training exercises, and to inflict destruction and damage to war materials which were stockpiled.

Bourne's commandos weren't unique even at this stage of the war. Other commanders looked to their own units to provide special means of defence. Gerald Templer formed what he called 'a special service group' in each rifle company whilst in command of the 210th Infantry Brigade in Dorset.

The Brigade Diary explained: 'The general idea was that it should form a mobile patrol of cutthroats, or, as the Brigadier [Templer] said with relish, "thugs" to deal summarily with any small or for that matter large band of enemy troops landed from the air or by sea, if in the latter event they should succeed in penetrating beach defences. These men were specially equipped for speed, silence and destructive ability, trained in fieldcraft and the use of the Thompson. They were all picked men, many volunteered but only a handful were chosen.'

Charles Newman and his company found their pleasant interlude in the Isle of Wight rudely interrupted once the Battle of Britain had begun in earnest. Suddenly someone in London remembered them, and they were moved off poste haste to Manston Aerodrome, and then to Ramsgate. Two days later there was another move. They were settled at Dungeness, at the sharp end.

This vast, flat expanse of grazing land, carved across by deep dykes and dotted with the famous Romney Marsh sheep, was not at all easy to defend. Most of the area is barely above sea level and it was easy to get lost. The marshes made an ideal area for smuggling until early in the 19th century, for only men born and bred there knew the routes through the maze of water channels.

119

The company of volunteers, trained to the peak of efficiency for raiding warfare, moved into a defensive mode. Newman deployed his men throughout Dungeness, behind coils and coils of Dannert wire. They manned recently completed pillboxes, dug slit trenches and laid their field telephone wire.

In late evening a mantle of heavy white mist would rise off the marsh giving the area an air of mystery and secrecy, while the company stood to in readiness to repel the invader.

The night sounds were punctuated by the loud creaking of the marsh frogs, the most recent invaders (a dozen had been imported from Hungary and escaped into the wild in 1935 where they soon spread throughout the marshes).

This was more than enough to excite the imagination of young soldiers, and, despite their training, many a night was spent in false alarms where sheep, moving like phantoms through the mist, were mistaken for German saboteurs or infiltrators.

The daylight hours afforded little opportunity for rest or relaxation. As the air battle reached its crescendo in August, Luftwaffe raids occurred daily and sometimes all day, the planes flying low overhead to strike at targets inland.

The company was housed in summer holiday homes that dotted the coastline and tracks inland. There were wooden huts in gay-painted colours, disused railway carriages specially converted by Southern Railways and 'parked' in convenient sidings off the branchline, that wandered through from Romney to Lydd and then to Rye.

Others lived in what Newman in his diary refers to as 'abodes of love' in peacetime. Newman shared a delightful old converted railway carriage with his man, Shears, who was in his element. He made it into a comfortable little home, and cooked marvellous meals on the primus stove.

Mines washed ashore were a particular hazard, especially on the flat headland of shingle which the Channel tides are still extending. Some were British, broken loose from their moorings in the patterned fields sewn to protect the Thames Estuary, others were enemy, dropped at night by low flying Dornier bombers, or dumped overboard from speeding E-boats. Two old salts, emergency reservists brought back under the war regulations, were quartered with the company. They spent their time unscrewing the deadly fuses and making the mines safe. District headquarters had published a standing order which dealt with the safety regulations in these instances. It advised that 200 yards should be the safety zone whenever one of these mines was beached.

It was about 8.00 p.m. one lovely evening in early August, when

Lieutenant Hopkirk called Newman on the fixed army telephone line that ran from his hut close to the seashore to Newman's railway sleeping car.

'There's a mine washed up just by my hut Sir. Could you send the old fellows along to do something about it?'

'They've done three already today, Hoppy, and are down the canteen with a pint or three inside them. How far from the hut is the mine?'

'About a hundred yards, Sir.'

'Oh, that's all right, quite safe. Don't worry about it. I'll send the old boys along first thing after breakfast.'

'Okay, if you're happy about it, Sir, I am.'

There was the most tremendous explosion and the land line went dead.

Newman dashed out of his carriage, across the grass and through the sand-dunes towards Hopkirk's hut.

Hopkirk crawled out from the smoke and dust pile that had been his home, covered in plaster and chunks of wood. Shaking like a leaf, he cursed the Germans, the war and was about to start on his commanding officer when he espied Newman. Fortunately he was none the worse for his ordeal, at least nothing which a couple of stiff tots could not remedy.

There was also one Jerry divebomber who appeared regularly every morning and dropped a bomb on Dungeness Point. The company were able to set their watches by him and take sensible precautions, so he was never able to cause any damage.

A bigger threat was posed by fleeing bombers, especially when airfields in the area such as Lydd were singled out for attack. The enemy running for home, and frequently harried by fighters, would unload their remaining bombs. Dungeness came in for more than its fair share of unwarranted dumping. The unit's anti-aircraft defences were paltry, just a couple of twin-mounted Lewis machineguns of Great War vintage which posed a greater threat to the gunners than to any aircraft.

A quite large bomb landed about 20 yards from one of the wooden huts, which in turn was just a short distance from the only public house in the company area. The pub was extensively damaged, windows blown and glasses shattered in the bar; but the hut bore the main brunt of the explosion. It was riddled with bomb fragments, and the doors and windows were all blown in by the blast.

The hut was home to a squad of soldiers who had only just come off duty. They were rolled in their blankets and asleep on the floor; it was that which saved them, for they were below the level of the blast. Rifles leaning against the wall were cut in two, and one man's large pack was completely severed with his best tunic and trousers inside. The ceiling fell in but as these were made of thin plasterboard they caused no injuries.

Newman himself had a couple of narrow escapes. He was strolling along the sand and shingle beach one overcast afternoon with Terry White, a platoon commander, when three fighters came tumbling out of the low clouds a little ahead of them.

'Spitfires,' gestured White.

'Look! A victory roll,' responded Newman, and as one plane banked towards them the words froze. Even in the hazy light the black crosses on the wing tip, etched in white, were unmistakable.

'Look out! they're MEs!'

The two officers dived to the ground and buried their faces in the shingle, hands clasped firmly over their heads in copybook fashion. The fighter was so low that its slipstream threatened to tear the tunics from their backs. Then came the muffled *crump* and the ground heaved and shook them free.

'You all right Terry?'

'Yes and you?'

'Yes okay.'

They stood up not a 100 yards from a large and still-smoking crater. Debris and shingle still fell to the ground about them. Terry White had a nasty gash on his forehead which was in need of stitching; Newman had a chunk taken out of his nose. It was a lucky break.

There were two further explosions, and a pillar of smoke rose from behind the sand-dunes. The two officers ran across to the scene.

One bomb had landed smack on a small café, a wooden affair run by a local family who had bravely stayed on to minister to the needs of the company, and make a little money which the emergency would otherwise have denied them.

There were seven men from the company having tea inside when the bomb struck. The owner and his wife were serving behind the counter. Soldiers and civilians were blown out through the walls as the building collapsed. Apart from cuts and bruises, one case of shattered eardrums, and the owner's wife scalded on the arm with hot water when the tea-urn burst, nobody was seriously hurt. If the building had been made of brick and masonry it would have been a different and more tragic story.

The company used the cookhouse at Lydd Barracks to prepare their meals. They shared facilities, and hot foot was transported out to the various positions. They suffered their only casualties during the Battle of Britain when Stukas divebombed the barracks, scoring a direct hit on the cookhouse. Many men were killed and maimed that day, including two dead and four injured from the company.

The Luftwaffe continued to make life extremely uncomfortable for the men who manned the defence positions at Dungeness, and few had reason to feel anything but loathing for the enemy. However, war does have the strangest influences on people's emotions. A Luftwaffe pilot was seen to bail out and land in the sea a mile or so off the point, where he immediately got into difficulties in the dangerous cross-currents. The Dungeness lifeboat was launched, and it was shorthanded. But there was no shortage of volunteers from the independent company to help crew the boat; after all, they had recently completed an intensive course on boatmanship!

Initially, at least, the Prime Minister was convinced that the great threat for the invasion lay on the east coast, and that this would be the main area of assault. Such a judgement was influenced by historical experience and the Wartime Cabinet leader's fairly recent memories. Throughout the Great War there was always considerable nervousness that the Germans might land in East Anglia; and substantial forces were stationed in the area throughout, to be held in readiness to counter-attack. Gradually, however, the mosaic of the intelligence picture was constructed from many different sources, headed by the master-codebreakers at Bletchley who monitored enemy radio chatter. Other pieces fitted the jigsaw, the invasion craft concentrated at Calais and Boulogne, and the fact that harbour facilities at Dover, Folkestone and other Channel ports were studiously avoided as targets.

The Germans had never intended the invasion beaches to be anywhere than those immediately across the Channel. As General Jodl, chief of operations section at OKW (*Oberkommando des Wehrmachts*), or the armed forces High Command, admitted in his trial at Nuremberg in 1945 'Our arrangements were much the same as those of Julius Caesar!'

It was not until early in September that sufficient evidence had been amassed to convince the War Cabinet to agree to a decisive increase in the defences along the south coast. Perhaps properly conducted small-scale raids, launched by MO9 would have helped to produce the conclusive evidence sooner. It is hard to reach a judgement, but it would have made more sense for MO9 to have directed its efforts to ways and means of countering the invasion rather than indulging in 'some of the grandiose' and totally unrealistic operations that it proposed at the time.

At the end of July 1940, No. 5 Commando was ordered to move from Bridlington in Yorkshire to reinforce the defences on the cliffs above Dover. The sense of urgency in the move was evidenced by the army transport system which brought them south, rather than commando initiative. Major Jack Churchill, as second in command, was responsible for the operation.

They were rather sad to leave Bridlington. The little resort had welcomed their presence, the men had been on the whole well-behaved and many a household had been glad of the extra income. With the menfolk away with the Colours, there was more than one heart broken by their departure.

As Newman had found in Dungeness, anti-invasion duty soon settled into a routine comprising long periods of boredom interspersed with moments of terror.

A major problem in the Dover area was bombardment from German long-range guns. By way of retaliation three old railway mountings dating from 1918 were resurrected, fitted with 13.5 inch naval guns from the French battleship *Paris* which was taken over by the Royal Navy, and sent to the Dover area. His Majesty's gun '*Gladiator*' manned by Royal Marines was one of the first in action.

Jack Churchill spent his off-duty hours at archery practice. He used the 'banks' or high ground above Dover as his butts, and this Olympic athlete invariably drew an appreciative audience.

The longest range at which an archery target had ever been hit was 22 miles. A German long-range shell burst over the banks and a fragment of the shell went through the blue ring on the target.

'Gentlemen,' said Churchill to the audience as they picked themselves up; 'This is the longest range that an archery target has ever been hit.

'And,' he continued amidst the gales of laughter, 'some unknown f-----g Kraut gunner in Calais has scored a "Five".'

As more of the newly formed commandos completed their training they too were moved into the danger areas and a high state of alert was sustained well into September until the onset of autumn spelled at least a postponement of Operation Sealion.

Before that time came, however, a new and highly secret outfit within the special forces was formed to deal exclusively with an invading enemy.

It was called Phantom Force and it had its headquarters at Richmond Park. This was a highly skilled officer-heavy reconnaissance regiment, which was to move forward and report on enemy strengths and deployments.

The phantom squadrons were distributed along the southern and eastern coasts. David Niven was posted to A Squadron which was attached to Fifth Corps, commanded by General Montgomery, and stationed in the danger area behind Poole Harbour.

Besides their primary function, they also made themselves ready to go underground. A large stock of disguises was earmarked for distribution should the invasion prove successful, and key men were trained or schooled in the roles they were to adopt.

David Niven was ready to re-emerge dressed as a parson.

---

[1] On Caesar's first raid in 55BC, he crossed from the Boulogne area and landed at Walmer north of Dover; on the second occasion in 54BC he again started from Boulogne and landed north of Dover and near to Sandwich.

CHAPTER SIXTEEN

Back to the Drawing Board

'I make myself detestable to everyone,' Churchill commented wistfully, 'except Roger whose dupe I am.'

August 30 1940

Even while the new commandos were being raised and then deployed alongside the independent companies, and the other oddities that came under the banner of special forces, there were changes at the top.

The failure at Guernsey was largely to blame. Monday 15 July was St Swithin's Day, and it poured with rain. This brought cheer to the farmers who had suffered a prolonged drought throughout the spring and early summer; and never before had the need been so great for a bumper harvest.

There was little to cheer the special forces. Churchill was furious with the failure of Operation Ambassador and called it a 'fiasco', and even the more optimistic Bourne could find little to present to the press; other than a travesty of the truth.

In the Prime Minister's opinion now was the time to put the house in some order. Espionage, sabotage, reconnaissance, raiding and all other forms of guerrilla warfare needed to be rationalized, roles and functions identified and resources allocated. Operation Ambassador and its failure was to be the vehicle of major change.

Churchill issued his Directive of 17 July which revised the terms of reference for all those units and organizations charged with attacking the enemy in Europe. In a series of late night visits to Churchill's War Chambers, his operation centre and bunker deep beneath Whitehall, by the various heads of intelligence and secret service, the new order was formed. Much of the discussion, and subsequent acrimony was over the vexed issues of hierarchies – namely 'who should report to whom', and boundaries – namely 'who was responsible for what'.

In the waging of irregular warfare against the enemy, two names were to figure prominently. The first was Hugh Dalton, the 'spiv-like', brash, dynamic and, in the event, rashly confident Labour member who was Churchill's Minister of Economic Warfare. Dalton had lobbied long and hard to get what one observer called 'a large finger into the sabotage pie', and such persistence was to be rewarded.

'Regular soldiers,' Dalton explained to the Prime Minister, 'are not the men to stir up revolution to create social chaos or to use all these ungentlemanly means of winning the war which come so easily to the Nazis.'

Dalton thought he was just the man. Churchill agreed and in the Directive appointed him the supremo of a new and 'fourth arm' of defence. Dalton was in charge of all sabotage and subversion in enemy territory. Up until then, this work had been undertaken by two separate organizations. The first was Department R of Military Intelligence (MIR) which we last met with Colin Gubbins waging guerrilla warfare, of a sort, in Norway.

The second was an older and more prestigious pillar of the establishment. Section D of the Secret Intelligence Service (SIS) had been happily employed fighting its own little war, trying to cause mayhem in the enemy-occupied territories (to date, it should be admitted, without much success).

The two departments were divorced from their respective patrons, and combined into a new organization. Under Dalton, they were to form the Special Operations Executive (SOE) or what Churchill was to call the 'Ministry of Ungentlemanly Warfare'.

There was another fellow 'hanging around Downing Street for employment'. Admiral of the Fleet, Sir Roger Keyes, MP for Portsmouth, hero of the Dardanelles and Zeebrugge, and close confidant of the Prime Minister was appointed Director of Combined Operations.

The appointment was a mistake, and a major error on the part of the Prime Minister. The separation of Special Operations Executive and Combined Operations has always been questioned by historians as unwise. The waging of the war against the enemy was now in the hands of two separate organizations where co-ordination and integration of effort would be even harder to achieve. The needs of sabotage and subversion on the one hand, with raiding on an increasingly large scale on the other, were exceedingly difficult to reconcile. Their separation made it well nigh impossible.

Originally it had been intended that the SOE should be responsible for small raids, i.e. those involving less than 30 men; but although agreed in principle, this was never implemented. SOE, as an 'intelligence organization', disliked and opposed raids, since they prevented the implanting of agents and held up the vital work of gathering intelligence.

Keyes's appointment and his terms of reference were ambiguous, although the Prime Minister's directive seemed clear enough:

> I have appointed Admiral of the Fleet Sir Roger Keyes as Director of Combined Operations. He should take over the duties and resources now assigned to General Bourne. General Bourne should be informed that, owing to the large scope now to be given to these operations, it is essential to have an officer of higher rank in charge, and that the change in no way reflects upon him or those associated with him. Evidently he will have to co-operate effectively. I formed a high opinion of this officer's work as Adjutant General Royal Marines, and in any case the Royal Marines must play a leading part in this organisation.
>
> Pending any further arrangements, Sir Roger Keyes will form contact with the Service Departments through General Ismay as representing the Minister of Defence.[1]

The appointment was made without any attempt to define the responsibilities and the hierarchy without which the military cannot function. The letter can be read to mean that Keyes will report through Ismay to the Minister of Defence, who was Churchill. This was the interpretation placed on the directive by Sir Roger Keyes. The service departments, not unnaturally, saw things differently. General Bourne's commitment was limited to training and conducting certain types of raid, but did not include large-scale operations. They saw Keyes as their servant and adviser.

Of course these affairs might have been of little consequence, given goodwill on both sides. The service departments however were of one mind with the War Office stance on irregular or special formations, so there would be no goodwill where the separation and the promotion of special forces as an arm of the service apart from the army was concerned.

Even so, all was not lost to the Whitehall warrior. Sir Roger was a veteran of the corridors of power, and the very ambiguities in the directive should have been turned to his positive advantage.

This required tact, diplomacy, charm and finesse, and above all a subtlety in approach.

Sir Roger Keyes was about as subtle as an air raid.

He was obstinate, arrogant and self-opinionated. He despised the chiefs of staff and made no secret of his views; and indeed treated them as his personal staff. Rather than co-ordinate, Keyes intended to empire build, and to use his directorate to greater things. Indeed one of his first steps was to divorce combined operations from the Admiralty and move it to 1A Richmond Terrace, right at the other end of Whitehall; this endeared him to few.

'We have suffered greatly in the First War from "dug outs",' commented one admiral, 'and here was the same tendency to bring back men for jobs they would have been ripe to undertake twenty years earlier.'

Admiral Sir Dudley Pound, the 63-year-old First Sea Lord, wrote to Admiral Cunningham in the Mediterranean, 'Roger Keyes intrigued himself into the position of Director of Combined Operations in spite of the protests of the Chiefs of Staff.' Pound was outraged by the appointment, but then the enmity between him and Keyes at a personal level was an unhealed scar that reached down to the bone.

The most charitable reaction to Keyes came from the Air Ministry and that was one of scepticism. The Prime Minister was fully aware that Keyes had his detractors, so why did he appoint him? There are no clear answers. Some say it was Keyes's willingness 25 years earlier to risk all at the Dardanelles by a renewed naval attack on the Narrows to force the issue, that had marked him out in Churchill's mind as a man of action and decision.

There is little doubt that Keyes had badgered Churchill for an appointment and on the basis of their long and lasting friendship. There are those, however, who have always maintained that it went deeper, that Churchill was repaying a debt. In May 1940 Keyes had appeared in the House of Commons, resplendent in the dress uniform of an Admiral of the Fleet, to denounce the Chamberlain administration for the Norwegian campaign and in particular the naval failures. Such a dramatic but vulgar castigation probably did hasten the downfall of Chamberlain; although one should remember that Winston Churchill was First Lord of the Admiralty. . .

The appointment also caused confusions within Special Forces, for it separated, at least by function, Combined Operations from smaller scale raiding. However, General Bourne seemed quite content. Far from taking offence, he instead asked to be relieved of his duties as Adjutant General Royal Marines, so that he might devote all his efforts and attention to being Keyes's deputy.

As for Dudley Clarke and Garnon Williams, they had hardly come to terms with Bourne's appointment when Keyes' appeared like a bolt out of the blue. For Dudley Clarke it reinforced old fears and brought new forebodings for the future of his raiding concept. He believed that Keyes might now attempt to force the pace beyond their capabilities. Clarke feared that the hero of the great Zeebrugge raid would hardly be content with the very modest programme of slowly expanding operations which was all that he had to offer through the summer and autumn.

The Prime Minister asked Anthony Eden, the Secretary of State for War, to consider ways and means by which raiding and combined operations could be related to sabotage, to produce the strategy to carry the war onto the continent.

On 22 July 1940 Eden sent the Prime Minister the following memorandum:

Stage One: Reconnaissance, sabotage and subversion, the experimental phase of coastal raids.

Stage Two: Guerrilla Warfare – 'constant smash and grab raids' by numbers of irregular troops and carried up and down the enemy's coast line.

Stage Three: Combined Services to make deliberate attacks upon important and well defended objectives.

Stage Four: The knock out phase, deep advances inland.

It was an honest attempt to bring some order into the present confusions, but quite unrealistic. Eden envisaged a tempo of operations in Stage Two which would allow two raids a week each using a minimum of 200 men and lasting anything up to 20 hours.

The Prime Minister rejected Eden's suggestions out of hand. 'It would be most unwise to disturb the coasts of any of these countries by the kind of silly fiascos which were perpetrated at Boulogne and Guernsey. The idea of working all these coasts up against us by pinprick raids and fulsome communiqués is one strictly to be avoided.'

Instead Churchill had already asked Keyes to plan medium scale raids using forces of up to 5,000 men and more during the winter months. The muddled thinking is apparent. The danger of invasion would recede with the onset of autumn and the deterioration in weather conditions, shorter hours of daylight and Channel storms. Yet the combined operations were required to launch raids involving a large number of men in exactly the same weather conditions. Indeed, the Prime Minister envisaged a rising crescendo of operations, so that, by the late spring and early summer of 1941, combined operations should be able to undertake 'large armoured eruptions' onto the continent.

Keyes guaranteed to meet the Prime Minister's requirements, and was taken aback when he discovered the true state of affairs in combined operations. General Bourne, Dudley Clarke and Garnon Williams explained where the weaknesses lay, and pointed out the absence of trained troops; to date none of the special force units was anywhere near their planned strength, and the specialist landing craft needed to carry them and their equipment. So long as these deficiencies remained, ambitions to launch anything other than smaller scale raids would remain ambitions.

However, Keyes did give Churchill a false impression of confidence in the capabilities of his new organization, so that within a month, when Churchill raised the question of another raid on Guernsey, Keyes replied that there would be no problem.

Keyes now introduced what for Dudley Clarke and his team in MO9 was a complete reversal of policy. It was bitterly resented. The whole idea of 'little and often' minor raids was abandoned, and a halt called upon all raids until the resources were available for a 'big show'.

The new policy directive did not earn MO9 any friends in the service ministries. Their co-operation had always been conditional on a quick and visual dividend, immediate raids. The promise of a longer term policy did not find favour. Dudley Clarke quickly found he was running out of support in Whitehall. Staff negotiations with the service ministries became bleak affairs, difficulties were emphasized, and co-operation discouraged from above. In the battles that were about to erupt between the feudal barons of the services over combined operations, MO9 had no friends, and its patron was not in the least interested.

Dudley Clarke was a skilled operator in the Whitehall scene, but he was the first to realize that with MO9's horizons still limited to small-scale raiding, and a Prime Minister angry over Guernsey, the writing was on the wall. Keyes had subsumed his authority over the 'commandos', and would not sanction the smaller raids. At the same time, Sir John Dill was utterly determined that Clarke should fulfil his commitment, which was a condition for the creation of the special forces.

This was a time when Churchill dominated the scene, and was probably at the height of his powers and his influence. Throughout August and into September, Keyes was the Prime Minister's constant companion, the favoured guest at weekend house parties at Chertwell, the close confidant on public visits and military demonstrations. Keyes was there when the occasions had nothing whatsoever to do with combined operations. But gradually the warnings from the Admiralty to the War Office and to the Air Ministry, of the suspicions about Keyes's personal ambitions began to take effect.

---

[1] Prime Minister to General Ismay and Sir Edward Bridges 17 July 1940.

CHAPTER SEVENTEEN

The War Office Offensive

From the very first Dudley Clarke and Garnon Williams held many discussions with members of the Admiralty Board and the Ministry of Supply on the design and the characteristics of assault landing craft. Boulogne and Guernsey had both pointed to the type of shallow draught craft which could be driven hard ashore, and then be able to return to the sea.

Some of the smaller British boat building yards were designing new prototypes, but it was taking a long time.

The breakthrough came about through a chance meeting. Senior officers like Dudley Clarke were required to do night duty at the War Office, in rotation. One evening in late July, Clarke was having supper at the Berkeley Buttery before going on duty; it was a favourite eating place. At the next table was another regular, Mr Dodds, the operations manager of the tanker fleet owned by British Petroleum.

The two men were on nodding terms, and Dodds enquired after Clarke's war wound. His head was still bandaged after the injury he sustained at Le Touquet. The conversation turned from the Boulogne raid to the subject of landing craft and Clarke went into considerable detail in describing the problem.

Discretion and security did not seem to have been a consideration in this open and very frank conversation with a civilian. Perhaps because Mr Dodds dined regularly at the Berkeley Buttery, he was 'the right sort of chap', and therefore a man to be trusted.

Suddenly Clarke found Dodds describing an American-built motor boat. British Petroleum had been looking at the craft to see whether it could service their drilling needs in swamps and shallow water.

Dodds had the specifications in his office and offered them to Clarke.

'How urgent is this?' he asked.

'The quicker we get the right boats, the quicker we can get on with raiding the enemy.'

'No time like the present,' replied Dodds. 'I'll go straight back to the office, and have them round to you by midnight.' Taxis were not the easiest things to come by in London at that time of night, but nevertheless Dodds managed to deliver the drawings to the War Office. Clarke, unable to contain his enthusiasm, telephoned Garnon Williams immediately and the two pored over the plans and specifications.

The craft was built by the Higgins Boat Company of New Orleans and called the *Eureka*. It seemed to meet their requirements precisely. The *Eureka* was designed for the Louisiana swamps of the lower Mississippi. The twin screws were housed in well-protected tunnels so that the boat could force its way through mud and tangled swamp water. It was designed with a shallow draught so that the boat could be driven directly onto a mud bank, and then relaunched by the simple expedient of putting the engine full astern to pull it free. It had a small turning circle which allowed the boat to leave land quickly and turn out to open water without the risk of broaching in the surf. There was a hinged bow ramp for easy unloading and an extremely reliable and already proven engine.

Clarke took the drawings to General Bourne first thing the next morning. He needed little convincing.

The directorate of Combined Operations designated the Higgins boat Land Craft Vehicle Personnel (LCVP). In a combat role it could carry 36 soldiers or a couple of trucks, and became the forerunner for a whole series of different and more specialist craft. Bourne realized the potential and was able to place a substantial order with the Higgins Boat Company through the Ministry of Supply. Then things came to a grinding halt. The problem was transportation. The first boats were 30 feet long and over 10 feet wide, and in days before prefabrication, a bulky cargo to deliver. In the convoys that were already being formed to deliver goods from the United States to England, there were other war materials and foodstuffs which had a higher priority.

One solution, which Mr Dodds offered, was to bring the landing craft across as deck cargo on the tankers. The latter were sailing fully-laden from the Texas oil ports, and New Orleans was en route to England. The landing craft were bulky but light, and the tankers had nothing 'up top' but deck space, so they could easily be transported without any sacrifice to their precious cargo of petroleum and fuel. Bureaucracy would have none of it, however, and the dead hand of officialdom ensured that tankers carried fuel and nothing else.

It was going to be some considerable time before the craft would appear in sufficient numbers to make their presence felt on this side of the Atlantic. There was no spare capacity in British shipyards, and what space could be devoted to combined operations was already fully occupied in another programme of improvization. This involved the conversion of ships to carry the troops and their landing craft to the invasion shores.

Two Dutch and six Belgian Channel packets were among the first to be completed. The more modern ships were designated Landing Ship Infantry Medium, LSI(M), and were equipped with British-designed landing craft which were carried in gravity davits. The older ships along with some ex-British Railway Company Ferries became Landing Ship Infantry Hand, LSI(H); their landing craft were carried in older hand-operated davits.

The old London North-Eastern Railway Train Ferries *Daffodil* and *Princess Iris* were converted, less successfully, to carry landing craft by their stern chutes.

A couple of large horse ferries were being built on Tyneside for the Turkish army. These were abruptly requisitioned and improvized into makeshift landing craft.

Finally a couple of larger cargo liners, instead of being earmarked for the now discredited role of armed merchant cruisers, were given over to combined operations and converted into large attack or assault ships. They had the capacity to carry many hundreds of troops with a full complement of landing craft.

All this work would take time. Churchill was already beginning to appreciate that it was one thing to fire off a daily broadside of memoranda to the harassed Ismay, demanding 'action this day': it was quite another to produce the result.

In the meantime, since the Prime Minister had outlawed small-scale raids, and so long as the resources necessary for larger scale operations were unavailable, the new formations of special troops could do little other than train and exercise, and then train some more. It was their inability to get to grips with the enemy that allowed the military establishment to organize opposition and launch a counter offensive against what they called 'Keyes's Corps d'Élite'.

Sir John Dill led the attack. He had the professional soldier's distaste for informality, and an abhorrence for the lax discipline which in his view already characterized the special forces.

General Allan Brooke joined the opposition, 'but for more practical reasons'. He saw these élite formations specifically appealing to young men with spirit, energy and talent. Brooke was under no illusions as to the quality of the post Dunkirk army, and he feared too many natural leaders would be enticed away from a field army where they were indispensable. It was Brooke's genuine belief and professional judgement that this was too high a price to pay for the new military formations which in any case were of dubious military value.

In October 1940, the establishment won an important victory. With the threat of invasion temporarily removed, the independent companies and the commandos were reorganized. They were now to be integrated into Special Service battalions as the spearhead troops for the big raids into Europe. The word 'commando' was deliberately avoided, and taken by MO9 as a deliberate snub.

There was an equally naïve disregard for the connotation 'SS', which the men, in their own snub to convention, called 'Suicide Squads'.

The Special Service battalions were grouped into a Special Service brigade. For recruiting and administration the new structure still came under the control of the directorate of Combined Operations. However, the War Office appointed an ex-Guardsman, Brigadier J. C. Hayden DSO, to train them and more importantly to command them in action. Keyes attempted to resist this latest innovation, but his opposition was to no avail; a more recognized military structure had been imposed, and some control reasserted.

The new measures marked the demise of the independent companies; although one other company was to survive for some time to come. The Axis between Germany and Italy focused attention on Franco's Spain. The fear in Whitehall was that Madrid would succumb to the temptation of joining a war-winning fascist camp, and throw in its lot with Hitler and Mussolini. We shall return to this question later for the implication to Britain of a belligerent Spain on neutral Portugal and the Atlantic sea routes, not to mention the balance of power in the Mediterranean and North Africa, which were more than enough to cause sleepless nights for the War Cabinet and the combined chiefs.

Immediately the fear was Gibraltar. So, though few tears were shed over the disbanding of the independent companies at home, approval was reluctantly given for a special company to be raised with volunteers from the garrison on 'the Rock'.

The new force, called Independent Company Gibraltar was raised in October 1940, and trained to meet two contingencies. The first was to provide guerrilla-style assault parties should Spain attack 'the Rock'. The second was to provide raiding parties should Spain declare war, but not press home an attack on the British garrison. Drafts of soldiers were dispatched to Scotland to train at the Irregular Warfare School. However, the landings by Americans and Free French in August 1944 in the south of France, removed the threat, effectively 'sanitized' Spain and allowed the company to be disbanded without having ever fired a shot in anger.

The disbanding of the independent companies at home presented their members with some hard choices. Should they opt for the new battalions, or return to their old regiments and the more conventional form of soldiering?

It wasn't an easy decision, for the pull of regimental loyalty, especially for these territorials was hard to resist.

Charles Newman was under pressure to rejoin his old TA battalion of the Essex Regiment.

They were overseas in Freetown West Africa, where they were to form the nucleus of the new African divisions with the expanding battalions of the Gold Coast Regiment. The battalion's second in command had been invalided home, and Colonel Gibson wanted Newman to replace him; so badly that he was pestered by telegrams.

At the same time Newman was summoned to meet Lieutenant Colonel W. Glendenning of the Welsh Regiment at Sandwich.

Glendenning had been given command of 1st Special Service Battalion.

'I want you to be my second in command.'

Newman was taken aback by this approach. As a long service territorial officer, he believed it was essential that a second in command and a commanding officer should like each other and know one another very well indeed for the partnership to succeed. He did not know Glendenning but he explained his opinions, and for good measure told him of the offer to return to the Essex.

'I know Colonel Gibson, and he knows me, but we two don't know each other at all!'

Glendenning, despite his regiment, was an Irishman, and now brought to bear all the charm of his race to win over the man he wanted.

'Well, look at me,' he said with a disarming smile. 'Here I am, do you like me? Will I do for you? You'll do for me, Charles!'

Newman thought quickly. Gibson's spit and polish, the regiment, its tradition, the band and drums, old friends and honest to goodness soldiering with the battalion, he had spent so many years in, preparing for war. The pull was emotional but strong enough to make him feel guilty – to feel a sense of desertion and betrayal. There would be no turning back. If he refused Gibson's offer, he would effectively cut the umbilical cord, and the chances of eventual command (which of course would be enhanced from being the second in command) would be squashed. Then as now the ceiling of ambition for every territorial officer was to command his battalion.

Newman looked across the table at Glendenning. Here was an unknown quantity offering him 'military employment' in an unknown force with at best its future prospects obscure.

'I'm on,' he replied, without even knowing why. Glendenning smiled broadly and clapped Newman on the shoulder. He then explained how the new battalion would be organized.

There were to be five special service battalions; each battalion would comprise over 1,000 soldiers and 50 officers, divided into two large companies each of five troops. Glendenning explained that the five battalions would effectively absorb all the various special force units in the United Kingdom. In this, however, he was wrong. No. 2 Army Commando continued its parachute training at Ringway, undisturbed by the reorganization taking place elsewhere.

The new amalgamations produced casualties. Nos. 5 and 6 Special Service Companies were combined into a single battalion under the latter's commanding officer. Pat Wood moved to the Special Service Brigade Headquarters, and the new CO, Lieutenant Colonel Fetherstonehaugh chose to keep his own second in command. This meant there was no place for Jack Churchill unless he chose to drop down to captain; or return to the Manchesters.

Churchill was livid and telephoned Charles Haydon.

'I'm very anxious to see you because I'm getting a raw deal from this man Fetherstonhaugh. He is pulling in everybody from his commando, and we're not getting anything, and most of all I'm not getting anything!'

Haydon was very tactful about the whole business, but he had no intention of losing Churchill.

'Well if this is so Jack, it seems quite wrong. Obviously you should have got command of A Company. Look, I'll see that you are not sent back to the Manchesters. How about a job in the meanwhile with Hughie Stockwell up at Inverailort?'

Churchill accepted the offer. It was either that or back to the Manchesters. Unlike Newman, the regiment did not exert the same emotional pull.

'Right, Jack, you get yourself up there and you can work something out with Stockwell. Tell him it will only be for a short while, but you'll be useful to them, very useful to them in some capacity.

While you're doing that job, I will see what I can work out with the battalions.'

Jack Churchill packed his bags and travelled north to Inverailort. Haydon had called Stockwell ahead of time and prepared the way; not that he needed much convincing. Stockwell and his hard pressed instructors were only too pleased to welcome a man of Jack Churchill's talents and reputation into their midst.

By the time he had settled into the new routine, the main 'customers' were the men from No. 2 Special Service Company, who, having completed their parachute training, were undergoing the rigours of the Irregular Warfare School syllabus.

Churchill joined in with gusto, and even considered applying to join the new parachutists, but all the officer slots were long since taken. He thought it better to wait for an opportunity elsewhere to return to active soldiering.

The First Special Service Company moved to the West Country. Half the battalion were quartered at Dartmouth and the remainder across the estuary at the bustling seaside resort of Paignton in the heart of the 'Devon Riviera'. Dudley Clarke's principle of private quartering with local families was allowed to continue for the present, if only because it eased the pressure on the War Office to find barrack space.

Battalion headquarters was established in a fine old country parsonage overlooking the Dart, and specially requisitioned. Glendenning and Newman became regular commuters on the ferry to Kingswear which linked with Paignton.

Newman busied himself writing the training programme for the battalion. Brigade headquarters was there if they needed special assistance, but Haydon had stressed to his COs that theirs was an independent command. The emphasis which Clarke had placed on the special service companies – his commandos – 'doing their own thing', was to endure with the new battalions.

The main weakness of the new formations soon became apparent. They were too big and unwieldy and it proved well nigh impossible to train the whole battalion at once. Newman split his training exercises into packages for companies and even troop size.

Brigadier Haydon did lay down one guideline by way of policy. He asked that his battalions devote as much time as was practical to familiarizing the men with the Royal Navy. Liaison officers from the Senior Service were provided for the purpose.

The First Battalion was ideally placed at Darmouth. Lieutenant Commander Pastle Beresford, a delightful and helpful officer, set up shop in Newman's office, and soon had a full programme of sea-going visits on the destroyers, escorts, and submarines that anchored in the Dart Estuary.

In November, Newman took a few days off from his desk and went to sea in the destroyer *Jupiter*. She was the temporary lead ship of the already famous Fifth Destroyer Flotilla under Captain Lord Louis Mountbatten.[1] The 'Fighting Fifth' was based in Plymouth but had just returned after screening the battleship *Revenge*, while she bombarded Cherbourg.

Mountbatten proved to be an excellent host, and showed great interest in the special service battalions. The epitome of a destroyer leader, Mountbatten delighted his audience by throwing the *Jupiter* around the Channel in a series of sharply executed turns and manoeuvres, all part of a simulated sub hunt, which tested the ship and his crew to the limits.

Just a week or so later, Newman was saddened to learn that *Jupiter* had been crippled in a night action against German destroyers. They had made some good friends amongst the crew of the *Jupiter* and the heavy loss of life was especially sad.

When not at sea, the First Special Service Battalion found realistic and useful training lay in acting as 'enemy' for the battalions and brigades who exercized on Dartmoor. However, their irregular warfare methods won them few friends, and there were frequent complaints that the methods employed were not included in the book of rules on war.

It proved all too easy for them to capture senior formation commanders. Brigadiers and divisional generals would fall into their hands through the simple expedient of a small group of 'commandos' lying up, and allowing the attackers to move 'over them', then emerging to attack the soft rear echelons.

On another occasion a troop ambushed a brigade's baggage in its rear area.

Amongst the plunder they made off with was a complete hot meal for a whole battalion. The troop fed themselves regally while the battalion cursed and fumed and went hungry.

Tempers boiled over when they hit the same battalion again that night. Their officers had bivouacked in a supposedly safe area. The raiders infiltrated the lax defences and 'killed' the lot, a decision confirmed by the duty umpires. The battalion officers remonstrated (but to no avail), that they had had a hard day's training, and should not have been disturbed during their only chance to sleep!

A few senior officers began to get the message. What was happening on Dartmoor was being repeated elsewhere. The damage that a handful of well-trained men could inflict behind enemy lines can be out of all proportion to the risks and costs involved. Others considered such antics as unworthy of the British character. 'Fighting dirty' was not the way to defeat the Nazis and still retain one's dignity. Fighting dirty was the enemy way.

The special service battalions trained hard, and gathered about them an aura and a reputation. But training whilst attracting new recruits to the cause was not inflicting damage on the enemy.

The absence of raids and the complaints from formation commanders on the 'outrageous' behaviour of the special service battalions on exercise, allowed Sir John Dill to renew the offensive. His one-time subordinate, Dudley Clarke, had failed to live up to his commitment, and now Dill's opposition was both petty and unrelenting. Clarke knew there was trouble coming. There were no raids planned to ease the pressure, and the Whitehall bailiffs were about ready to move in on his domain.

Dill called a halt to further recruiting into the special forces. The chiefs of staff concurred and Keyes protested vigorously. The Prime Minister demurred pending a War Office investigation into the role and future of the special service battalions.

Field Marshall Sir John Dill chose to investigate the lodging allowance; which, for some reason best known to himself, he abhorred.

In late November 1940, the five special service battalion commanders and the commanding officer of No. 2 Commando were called to London and a conference at the War Office. All the senior special force officers and the combined operations were invited to send representatives as observers.

The critics of the lodging allowance met with a support for the experiment that took even Dudley Clarke, its author, by surprise. It was the unanimous opinion of the commanding officers that the billeting arrangements did more than anything else to instil self-reliance and initiative. This in turn left the men free to devote their whole time to training with none of the irksome chores of guard, barrack duties and parades.

Indeed Clarke knew that it was these less palatable features of regimental soldiering that were proving one of the biggest incentives for men to volunteer to the special forces. Dill conceded the point and accepted that the lodging allowance should remain. However there was a price to be exacted. In return for War Office approval not only of the special service battalions, but the large measure of independence invested in them, there could be no role or purpose to MO9.

The logic was inescapable. Any small scale raiding could be handled at troop or company level with the special service battalion.

Planning for such raids could be undertaken in the directorate of Combined Operations, and operational control through Brigade headquarters.

Given that small-scale raiding was no longer the priority, it did not need a separate department.

None of the special service officers, probably relieved at winning concessions, was prepared to defend Dudley Clarke's organization.

Admiral Keyes and General Bourne were now fully involved in the big operations, and Garnon Williams had already joined them.

The War Office ordered MO9 to be placed under sentence of early liquidation.

Dudley Clarke took the only action that was open to him. He resigned.

It didn't take very long to hand over to his successor, who was appointed simply to preside over the dissolution.

Within 48 hours Dudley Clarke was out of the War Office and en route to the Middle East and a new job.

---

[1]The flotilla leader, HMS *Kelly* was under repair on the Tyne after having lost her bows to a German torpedo while on patrol in the North Sea.

CHAPTER EIGHTEEN

Commandos at Last

Throughout the autumn of 1940, Sir Roger Keyes still remained a force to be reckoned with in Whitehall. At first he was a welcome guest of the Prime Minister and still accompanied him on numerous visits around the country. For the time being Churchill's patronage was sufficient but it was on the wane. And a number of people equally close to the Prime Minister were joining the ranks of opposition to Keyes.

General Ismay, as Churchill's chief of staff, was at the very centre of affairs. At first, and by using all the skill in diplomacy for which he was to become renowned, Ismay sought to contain the situation. After all, Churchill was a prime minister who surrounded himself with a galaxy of talents as his advisers, and there were bound to be jealousies and infighting 'amongst the Court'. The problem for Ismay was that he could not contain Keyes's ambitions, especially when his intentions were displayed in such unsubtle ways. Ismay and the other military members of the inner sanctum were appalled at the sheer effrontery of Keyes when he suggested to the Prime Minister that he should be appointed 'his deputy' to preside over the chiefs of staff!

A successful raid or two in line with the exploits of a Drake would have helped Keyes's cause. Until the landing ships were made ready, the specialist crews trained to man them, and the raiding forces exercised in their use, nothing could be attempted. So the dream of the Prime Minister for large-scale raids across the Channel remained a dream. Keyes in turn had only the future promise of his directorate and his own past reputation, as hero of another war, to use to his own advantage.

Plans for the new year were being made, and attention, from October onwards, began to focus on Italy and the Mediterranean. Garnon Williams presented a scheme which he called Operation Dudley. Directed against Italy it dispensed with half measures, and went straight to the core of the problem. The objective was to knock Italy out of the war, and in a single stroke. This would be achieved by landing 5,000 special service troops at the Lido de Roma, or the estuary of the Tiber, and capture Rome. This Garnon Williams believed would paralyze Italy, and allow the anti-war, anti-fascist opposition to assert themselves. Together with the special service troopers they would topple Il Duce and take Italy out of the war, or even perhaps declare for the Allies! If it failed, the British had gambled and lost just 5,000 troops . . .

It is surprising to think that such a scheme was ever placed for consideration to the chiefs of staff, leave alone before the War Cabinet. To learn that Operation Dudley was viewed as a serious option is staggering. It was shelved finally with the arrival in 1941 of the Luftwaffe in Italy and Rommel in North Africa. The planners had enough sense to appreciate that a significant German presence ruled out any intrigue in Italy with a national dimension. The tragedy is that the same conclusion was forgotten three years later when the Italians tried to surrender and change sides.

In October, attention also centred on Pantelleria, a small rocky island about 150 miles north-west of Malta. Together with its smaller sister, Lampedusa, it had been heavily fortified by Mussolini. Both were held in strength but Pantelleria boasted an airstrip and underground hangars with a capacity for 80 fighters. The numerous caves and grottoes were converted as refuelling and resupply bays for submarines and torpedo boats.

In Operation Workshop, Keyes proposed the capture of Pantelleria by the special service battalions. Its capture, he argued, would inflict a resounding psychological blow on Italy, perhaps enough to bring about the downfall of Mussolini in time. Militarily its capture and retention would cut the Axis line of communication with North Africa.

If Pantelleria could have been captured, it would have had a significant psychological influence on the Italians. Its military utility to the British is more open to question. Malta was already proving more than effective in its role of interdicting Italian communications. Secondly the garrison would have to be fed, watered and supplied, for Pantelleria was not self-sufficient; and Keyes's 'guerrillas' could not live off the land. With the bulk of the northern shores of the Mediterranean if not hostile, then 'belligerently neutral', the convoying of supplies to Pantelleria seemed a high price to pay in return for moving the base of operations 150 miles nearer. The Italian fleet was a formidable opponent with more, and more modern ships than the Royal Navy had at its disposal in the Mediterranean.

The Prime Minister was much taken by Operation Workshop; he saw it as bold and imaginative with the right ingredients for a grand historical gesture. He was largely opposed by his service chiefs who still feared the implications of Franco joining the Axis. Gibraltar could not withstand a prolonged siege, and a hostile Spanish coast would open up yet more ports from which the U-boats could operate. Loss of Gibraltar meant the Straits would be lost too and our armies in the Middle East could then only be supplied, and under even greater difficulty, via the long Cape route.

The Italian surface fleet would no longer be bottled up in the Mediterranean. Portugal's neutrality would be compromised if Spain became a belligerent.

Contingency plans were prepared. If Franco declared for the Axis, Britain would have to consider taking the Azores, Madeira and possibly Cape Verde Islands from Portugal, and the Canary Islands from Spain. Such contingencies required a 'fire brigade' force of troops trained in amphibious warfare. At that time there were neither the ships nor the special service battalions available for two major operations.

If this wasn't enough, the Admiralty had a pet scheme of their own for 'Keyes's Private Army'. The naval staff fancied a show of strength in the eastern Mediterranean and proposed that Keyes seize Rhodes. This, it was believed, would bolster the Greeks in Albania, and encourage the Turks to come off their neutral fence and declare for the Allies.

The merits of these different operations were considered, but in the murky context of intrigues and mutterings against Keyes. In such infighting he was not at all well equipped. He had a temperament which did not allow him to handle the senior staff officers with any tact or skill. Worse, Keyes had the kind of ego which persuaded him that he alone knew all that was worth knowing about raiding and combined operations. Neither could he conceal his desire to have a battle command, to lead his special service troops on Operation Workshop; and thereby to repeat his exploits of Zeebrugge. Perhaps if Sir Roger had concentrated on building up his raiding forces, their training, administration and organization, and left command to a younger man, then life might have been easier. Brigadier Haydon had already been appointed to the battle command, and Keyes's attempt to have that decision reversed simply stirred up even greater resentment.

By November, Sir Roger Keyes in his dealings with the chiefs of staff was locked in a battle largely of his own making. Even those on his own staff who dared to challenge his grandiose schemes earned his wrath. One such officer was Captain Mound RN who had been appointed in the early days to head the naval staff under General Bourne.

Mound opposed Keyes's schemes and the admiral summarily dismissed him, which was a draconian step to take against any senior officer. Dismissal under these conditions could have an immediate consequence on the subject's career. It did on Mound's. The Admiralty promptly awarded him command of the carrier *Ark Royal* in the Mediterranean.

On 12 December 1940, the decision was taken to postpone Operation Workshop.

Keyes was not party to the decision-making, and was only informed about it afterwards.

The Prime Minister, however, must have anticipated a few problems, and deliberately excluded Keyes from the Chertwell guest list that weekend. Sir Roger was furious, so furious that he turned up unannounced and demanded to see Churchill.

The Prime Minister was indignant, but eventually did agree to see his Director of Combined Operations; but Operation Workshop was not reactivated.

Keyes had presumed too much on his friendship with the Prime Minister. Churchill's private office were thunderstruck at Keyes's audacity. He had, according to John Colville, 'carried the Zeebrugge spirit too far into private life'.

Despite all these intrigues, combined operations had at last succeeded in building up a sizeable 'brigade of special troops', but the battalions were still short of the fully-trained manpower. However, by this time, the Royal Marine Brigade had completed its training and was available.

Ships were available too with the conversion of HMS *Glengyle*, a 13,000-ton, former fast cargo liner into a Landing Ship Infantry Large or LSI(L). She had the capacity to lift 1,000 troops and was intended as the first, and in the event, very successful, class of warships.

Although the choice for an operation did differ, there was a consensus that the Mediterranean offered a better prospect for raiding operations than the Channel. Keyes was instructed to retain a sizeable contingency force for Spain and to equip a major expedition for the Mediterranean.

In the new year of 1941, three understrength special service units under Colonel Bob Laycock and called 'Layforce' left for the Middle East in a convoy headed by HMS *Glengyle*. They arrived in Egypt in March, just as Rommel's defensive in the Western Desert was gaining momentum, and the German Panzers were rampaging into the Balkans.

There was time too for other changes. At last in February 1941 what many had known for some time was officially acknowledged: the special service battalions were too big and too unwieldy. They were to be divided into smaller formations called commandos each comprising six troops.

Reorganization at long last gave Charles Newman his chance of an independent command.

No. 1 Special Service Battalion was split. Glendenning took A Company and formed No. 1 Army Commando, and Newman had B Company which became No. 2 Army Commando. It meant immediate promotion to lieutenant colonel and the opportunity to put into practice all the ideals and objectives which he had long considered should characterize special forces.

Lieutenant Colonel Newman raised his commando at Paignton and weeded out the undesirables, who hitherto had evaded detection in the mass of the big battalion.

Newman adopted the 'SS' for 'Special Service' as the shoulder flash, with a fighting knife with which everyone was armed.[1] Like other commando leaders he saw that the individuality of the insignia would set them apart from other units in the army, but, more importantly, he tried to foster an *ésprit de corps* for Special Service.

The Special Service was voluntary, but Newman was ruthless in his determination to rid himself of any man, officer or soldier who did not have the *offensive spirit*, the desire to go anywhere, and do anything that struck at the enemy. Officers and men were much closer than in the field army, and there was a degree of informality not to be found in the more conventionally minded battalion or regiment. The level of understanding and mutual confidence reached a very high degree.

In these early days the commandos were autonomous under their commanding officers. Volunteers were given initial training now at Inverary, but thereafter additional skills were down to the units. The result was that there were good and not so good outfits. The variations were those that one would expect to find in any army, except that the *mean standard* was so much higher. Newman from the outset laid down a veritable 'catechism' of standards and attainments,[2] by which he set great store in moulding 2 Commando into 'a very special force'.

This second reorganization of the commandos was completed by mid-March, and Jack Churchill too found a home. Charles Haydon telephoned him at the School of Irregular Warfare in Inverary.

'Jack, I've just the job for you.'

'Really, Brigadier.'

'John Dunford Slater, who you may know, is a gunner.'

'No, I didn't know.'

'Well, look, he's in command of 3 Commando at Largs and he has just sacked his second in command. So there's a vacancy there. Would you like to go and see John and sell yourself to him?'

'Certainly – this is marvellous.'

Jack Churchill telephoned John Dunford Slater without delay.

'Can I come and see you?' he began. 'I have been told by Charles Haydon that you want a second in command. I was unhorsed by that bloody man Fetherstonehaugh and his caper. Can I come and see you to see if I am suitable?'

Newman worked his commando hard from the outset, but the Paignton area no longer held any surprises for them; they had trained over every yard of the neighbouring countryside and there is nothing worse than soldiers who are bored on exercise.

It was time for fresh fields. Newman called Brigadier Haydon and gained his approval to move his commando to Weymouth. This would make a pleasant change. Haydon, helpful and supportive as ever, offered to arrange transport to move the commando to its new town. Charles Newman graciously declined, and decided that the commando would move itself.

They had a tiny administrative tail, and this included a few army trucks. These were loaded with their stores, the mens' kit bags and the officers' baggage, and convoyed to Weymouth.

Newman and the commando marched the 120 miles to Weymouth, sleeping where they arrived each night, and bivouacking in the nearest fields. Four days later, footsore and weary, the commando shouldered arms and there was a spring in their step as Newman led his men straight down the main high street. The second in command had driven ahead, arranged the lodging and greeted his colonel on the town hall steps. Newman brought the commando smartly to a halt before the mayor and town council.

They had a month of solid training in the rolling downs and then it was time to move on again. War and the prospect of action beckoned.

On this occasion Brigade Headquarters did intervene and 2 Army Commando were transferred northwards to Inverary, where the instructors put them through a crash course in amphibious operations. Rumours were rife that a job was coming up. But London was dithering again.

All the hard evidence indicated that Spain might be on the point of renouncing its neutrality and joining the Axis. Contingency plans had to be activated. The result was that for a month and more the commandos were put through the hoop while Whitehall waited in dread anticipation.

The course at Inverary was abruptly terminated, and 2 Commando hustled down to the Clyde. There they moved into a makeshift transit camp at Gourrock along with other troops, and in the most spartan conditions. A force was gathering for something; there were marines and other commandos, tanks and guns in support, together with a couple of line battalions of bemused infantry.

Fortunately the transit camp lasted only a couple of days. Any longer and there would probably have been wholesale riots. No decisions were taken in Whitehall, but the troops were moved to their ships. No. 2 Commando settled into the recently converted HMS *Ulster Monarch*, where they were told to prepare for a long voyage, so perhaps it wasn't Spain after all. While the men found their way around the ship, and that didn't take long (for this one time Irish sea packet and now new LSI(H) was a small affair), the staff took over. There was a complete issue of clothes and uniforms, pith helmets and tropical gear, scale maps were locked away in the ship's safe; tables for next of kin revised and the commandos urged to put their affairs in order.

The task force put to sea for a week's exercises. Three rehearsals for the landings were carried out with the order of battle and sequence of landing practised thoroughly.

It was exciting. There was a purposeful feeling to things, and the commandos paid very careful attention to even the smallest details. Nobody of course knew where they were going or what the eventual target would be.

Rumours continued to spread around the fleet. And General Sturgess, who was in command of the Marine brigade had to order his men to stop gambling on the location of the raid; this of course had the reverse effect and served only to fuel speculation.

Almost as if in punishment, the fleet returned to Gourrock and the official word this time was that the operation was postponed. Troops were disembarked from the ships and dispersed to their bases.

HMS *Ulster Monarch* was in need of a quick refit. The previous week had proved rather traumatic. There were repairs to be made and alterations to the accommodation after the experiences of carrying troops for the first time.

Brigadier Haydon instructed Newman to leave all his stores on board, together with a rear party, while he settled the commando into Dumfries; so the delay could only be temporary. Sure enough, within the week, the commando had returned to the *Ulster Monarch*, and the other ships made ready to receive their troops. Everyone was convinced that this time it would be 'the real thing'.

The task force set sail. Once the docklands of Clydeside had disappeared the commandos rushed below to try on their new tropical uniforms. The result was that very few were on deck to witness that the fleet 'turned right', and headed northwards up the Scottish coast.

Two days later the ships dropped anchor at Scapa Flow; the northern anchorage of the Home Fleet in the Orkney Islands.

There was another full-scale landing rehearsal at Scapa. This one was masterminded by Keyes and watched by the King. It did not go at all well, which pleased the establishment and discomfited Keyes.

Newman's commando landed on a beach near Kirkwall, and marched through pouring rain to a service canteen in the naval base, where they spent a miserable night brewing tea. Nobody witnessed their part in the production and the next morning they marched all the way back, still in the pouring rain, to the *Ulster Monarch*.

By the end of the day, the fleet had weighed anchor, and along with its escort sailed south to the Clyde. For two days the troops were confined to the ships and some still believed that an operation was imminent. But when the official word came, the operation was postponed.

The commando returned to Dumfries. The soldiers had been promised action. They were angry, disappointed and frustrated. Newman knew there was bound to be trouble, for you cannot keep a thoroughbred horse on top of his form unless you actually give him a run.

Brigade headquarters moved them on from Dumfries, which was a pretty dismal place, to Perth, but the commando found they were not welcome in Perth. This was a new experience. The image had been carefully fostered that these were the specialists, shock troops of the new order, full of derring-do and very special.

Perth was full of Free Poles. They were romantic, ardent lovers, had been there a long time and, by now, had the locals well-trained.

After three nights, during which the commandos found their charms wasted at the local Lyceum Ballroom, their patience was exhausted. The girls would not even dance with them. Enough was enough; Kirkwall, King, the *Ulster Monarch,* and Newman too, came together on a collision course with the Poles.

Nobody is quite sure how it all started, but within a very short time there was the most enormous scrap. The commandos gave vent to their fury, and all Mr Fairbairn's little tricks were given an airing. The Poles, who have often been likened to the 'Irish of Eastern Europe', love a good fight, and they were not slow in coming forward.

A score of Poles had been laid out and a number of commandos injured with stab wounds, before the military police appeared on the scene. That was an unwise step. The appearance of the stick-wielding Red Caps en masse was more than sufficient to unite the antagonists.

Poles and commandos laid into the police with gusto.

The band, which had at first tried to play as if nothing was happening, attempted one last strategem to restore order. They struck up 'God save the King'. The battle ceased, and the protagonists to a man stood ramrod-stiff to attention. However, immediately the last bar of the national anthem died away, they were at it again, until by sheer weight of numbers the military police battered the miscreants into submission.

The commandos (as the newcomers) were blamed. The dance hall manager was around to see Newman the next morning, demanding restitution. The provost marshal in Perth instituted a court of inquiry which eventually found the commandos guilty.

Newman, meanwhile, had paid several 'token of friendship' visits to the Poles at their headquarters and the affair was soon settled. Some of the commandos felt that using knives was over the top, and there was the odd reprisal, but within a couple of days, Poles and commandos were fraternizing all over Perth. They became the best of friends and both sides had really enjoyed the scrap.

Those in authority thought differently. The provost marshal's report made its way through the channels via district headquarters to Scottish Command at Edinburgh Castle. Perth was not big enough to contain the super-physical commandos and the temperamental Poles. The former would have to leave.

The Poles gave the commandos a genuinely embarrassing send-off. The Polish general insisted his men line the streets in salute while Newman marched by at the head of his commando. The band from a Free Polish cavalry regiment led the way, marching to the tunes 'There Will Always Be a Poland', 'The Girl I Left Behind', and for a reason which Newman couldn't fathom, 'The Red Flag'.

The commando now settled at Ayr for more training. Newman commuted regularly to Richmond Terrace and received more plans. He realized that unless they had a raid soon, the quality of his commando would deteriorate. There could be no gradual approach as with the line battalions, where it was possible to train through exercises with larger and larger formations.

Newman saw Haydon, Bourne and even Sir Roger Keyes. All sympathized, but then they had heard it all already. From other commando leaders.

---

[1]The men wore regimental badges in their headgear. The distinctive green beret was not introduced until the late summer of 1942.

[2]Newman's 'catechism' which he produced at length in his journal – is to found in the Introduction on pp. xv-xvi

CHAPTER NINETEEN

Operation Colossus

PREPARATIONS

The third raid after Boulogne and Guernsey, the first under Keyes's stewardship, had already occurred. Operation Colossus was mounted in the greatest of secrecy by another unit called No. 2 Commando.

In the autumn of 1940 the then No. 2 Commando emerged as the first parachutist-trained unit in the British army. While Lieutenant Colonel John Rock worked feverishly to establish a training school at Ringway, a commando CO was going through the unique experience of sifting his men by having them volunteer twice. Lieutenant Colonel Jackson had been in the Royal Tanks and knew little about the requirements of his new job. All the men under his command, having volunteered for the commando, were then asked to volunteer for parachute training. Those who weren't too keen on the idea were transferred to a 'land commando'.

Training proceeded in two distinct phases. Commando training was conducted at Inverary under the tutelage of Hugh Stockwell and his team of instructors. Parachute training was the province of John Rock, but there was no expertise, no knowledge of parachuting within the army. When Rock arrived at Ringway the first equipment he was given, or to be correct signed for, was a parachute and jumping helmet, captured from the Germans.

Rock had to start from scratch, writing his own book of rules as he went along. The first instructors he recruited were army PT specialists and air force tradesmen who packed parachutes. None had ever jumped and they trained alongside Anthony Deane-Drummond and the first batch of commandos. It must have been one of the very few occasions when instructors and students were on the same course.

Learning the basic mechanics of parachuting was just a first step. The tactics and techniques involved in parachuting en masse, or even with a small group, was something else. How do men exit from an aircraft quickly? At what height and speed should the aircraft fly in order to ensure that the parachutists are not dispersed on landing? Rock needed the help and support of the air force. Unlike the Luftwaffe, which had the tri-motor Junkers 52, the RAF had no equivalent tactical transport. So a bomber which had the necessary range and endurance would have to be used; but this was a national emergency and bombers were required for more pressing duties.

For a while, Rock had to make do with what was available. This took the form of an obsolete Bombay which happened to be hanging around Ringway. However, Sir Roger Keyes intervened, and influence was brought to bear in the right quarters, with the Prime Minister asking the odd, pertinent question, before the air force could be levered into releasing something better.

In November 1940, a couple of Whitleys arrived. The Armstrong Whitworth Whitley was a long slab-sided, underpowered but tough, heavy bomber. It was the best available but it was far from ideal. In the Bombay, the parachutists exited from a door in the fuselage; but this was not possible in the Whitley. They tried removing the rear turret and 'jumping off the back', but this didn't work either.

The only solution was to cut a trap door in the floor of the aircraft. By trial and error the technique was developed which allowed four men to exit quickly and a fifth immediately after. The four would sit around the hole with their feet dangling and then drop through in turn.

The fifth would stand behind and act as 'despatcher', before jumping through himself. He had to be very quick off the mark since the slightest delay would mean miles off the drop zone on the ground. The jump had to be performed precisely by the book which meant that the parachutist had to drop out upright. If he leant forward the slipstream would blow him across the hole and he would hit his face on the outer rim as he exited. This was called the 'Whitley kiss'.

The introduction of a static line was an early improvement, for the men need not be concerned with opening their parachutes. It was done automatically. Canisters were designed to carry equipment; the early ones were particularly awkward, because they had to conform to the configurations of the Whitley's bomb-bay where they were stored.

It all took time, but gradually Rock attracted some specialists onto his staff of instructors. There were stuntmen from the film world who had experience in parachuting. And two professional parachutists, Henry Ward and Bill Hare, from Sir Alan Cobham's Air Circus also arrived on the scene.

These specialists could in turn advise the Whitley flight crews on altitude and speed for a parachute drop. The Whitley pilots were used to dropping bombs from a service ceiling of about 17,000 feet. The parachutists needed an altitude of about 400 feet, which did not please the pilots at all. At that low altitude the Whitley was a pig to fly, the navigators were not trained to operate at such low altitude and the aircraft might manage about 200 m.p.h. She was a big plane, and, at that height and speed, desperately vulnerable. Over the dropping zone the instructors asked the pilots to throttle back to about 100 m.p.h., a suggestion which left the 'Brylcreem boys' speechless.

In turn, local defences had to be warned about the training, for it was a time when the invasion scare still lingered and there were an ever-increasing number of gun batteries deployed in the anti-aircraft defence at Manchester, Liverpool and Merseyside.

And some Home Guard platoons needed a lot of convincing that any parachutists could be friend, not foe.

After a commando had completed six parachute jumps he was sent north again to the School of Irregular Warfare; and a more advanced course.

Lieutenant Deane-Drummond thoroughly enjoyed the six weeks he spent on his second course at Inverary. Mr Sykes and Mr Fairbairn, one short and portly, the other tall and thin, were for all the world like a pre-war music-hall turn.

'Remember gentlemen – go for the eyes, ears or testicles,' was Mr Fairbairn's parting message.

They spent time in the heather learning how to stalk deer. Jack Churchill had introduced this into the curriculum and recruited local ghillies from the Duke of Argyll's estate as instructors. The message to Churchill was crystal clear, stalk a deer and you can stalk a man.

Not all the training was held outdoors, or was even of a practical nature. A strange-looking little man came to lecture. Dressed in civilian clothes, the suit shiny with age, with lapels that looked as if they had been shaped with a curling tong, he wore thick-rimmed pebble-lensed spectacles, and spoke in a soft voice. The man never gave his name, but most troopers thought he was a university professor, and he held their attention with effortless ease. He had been an officer with the International Brigade during the Spanish Civil War, and was reckoned to be one of the leading experts on street fighting.

By December 1940, some 300 men had successfully completed both the parachute and commando courses. It was time to put the experience to test with a target which would inflict significant damage on the enemy, and prove the effectiveness of the parachutists as a raiding force. The target was chosen by combined operations in Richmond Terrace. Germany, Occupied France and the Low Countries were dismissed as too tough a nut to crack at this time. The raiders might break in, and inflict heavy casualties in the process, but they would never escape. The German army was considered too strong and the local population too docile. Nobody wanted to contemplate a suicide mission.

Italy looked a more encouraging venue. The best of the Italian army, it was reckoned, was abroad fighting in Africa and the Balkans. Intelligence estimates considered home defence to be minimal, thin on the ground and ill-prepared.

Nowhere in Italy is very far from the sea and the long, exposed coastline presented ample sites from which to rescue the raiders once they had completed the operation.

The intelligence staff chose an aqueduct as a most suitable candidate for destruction. It spanned the Tragino Valley about 30 miles inland from Salerno and deep in the mountainous interior of Calabria, the ankle of Italy. This was an important aqueduct, serving the needs of Brindisi, Bari and the airfield complex around Foggia.

So if it was that important, why not send bombers from Malta to bomb it?

The Whitleys and Wellington squadrons would have included it on their target list but for two considerations. First an aqueduct is long and thin and doesn't present much of a target. Second, hidden in a mountain range, it was impossible to get a bombing run into the target even if the crews were good enough. Sabotage was the only alternative. In an enemy country such an undertaking would have to be a 'guerrilla style' raid.

There was a final factor which favoured this target above other 'candidates'. The aqueduct had been completely rebuilt before the war, and a British firm of consulting engineers had been involved in the contract. Sworn to secrecy, the engineers were able to furnish the raiders with detailed drawings, plans and specifications. The aqueduct was made of cement, which allowed the Royal Engineers to plan how much explosive to take, and to pinpoint where it should be planted to ensure total destruction.

The raiding force was to comprise 36 men. Major Trevor Alan Gordon Pritchard, a regular officer of the Royal Welch Fusiliers and the commando second in command, was chosen to lead the raid. He was a big man to trust his weight to a parachute.

Two hundred pounds and six feet tall, he was, as one would expect from that regiment, a keen rugby player and heavyweight boxer. Five other officers were selected, and Anthony Deane-Drummond was delighted to find his name included.

In true 'commando fashion', each officer then had to select five soldiers. This was not an easy task since all the men were qualified, and everyone volunteered.

Early in January 1941, the selected band of raiders were completely segregated from the remainder of the commando. Together they formed X Troop, gave up their cushy billets in the town, and were quartered instead in some Nissen huts on the airfield at Ringway.

It took an awful lot of persuasion and the personal intervention of the Prime Minister before the Air Ministry would release a flight of Whitleys for the operation. The bombing offensive against Germany was in full swing, and not going at all well so there were precious few aircraft to spare. The operation required absolute accuracy, and navigation which could only come from experienced crews, and they were much in demand.

Eight Whitleys were needed, six to carry the paratroopers and two to bomb Foggia as a diversion and keep the Italian defences occupied. The Whitley pilots had to be indoctrinated into the strange world of carrying parachutists, and they too blanched at a low-altitude low speed mission over enemy territory.

Bomber Command's losses were still less than two per cent of the sorties despatched, as the squadrons struggled over Germany; but the pilots were all too aware of the attrition rate. Although only a tiny proportion of the crews were bombing within miles of the target, to date they were the only offensive arm carrying the war into the enemy homeland.

Major Pritchard took X Troop back to Scotland for a short intensive course in mountain walking. Richmond Terrace had decided that the Western Highlands were broadly similar to the Appennines and a little acclimatization would not go amiss.

Specialists now joined the team of instructors. Major Lindsay had won renown as a Polar explorer. An expert on survival techniques, he introduced his tricks of the trade to X troop and helped oversee the preparation of survival rations.

Even at this stage, very few men knew the full details of the complete operation, and this was as it should be. The plan was, like all good plans, relatively simple. The raiders would be flown to Malta, strangely not in the aircraft dedicated to the operation. From Malta the Whitleys would fly into Italy and drop the parachutists over the selected zone in the Tragino Valley. The aqueduct would be seized and destroyed. The raiders were then to march to the sea where, four nights later, a submarine would be waiting.

On 24 January 1941, Deane-Drummond left for Malta. He was to make the arrangements for the arrival of the main party.

Ten days later Major Pritchard led X Troop out of Ringway for the last time. On 3 February they were convoyed across England to RAF Mildenhall in Suffolk, whence they would be flown to Malta. Their Whitleys left the same day to fly direct to Malta. It was within range, provided they flew in a straight line, across enemy occupied Europe to the Mediterranean.

In Suffolk, the final preparations were completed in the rush for departure. The commandos were given a new issue of 'protective clothing' – a cumbersome three-quarter length leather overcoat worn over battledress, the sort of garment much favoured by motorcyclists of the time. They had army-issue Balaclavas, and a flying helmet which had ear guards and fastened under the chin. Their battledress blouses were taken away for modifications, and special items were sewn and secreted into various nooks and crannies. Every man had 50,000 lire, sewn into blouse, waist band or collar. The idea was that if the enemy should capture some and find the money in one place, they wouldn't look elsewhere.

As well as the paper lire, officers had ten gold sovereigns sewn into their blouses; should they find themselves in another country. Everybody had a fine hacksaw blade sewn into the seam above the left breast pocket for sawing through bars on a cell window. In the sleeve linings were secreted silk maps of Italy. The right sleeve contained southern Italy, the left the north.

Finally, every man had a brass collar stud with which to fix his collar and tie. The men were, after all, to be properly dressed for the operation.

Scrape the metal off the head of the stud and inside was a miniature compass.

On 6 February Pritchard briefed X Troop on the operation and how they were to get out of Italy. Listening to his reasoned account none could have given themselves better than a 50–50 chance of making it home.

On the fifth night after the raid, HM submarine *Triumph* would surface in Salerno Bay, directly off the mouth of the Sele River. It had to be at least 60 miles from the aqueduct to the Sele. The men could only travel at night, and even then it would be hostile with a full hue and cry after them; and it was winter.

The prospects for making better than 15 miles a night under those conditions, and lying up during the day when they would have to remain alert, were not good. Yet none had second thoughts, or if they had, did not reveal their doubts. They were young, fit members of an élite organization, proud of their prowess and skills.

Pritchard now paraded X Troop with full kit in a large hangar at Mildenhall. Behind them stood the Whitleys that would ferry them to Malta.

Admiral Keyes came to inspect the parade and see them off. He moved along the ranks as Pritchard introduced each member of the party, having a quiet word with each and every one.

Returning to the front, Keyes addressed the assembled men. 'You are setting off on a very important job. I should like you to know that I have been assured that no better, fitter or braver men could have been selected than you to play the role.'

The admiral wished them goodbye and before Pritchard could bring X Troop to attention, Keyes saluted them. This was not lost on the troop. It was a gesture from a man given to the dramatic, or perhaps their chance of making it back was slimmer than they had appreciated.

THE RAID

Operation Colossus was mounted from Malta on the night of 10/11 February 1941. Five of the six aircraft made it to the correct valley and the paratroopers jumped onto the DZ and landed all over the valley. The two diversionary aircraft performed their tasks without a hitch and bombed the airfields at Foggia. Thereafter it started to go wrong.

Whitley B for Baker carried Captain Daly, who was the senior engineer officer, and five men along with the bulk of high explosive. The pilot, in evading what his rear gunner confidently asserted was a night fighter, lost his way and dropped the men in the wrong valley.

Meanwhile, Pritchard had to make do with what was available to him. They were well behind schedule by the time the men had staggered in from all points in the valley, although there was only one casualty; a man with a broken ankle.

Worse still, the canisters of high explosives, equipment ropes and ladders, were as dispersed as the men, and in the dark the very

159

devil to find. Not all the canisters were dropped. Some were carried in the bomb-bays and others slung beneath the inner wings on makeshift racks. All the planes that returned to Malta arrived with at least some canisters still on board.

But there was no garrison on the bridge, and that was about the only mercy to come their way.

There were a number of small farms in the valley and despite the lateness of the hour the descent attracted a lot of attention. With five Whitley bombers thundering down the valley at about 400 feet, it was not surprising. The Italian farmers were all roped in to act as porters, bringing in the heavy boxes of explosives. They were docile and co-operative.

Lieutenant George Patterson, Royal Engineers, did a splendid job with the materials to hand, but there was a major problem. The aqueduct was not constructed out of cement. It was reinforced concrete.

The British 'consultants' had got something else wrong as well. The dimensions of the main supporting piers were quite different. Either the Italians couldn't follow a set of drawings or they had introduced their own modifications. It was an all or nothing situation. With all the confidence of youth, Patterson strapped the available explosives around a single pier of the aqueduct in the hope that its destruction would topple the lot.

Captain Daly and his group were scrambling out of their valley when they heard the explosion. They must have been 10 miles away but sound carries a long way at night especially when it is made by 600 pounds of high explosive.

Patterson had indeed done a superb job. Half the aqueduct was down and one of the two main piers had gone altogether. The second pier, unable to sustain the weight, leaned at a crazy angle, while from the concrete waterway above, shattered and fractured in a dozen places, water cascaded into the valley.

In the other valley Daly called a halt. Like all the officers he knew the precise grid reference for the rendezvous with the submarine at the Sele Estuary. There would be no point in linking up with Pritchard and the main party; perhaps every virtue in being separate. Daly set a course across country for the beach.

Meanwhile Pritchard collected his men together.

There were perhaps three hours of darkness left, and, although they had been unmolested in their destruction, the local Italian security forces were bound to be on the scene in a short time.

There were 29 men fit to march. Pritchard divided them into three teams in the belief that smaller groups might more easily escape detection. It was a sound decision but his next one was very questionable.

Speed and time were of the very essence, which could not be denied. He ordered the men to abandon all the bren-guns. Each group was allowed one Thompson, otherwise the men only had their pistols and a few grenades. The emphasis would have to be on evasion, for there was no way they could blast their way out if they became embroiled in a fire fight.

Lance Corporal Boulter had suffered a broken ankle, and he knew the rules. The third and final decision which Pritchard made as leader was unavoidable. All the commandos knew and understood that in an operation, there could be no pity on the wounded. If a man could not march he was abandoned. Anthony Deane-Drummond herded the Italians into a single farm house. One of the commandos spoke Italian, and it was made crystal clear that if anybody moved they would be shot; for sentries were to be left behind as a rearguard. They could only hope the bluff would work, but the explosion would have raised the alarm anyway.

Pritchard wished his raiders well, as they prepared to separate.

'Don't get involved with the Italian army and don't take prisoners.

'I will see you at the RV,' he concluded almost as an afterthought.

Boulter accepted his fate with dogged courage. They bound his wound, placed his leg in a splint, bade their farewells and left him to his own devices.

PURSUIT

The march to the sea was a nightmare; and one for which they had not been well prepared.

In the Scottish Highlands there were more deer than people. The southern Appennines were quite different, and the main problem for the fugitives were the farms. No one had appreciated just how heavily populated this part of Italy was, and the frequency of the settlements proved a real obstacle to progress. The fleeing raiders could not use the tracks, and every house seemed to deploy half a dozen guard dogs.

The weather proved the real enemy. In the Highlands they had exercised through good clean snow. It had been the worst recorded winter in Italy and the thaw had already set in with a vengeance. The valley floors and mountain sides below the snowline were coated in thick, oozing, boot-clogging mud; little streams had become raging torrents, and it rained in the valleys and fell as driving sleet on the hill slopes, without ceasing.

Including Captain Daly there were four groups heading for the coast through a countryside which soon swarmed with frenzied search parties. The local military garrisons were turned out in force while the Carabinieri co-ordinated the whole operation. It wasn't difficult to work out that the raiders would have to make for the coast. As luck would have it, a battalion of élite Italian Alpini infantry was exercising in the area. They were quickly drafted into the dragnet.

Anthony Deane-Drummond travelled with Major Pritchard's group. They marched through the remainder of the first night, huddled in a ruined barn during the day, and marched through a second night. Dawn found them searching frantically for cover on an exposed hillside. The map showed a copse of trees, the reality was a new plantation, where the trees were 18 inches high.

There was a settlement in the valley beneath and they were spotted. The men were too exhausted to flee and in any case the Italians quickly threw a cordon around the hill.

The Carabinieri and a couple of squads of Alpini advanced up the hill. Pritchard, Deane-Drummond and the commandos prepared to do battle with side arms, grenades and a single Thompson.

The advancing foe grew in size and a shudder went through the commandos, like a collective moan.

The Italian military herded a small crowd of civilians, children and women for the most part, as a shield before them. Either the man in charge had the most cynical disregard for life, or he knew his enemy extremely well.

There were no orders given. The commandos dismantled and destroyed their side arms and prepared to surrender without a shot being fired.

Then came the humiliation.

The prisoners were fettered with ball and chain and herded in a shuffling jumble to the local police station. The villagers relieved their fears by shouting abuse and lashing out with sticks and anything else that came to hand.

Lieutenant Patterson travelled with the group that had been caught late on the previous day. They had made painfully slow progress in the two night marches, so much so that the leader, Captain Lea, knew there was no hope of reaching the rendezvous in time on the third night's march.

They gambled and lost, but it was a cheeky throw for all that. Lea marched the men down the road towards the sea in parade-ground style. He passed his tight, disciplined group off as Austrian troops on exercise and got away with it until they encountered a road block manned by Alpinis. The Italian Tyrolean troops knew their counterparts, and the men who stood before them were not Austrians.

A third party were trapped in similar circumstances to Patterson. All were chained and fettered as soon as they were taken.

Captain Daly's group almost made it to the Sele Estuary, perhaps because the Italians were not aware of their existence. On the third evening, they picked up the line of the Sele, came out of the hills and marched parallel to the river across its flood plain to the sea. The men could smell the sea when they rounded a bend in the track, and walked straight into a company of Italian soldiers.

It was probably as well that none of the commandos made it to the rendezvous: HM submarine *Triumph* had never left port.

The second of the two Whitleys which had attacked Foggia developed engine trouble on the way back to Malta, over the Italian mainland. In simple code the pilot radioed Malta that he intended to crashland his plane on the sand banks at the mouth of the Sele River; and asked for a rescue operation to be mounted.

None of the RAF crews knew the escape plans of the raiders, for obvious reasons, and so it was only by the strangest quirk of fate that the pilot had chosen the exact grid reference as the *Triumph*'s rendezvous with the raiders.

Convinced that the Italians would break the code and descend upon the point to lay in ambush, Malta believed the operation was compromised and cancelled the sailing orders for *Triumph*. Some have since maintained that the authorities, if not in Richmond Terrace, then in Malta, did not rate very highly the chances of X Troop making it to the sea, and certainly not highly enough to warrant placing at risk a valuable submarine in enemy coastal waters.

The saga of the Whitley was a nice way out of a dilemma.

AFTERMATH

The Italians repaired the aqueduct and within a month it was providing water once again to Brindisi, Bari and Foggia. That wasn't important. In guerrilla warfare it is the psychological impact which matters, more than the material cost.

Psychologically, Operation Colossus was a resounding success. The Italians had been frightened witless and now diverted manpower and resoures to the protection and defence of every vulnerable point in the country.

Richmond Terrace knew the raid had been a success, photo reconnaissance missions had shown the damage, and the impact on enemy morale was carefully monitored. It was more than enough to vindicate the experiment. No. 2 Commando at Ringway was disbanded to form the nucleus of the Parachute Regiment, at about the same time as the special service battalions were being reorganized.

The commando lived on with Charles Newman.

Finally, what of the raiders?

One man was executed by the Italian authorities. He was an Italian waiter who had joined the commando operation as an interpreter. Everybody else was under sentence of death, but the fact that the raiders wore military uniform caused the Italians to abide by the Geneva Convention.

They could not be shot as spies, saboteurs or fifth columnists. Instead the commandos were packed off to prison camp where they were reunited with Corporal Boulter.

Some immediately planned to escape. Anthony Deane-Drummond broke out and was caught. He had a second and successful attempt, which after many adventures took him into Switzerland. From there he joined the underground route through France to Gibraltar and home. Within months he was appointed signals officer of the newly formed Second Parachute Brigade.

CHAPTER TWENTY

A Nice Morning Ashore: The First Lofoten Raid

Even as Anthony Deane-Drummond was coming to terms with the humiliation of capture and imprisonment at Naples, another and much bigger raid was being launched. Operation Colossus and X Troop were now history, and Richmond Terrace concentrated all its attention on Norway and the first big commando raid of the war.

Over the next three years a number of significant raids were targeted on Norway. The reasons for such operations were primarily economic. There was never any serious intention to launch the Second Front in Norway, so the raids were not about battlefield intelligence in the accepted sense of the term. Of course, if the enemy could be convinced into believing that the Allies were seriously considering Norway, and thereby diverted significant numbers of their best troops to meet such a contingency, then that was an added bonus.

Such a bonus did come in the dead hand of Hitler. Unable and unwilling to let his High Command make its own deductions on high strategy, he insisted that the Allies could come through Norway to Berlin.

Norway was now to be hit more frequently because it was easier, not militarily but bureaucratically. Cross-Channel raids were tightly bound in red tape and hierarchies of command. They needed permission from the local army commander opposite because it was on 'his patch'.

Norway was a naval preserve. It came under the bailiwick of the C in C Home Fleet at Scapa Flow; and there were no local jealousies to protect. The navy were also attracted to Norway for other reasons. It was the scene of their early war, success and humiliation. Besides German capital ships might be induced to fight. The fleet was bored rigid in Scapa and thirsted for some action, if only as a break in the monotony and routine of harbour life.

The target which had been identified by Richmond Terrace as most suited to the raid was the southern chain of islands that make up the Lofotens. The commandos were to raid the four small ports of Stamsund, Hemmingvaer, Svolvaer and Brettesnes. At each was a factory that processed the herring and cod oils from the local fishing fleet. Together the four factories accounted for just about half of Norway's total output in fish oil, all of which now went to Germany.

Glycerine, vitally important in the manufacture of explosives and munitions, is extracted from fish oil. Another by-product was vitamin pills. The Wehrmacht supplied vitamin A and B pills to its front line troops and these came from Norwegian fish oil.

If the factories were that important, why didn't the air force bomb them? There was always the high risk of inflicting civilian casualties in a bombing attack, but a commando raid had other appeals. An operation of this nature could bring comfort and encouragement to an oppressed population, drum up recruits for the Free Norwegian Forces, punish Quislings, and thereby discourage collaboration with the enemy.

Combined Operations Headquarters under the direction of Keyes planned the operation. Haydon, the brigade commander, led the force, much to the chagrin of the admiral.

Two commandos were used; No. 3 under John Dunford Slater and No. 4 led by David Lister. Lister was considered by many to be a bit old for the business, but this regular officer in the West Kents, and one-time army heavyweight boxing champion, would not be persuaded otherwise.

There were some sappers to handle the demolitions and about 50 Norwegians to act as interpreters and liaison officers.

The days leading up to their departure were hectic in the extreme. Jack Churchill, as befitted a second in command, busied himself with the loading tables and accommodation scales for HMS *Princess Beatrice*, their converted landing ship. Lister's commandos sailed in HMS *Queen Emma*.

They went first from Gourrock to Scapa, under a local escort of five smaller destroyers. At Scapa they spent a week in planning conferences and some reorganization before setting sail for Norway.

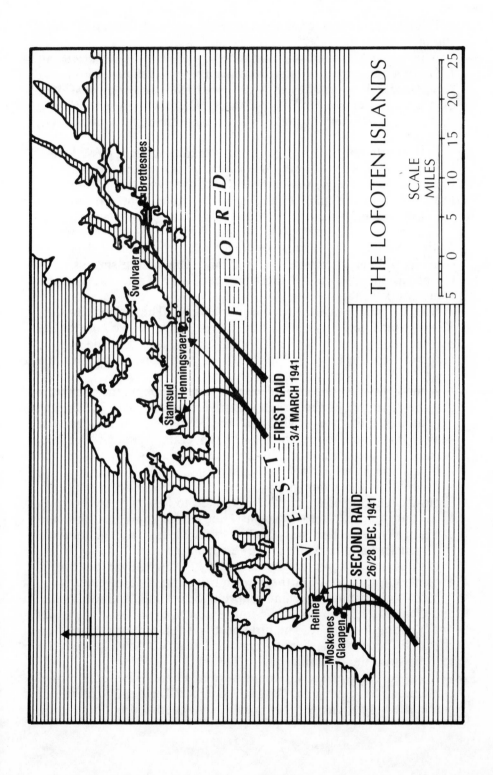

THE LOFOTEN ISLANDS

SCALE
MILES

5   0   5   10   15   20   25

FIRST RAID
3/4 MARCH 1941

SECOND RAID
26/28 DEC. 1941

V E S T   F J O R D

Brettesnes
Svolvaer
Henningsvaer
Stamsud
Reine
Moskenes
Glaapen

The fleet came too, or at least a hefty wedge of the capital ships stationed in home waters.

A posse of Tribal-class destroyers *Somali, Bedouin, Tartar* and *Eskimo* joined the close escort while the battleships *Nelson* and *King George V*, with cruisers *Nigeria* and *Dido* and their destroyer escort, shadowed the force at a distance. There was always a chance that the German battle squadron might be tempted into interdicting the raiders.

In the early hours of 3 March 1941, the raiding force passed close by HM submarine *Sunfish*, the beacon ship at the entrance to the great *Vestfjorden*, that sheltered channel which separated the Lofotens from the mainland. The capital units beat a patrol line over the horizon, tempting the Germans to come out to give battle.

The raiding force met a Norwegian fishing fleet on its way out to the grounds, and a burst of tracer from the leading destroyer convinced them to stay put for the day. The fishing smacks hove to, raised the Norwegian flags on their masts, and cheered the commandos ashore.

One German warship tried to intervene. The armed trawler, *Krebs*, which acted as the islands' patrol put to sea to contest the passage. It was an act of incredible valour on the part of the skipper and crew, and in keeping with the finest traditions of the German navy.

Armed with just one small deck gun, *Krebs* took on the combined fire power of five of the largest destroyers serving with the fleet.

Although quickly overwhelmed, the *Krebs* did not sink but her skipper managed to beach his stricken craft. Whether this was because of the impotence of the Royal Navy's gunfire or the seamanship of the German, we cannot say.

Thereafter, the landings in all four ports proceeded as an anti-climax. Commandos are ruthlessly trained to fight, not the enemy's best, but the rear-area echelons, lines of communications and garrison soldiers. This was the first principle of raiding, to avoid the front line and strike fear and terror in the rear.

It does help, however, if the enemy, of whatever quality, is present. On this occasion there wasn't a German to be seen.

Most of 3 Commando came ashore at Stamsund. Dunford Slater and Churchill led the first wave to the beach, weapons at the ready and bursting for a fight. The little port was full of Norwegians who cheerfully secured the landing craft and reached down to help the men up onto the quayside.

It was just as well the Germans were nowhere to be seen, mused Churchill. The intelligence boys at Richmond Terrace had identified gentle shelving beaches. They would have been sitting ducks if the port had been defended. Churchill thought a quiet word with the appropriate authorities in Richmond Terrace would be in order upon his return.

Once ashore and beyond the jubilant locals, the men in Stamsund spread about their allotted tasks. The story was the same everywhere. The local Quislings were rounded up and the factories were made ready for destruction. Tons of foodstuffs and comforts were brought ashore in the belief that the locals were suffering from the 'jack boot of the oppressive Hun'.

Richmond Terrace had got it wrong again. The local people appeared to be better fed and clothed than the commandos. It was they who rushed home to cook the soldiers eggs and delicious cakes, delicacies the commandos hadn't tasted through the winter months.

There was some time in hand, so a few of the men moved further inland. Then Lord Lovat, who had recently joined Lister's commando, caught the local bus out of Svolvaer to the sea plane base. There he stopped off and single-handed captured the local German staff. Their commander was outraged, and couldn't believe Lord Lovat's audacity. All the way back in the truck which Lovat had commandeered, he complained long and loud. Indeed he threatened to inform the Führer of Lord Lovat's unwarlike behaviour!

One of the raiders did indeed contact the Führer: Lieutenant Richard Willis, a troop officer in 3 Commando had been assigned to capture the vitally important telephone exchange at Stamsund. In the absence of an enemy, this had been accomplished with consummate ease and he was now thoroughly bored, so he sent a telegram addressed to 'A Hitler. Berlin'.

> You said in your last speech German troops would meet the British wherever they landed. We are here. Where are your troops?

Shortly after midday the commandos began to evacuate the ports and return to the landing ships. There had not been a single commando casualty and already 18,000 tons of shipping including the 10,000-ton freighter *Hamburg* had been sunk.

The task of destroying the fish oil factories proved more difficult. At Stamsund, Jack Churchill had been frustrated by the antics of the local population, who rushed into the buildings to loot whatever was of value before they were put to the torch. Given that their livelihoods were about to go up in flames, it was a reasonable course of action on their part.

Some of the commandos had been given Norwegian currency in

case of emergency, although there were no hacksaw blades sewn into tunics and battledress blouses. A sergeant, whom we shall call Smith, took a very liberal interpretation of the word emergency, which only came to light when he had to account for the shortfall in his currency.

With 30 kroner he purchased the favours of a particularly attractive flaxen-haired Viking lady.

Thereafter he was always known in the commando as 'Sergeant Thirty-kroner Smith'!

Churchill had the provost sergeant round up all the Quislings in the Stamsund area, and they were marched into a hut where John Dunford Slater had established his headquarters. The CO and Churchill debated what to do with the collaborators who were under the watchful eye of the provost sergeant, a man called Chitty.

The problem with the early Thompsons was that the safety catch often failed if a full magazine was engaged. The sergeant had a Thompson cocked and loaded, slung low under his shoulder; he covered the Quislings while the two officers debated their fate.

Chitty inadvertently loosed off his Thompson, and a burst of shot riddled the floor boards between the feet of Dunford Slater.

'Yeah, well Sergeant Chitty, you want to be more careful of those bloody things. They're dangerous.' He then continued his discussions with Churchill.

Both doubted whether the majority of the 20 or so Norwegians who cowered before them in anticipation of a sentence being passed were dyed-in-the-wool Quislings. Some had probably been denounced by business rivals, others because of old family scores. None in Churchill's opinion warranted a free trip to England, or food and lodging for the rest of the war as the guests of His Majesty.

John Dunford Slater agreed, and turned to the Norwegians, adopting his 'tough man stance', which his own men had come to know so well. Legs apart, thumbs hooked into his webbing, he fixed the miserable crowd with a hard stare.

'Yeah, well I don't want to hear any more of this bloody Quisling business. It's no bloody good I'm telling you. If I hear there's been any more of it, I'll be back again, and next time I'll take the whole bloody lot of you. Now clear off.'

It was indeed time to leave. Perhaps the commandos had already stayed too long, judging by the flurry of activity from the patrolling destroyers whose aldis lamps chattered incessantly. There were more than enough air bases in the area for the Luftwaffe to make life difficult on the way home – if only to compensate for their failure so far.

The prisoners were rounded up along with those Norwegian men and women who wished to volunteer for their forces in exile. One soldier appeared at the quayside in full kit, his well-kept green uniform and top coat neatly pressed, complete with pack rifle and ammunition. At the end of resistance in 1940 he had simply discharged himself, but now he explained to the astonished commandos it was time to join the war.

For those who stayed there were farewells to be said although no one, Norwegian or commando, spoke about their real fears, namely that the Germans would return to exact a terrible revenge.[1]

The raiding force returned without incident to Scapa Flow and a rapturous welcome from the anchored units of the Home Fleet. It was all a bit embarrassing, and Churchill felt that they should at least have gained a major victory over the enemy to be worthy of such praise, but the sailors were bored.

Before the commandos continued on to Gourrock, a proper tally of the raid was made and recorded. Besides ships sunk and factories fired, 800,000 tons of fish oil stored in reservoir tanks had been destroyed. Sixty Quislings from the other ports were brought back to face justice and King Haakon's exiled forces gained 300 new recruits.

Two hundred German prisoners, for the most part merchant seamen, were brought back to the stockades.

Except for some smaller operations, mostly in conjunction with the SOE, the commandos, who had been so carefully raised and nurtured, spent a frustrating spring and summer.

There were plenty of suggestions for raids on a large scale. St Nazaire was discarded after an initial study because the shoal waters and mud flats of the Loire Estuary were considered too hazardous.

Dieppe was in favour for a while and then dismissed by the planners in Richmond Terrace. Any enemy port was bound to be too heavily defended and should be avoided at all costs. How right they were.

Meanwhile, the opposition gathered to make another attempt to 'disband Keyes'.

The army was in trouble in 1941, because of the quality of its officer corps and senior NCOs. Such was the glamour and attraction of the commandos, particularly compared with the soul-destroying tedium of the battalions stuck in England, that the brightest and the best were leaving.

Young officers pestered their superiors into releasing them into commando service, and many young soldiers and NCOs who were themselves officer material went too, many willing to take a reduction in rank to escape.

171

The operative word was 'escape', for it was the weakness of the army that encouraged those that really cared to get out into something which offered a little more excitement.

Partly in order to stop the rot a very concerned General Alan Brooke as C in C Home Forces approached the chiefs of staff to be allowed to conduct raiding operations on the coast between Ostend and Cherbourg, and with forces at his disposal.

Brooke gained the support he needed but the chiefs did suggest that it might be polite to agree this course of action with Admiral Keyes. They spent three days together at Inverary while Brooke studied commando methods. His report speaks for itself:

> The whole of my visit to Roger Keyes was an attempt on his part to try and convince me that our Commando policy was right. He failed to do so and I remained convinced until the end of the War that the Commandos should never have been divorced from the Army in the way they were. Each division should have been responsible for maintaining a divisional battle patrol capable of any Commando work that might be asked of it.[2]

Brooke's report found one ally in Admiral Sir Dudley Pound, and Keyes's particular *bête noir* on the chiefs of staff. He wrote: 'I'm sorry to say but I firmly believe the only thing he [Keyes] cares for is the justification of Roger Keyes.'

Brooke's most damning criticism was reserved for his observations on the training he had witnessed at Inverary, which he found to be 'too stereotyped to fit in with varying conditions of our possible operations; they are still thinking much too small.'

Lack of resources and Churchill's passion for the commandos thwarted Brooke's plans, but Keyes had not emerged unscathed either and events in the summer and autumn conspired against him.

General Brooke was instructed to set up a feasibility study to mount a major cross-Channel raid timed for the spring of 1942. This was a major rebuff for Keyes and his staff at Richmond Terrace, whose monopoly of combined operations now looked a bit sick. Brooke left the army planning to Lieutenant General Bernard Montgomery in South-East Command, another of the rising generation of senior officers who had scant regard for Special Forces of any description.[3]

Brooke's raid promised to be bigger than anything which Keyes could organize; but then of course he had the full resources of the home army as well as the carefully cultivated co-operation from the other services. Keyes's abrupt manners and brash arrogance had come home to roost, as his directorate was left out in the cold.

Sir Stafford Cripps was the British ambassador in Moscow. In June 1941, the Germans invaded the Soviet Union, and by that act the Russians joined the Allied cause. Sir Stafford proposed a raid and occupation of the coal-rich Spitzbergen Islands, which hitherto had been a joint Soviet/Norwegian condominium.

The War Cabinet favoured the scheme, but the islands' distance and isolation from Britain ruled out any planned occupation on a permanent basis.

There was by this time a surfeit, in more senses than one, of Canadian troops in Britain, and so it was from their ranks that the 'raiders' were to be chosen. A battalion of the Edmonton Regiment together with another from the Saskatchewan Light Infantry were given a quick course at Inverary on landing techniques, and that represented the sum total of the combined operations directorate's involvement.

The Canadians, together with some sappers and Norwegians, sailed to Spitzbergen in the *Empress of Canada*, together with a small escort; for there would be no enemy to resist the invasion.

The operation proceeded according to plan. The Russian miners together with their families, some 2,000 people in total, were rounded up and sailed in the *Empress of Canada* to Archangel, while the troops remained to destroy the installations. Nine days later the liner called back at Spitzbergen to collect the soldiers who had completed their work and returned safely to the United Kingdom.

The fact that this operation had been successfully completed quite adequately by so-called ordinary soldiers, who had received the minimum of special training, was not lost on those in authority.

Admiral Keyes laid on another full-scale demonstration of commando skills before the King, Prime Minister and a galaxy of talent from the Military High Command. Richmond Terrace worked exceedingly hard to ensure that every detail of the exercise was catered for and covered.

It all went wrong. Two days had been set aside at the end of August 1941. The weather was foul, the landing craft delivered troops to the wrong beaches and the exercises fell hopelessly behind schedule.

The United States, although still neutral, began to mobilize its forces in the summer of 1941. There were frequent 'military conversations' and visiting delegations, mostly on the part of Americans anxious to learn about this war and in a hurry. A group of high ranking US Marines visited Richmond Terrace, where Keyes's behaviour proved to be outrageous.

Dominating the discussions from the outset, Keyes rode roughshod over the opinions of others, and held forth vehemently and at length on concepts which even the Americans knew were hopelessly out of date.

The concepts were those inspired by his personal feats in the past, and had no place on the Second World War battlefield.

The Americans returned bemused, at a loss to explain how a man with such outmoded ideas could occupy a position of influence.

Members and representatives of the chiefs of staff who attended the meeting left more determined than ever to ensure that Keyes should go.

In September, General Brooke succeeded in reducing the independence of the commandos and the power of Keyes. Winston Churchill agreed that amphibious operations would not be mounted from the United Kingdom without the express authority of GHQ Home Forces. This in effect meant that the operational control reverted to the army; and from now on, combined operations would only plan (with approval), train and advise. The Prime Minister had most effectively drawn the power away from Richmond Terrace and 'its tenant in chief'. He wrote the following letter to Keyes with a new directive and offered him the title of Adviser Combined Operations.

My Dear Roger

I hope that you will find yourself able to come to an agreement with the Chiefs of Staff upon the modification of your original directive. Your title 'Director' does not correspond with the facts. Special Operations once decided upon in principle must lie in the hands of the Commanders chosen, who have to back them with their reputations and their lives. I am convinced that excursions from this country to the continent, unless entrusted to specially chosen Commanders, must have behind them the authority and resources of GHQ Home Forces. In both cases the responsibility for advising the Defence Committee and the War Cabinet can only lie with the Chiefs of Staff. These are facts which must be accepted.

It seems to me that very large spheres of important and interesting work will be open to you as Adviser under the new management. I should find it very hard to resist the advice of all my responsible experts. I trust therefore you will fall in with the plan that has now taken shape.

Yours very sincerely,

Winston S. Churchill.

30 September 1941

But Roger Keyes would not 'fall into line'. He had been outmanoeuvred but could not see it. Instead, he tried to bluster and bully his way out of a cul-de-sac, which had been largely of his own making.

On 4 October, Churchill told Keyes in blunt terms that he was arranging his relief. The Prime Minister had little choice other than to sack Keyes. Everyone was against him. Even if Keyes had been in the right, he still would have to be dismissed, for nobody would work with him. He was also 70 years of age, and, whatever his virtues, it would have been time to make way for a younger man. Admiral Pound was particularly relieved to see him depart, and typically scathing in his comments to Admiral Cunningham: 'He never had much brain and what he has got left is quite addled.'

Keyes's dismissal was not received kindly by the majority of his staff and those officers who came into contact with him. The side of his character which had provided the tensions with the chiefs of staff, his arrogance and ambition would have been largely unknown. Instead they saw Roger Keyes as the leader, a big, bluff, decent man, a man of honour, and able to command affection, respect and loyalty.

Thus, the successor to Keyes would not find himself in the most enviable of positions.

---

[1] In the event they didn't, at least directly. The occupation was stepped up and made more visible, but remained a benign affair. Maybe Hitler saw an opportunity to still win the Norwegians over to his side; for even those families whose sons had left with the commandos were not singled out for punishment. Norwegian officers still held as prisoners of war, however, did have a rough time for a while.

[2] Arthur Bryant *Turn of the Tide 1939–43*, pp. 255–6, Collins, London 1957.

[3] General Paget succeeded Brooke in November 1941 and later produced a report which proposed a raid for September 1942. Codenamed Sesame it led directly to the massacre at Dieppe – but by then of course Montgomery had left for North Africa.

PART FOUR

MOUNTBATTEN'S TENURE

CHAPTER TWENTY ONE

Under New Management

Churchill's choice for the new supremo of combined operations was Captain Lord Louis Mountbatten. He was as young for the job as Keyes had been old.

In June 1941, Mountbatten lost the *Kelly*. The destroyer was bombed and sunk from under him in the desperate battles for Crete. The 'Fighting Fifth' destroyer flotilla was dismembered and Mountbatten came home. Already a national hero in the making, he was given command of the aircraft carrier *Illustrious*, herself a refugee from the Mediterranean and the Malta convoys, and now undergoing an extensive refit in a neutral American shipyard.

Mountbatten was despatched to the United States in August. While Lady Mountbatten toured the American Red Cross, Lord Louis waved the flag and met the rich and influential. He lectured to the midshipmen at Annapolis, dined at the White House, met congressional leaders and visited Pearl Harbour. By his own admission he was on course to emulate his father. Command of a capital ship like the *Illustrious* would be the best sort of stepping stone to the Admiralty Board.

Thus he was not exactly delighted to be told that his tour had been cut short, his command cancelled, and that he was to report to London as soon as he could disentangle himself from the most important of the outstanding engagements.

This 'semi-royal' regarded Richmond Terrace as second best, and this attitude was not helped by the legacy of bitterness and resentment which he inherited. Although promoted to commodore, it did not help matters for Mountbatten to be outranked by almost all of his senior staff.

Mountbatten was 41 years of age, his chief of staff in the headquarters was 57 years old and two ranks his senior; Bourne, as his 'number two', was out of sight in the promotion pyramid.

Whatever his misgivings and disappointments, Mountbatten tackled the challenge head on.

Drive, energy, zeal and enthusiasm were the hallmarks of a personality which breathed new life and a sense of purpose into Richmond Terrace. The 'royal connection' did not go amiss either. The chiefs of staff might still distrust and even resent combined operations as an entity, even though with a commodore at the helm, the situation was reversed and they outranked its director.

Mountbatten's connection with the royal household was something which could more than compensate for his youth and lack of seniority. Even Sir Dudley Pound, a product of the old school who believed that 41-year-old destroyer captains should serve their time before sitting at the councils of admirals and generals, had to tread warily with one who dined regularly with the King.

In addition, the chiefs had in Mountbatten a man of glamour, and a national hero of the war to contend with, soon to be immortalized by Noël Coward in the film *In Which We Serve*.

Lord Louis also had the ear of the Prime Minister, and none of the chiefs was present when Churchill discussed his appointment with him.

Mountbatten's 'power' and the limits of his authority were laid down in a Prime Ministerial directive and approved by the chiefs of staff.

The directive allowed Mountbatten to mount operations, and to retain operational control of those raids which were undertaken by his own special forces personnel; these were the commandos. On paper they numbered 5,000 élite troops. The reality was well short of this figure.

There was one last raid under the auspices of the old regime. A hundred men from Ronnie Tod's 9 Commando were to attack a four-gun battery on the French coast near Houlgate. Some men were landed, but, on a beach 400 yards away from their intended site, most failed to get ashore. None was able to cause mischief, leave alone attack the battery before the Germans were onto them with a vengeance. Having succeeded only in thoroughly alerting the coastline, the force was extricated with difficulty.

The raid was a failure, and Mountbatten was determined there were to be no more failures. He asserted his authority and instituted changes. Many officers on the staff were quietly relieved and replaced. This was no bad thing since they largely comprised Keyes's cronies, and they were of an age where they could be retired with dignity.

In December 1941 the commandos prepared for a return visit to Norway. The target was a town called Sör Vaagso, and the Lofotens was the venue for a secondary diversionary but vaguely determined enterprise.

Vaagso is an island, part of the outer chain, the Indelred which stretches along so much of the Norwegian coast. This provides a sheltered channel through which ships can sail, protected from the worst of the Atlantic gales. The Indelred is not continuous, and where there are breaks the storms can be at their most severe. There is such a break at the north of Vaagso Island where ships have to negotiate Norway's most westerly peninsula of Staadlander. Coastal shipping gathers in the narrow channel between Vaagso and the mainland known locally as the Ulvesund, and waits for fair weather.

Sör Vaagso's prosperity was based on the sea, and was directly related to its sheltered anchorage. There were two hotels which catered to the sailors, a wharf for repairs, and warehouses offering bunkering facilities. The town boasted its own fishing fleet and there were the associated fish oil factories.

The town was of importance regionally, and this was reflected in the German garrison and the coastal defences. In midstream in the Ulvesund and opposite Sör Vaagso is the tiny island of Maaloy. Measuring only 500 metres by 200 metres it was garrisoned and armed with four Belgian-made 75mm coastal defence guns.

Maaloy protected the anchorage and guarded the town. A mile to the south and running at right-angles to the Ulvesund was Vaags Fjord and the open sea.

There was another island which guarded this approach. It was called Rugsundo, similarly garrisoned but with four larger calibre coast defence guns taken from the Maginot Line. Their field of fire lay westwards down the Vaags Fjord.

The target then was an economic one. Fish oil processing plants, a fishing fleet, a small base, and warehouses to be sacked, and whatever shipping sheltering at the time sunk. Unlike the previous Lofoten raid this economic target was defended.

The Wehrmacht, unlike the British or the Americans, graded their infantry divisions according to quality. Whereas the Allies tried at least in theory to ensure that all their infantry divisions were of equal quality, the Germans did not. Some were poor, and they were kept that way. The 150 soldiers who were at Vaagso came from the low grade 181st Infantry Division. This was a garrison division comprising the more elderly, less physically fit specimens of the Third Reich. There were also some naval personnel and about 100 men from a harbour unit. This was all known by Richmond Terrace, and fitted into the context of standard raiding policy. The plan, codenamed Operation Archery, was to hit the enemy on 26 December, Boxing Day, when the local garrison ought to be nursing monumental hangovers, and paying little attention to their duties.

What the planners did not know was that another company of soldiers from a top grade mountain division was on the island. They were about to learn that even so-called low grade German divisions can give a very good account of themselves.

Brigadier Haydon again called on Dunford Slater's 3 Commando to lead the operation. Newman's No. 2 Commando was to lend two troops' worth of soldiers to bolster Dunford Slater. There were also Royal Engineers for demolition, some additional medics to cope with the expected casualties, and a Norwegian detachment under the popular commando-trained, and very highly regarded Captain Martin Linge.

Brigadier Haydon was to be in overall command of the operation and he had under his direction 51 officers and 525 other ranks. These figures provide an interesting insight into the commandos at this time.

There were to be ten commandos each of just over 500 men. Dunford Slater, with Newman's two troops, would have the equivalent of nearly one and a half full commandos plus additional engineers and medics. Yet the total force, to include Haydon's staff was less than 580 men! It is interesting to note, with all the commandos clamouring for action that Dunford Slater and his No. 3 were selected yet again.

The naval task force was commanded by Rear Admiral Burroughs in the cruiser *Kenya*. Her 12 6-inch guns would provide the main fire support. The destroyer escort comprised three brand spanking new fleet boats *Onslow*, *Offa* and *Orbis*, together with HMS *Chiddingfold*, a Hunt class destroyer escort.

Air Force Hampdens were to provide close air support for the landings, while Blenheims and Beaufighters would attack Luftwaffe bases in striking distance of Vaagso and attempt some form of air cover for the fleet.

In fact this raid was going to be the first against a known enemy opposition and, more importantly, the first which would be a truly combined operation involving all three services. Whilst the navy and air force were to provide the artillery, commandos were to land and kill the enemy and sack the town; a sort of Viking raid in reverse and ten centuries later.

Between them Haydon, Dunford Slater and Churchill worked out a comprehensive but simple battle plan which just about covered every eventuality.

Round the corner and out of sight in a secluded bay in Vaags Fjord the Commandos would embark into their landing craft. They were divided into five task groups. Group 1 were to come ashore first at a little hamlet called Hollevik, about a mile and a half from Sör Vaagso to sweep up any isolated outposts and move into the town as a reserve. The main force in Group 2 were the assault group on Sör Vaagso itself, and led by Dunford Slater. Maaloy Island and its batteries were the objective for Jack Churchill and the third group. They were to land slightly ahead of Dunford Slater so as to keep the island's garrison busy – otherwise the enemy would have a clear view of Dunford Slater's back.

A floating reserve were to be kept in the landing ships ready to support either Dunford Slater in the town or Churchill on the island. Once the island had been secured, the destroyer *Oribi* was to slip through the narrow quarter-mile channel and into the Ulvesund. Her commandos, Group 5, were to land north of Sör Vaagso, near to the Kapelnoes Point to provide a rearguard or backstop in case the enemy from elsewhere tried to intervene.

Once the commandos were landed, the destroyer was then free to set about the enemy shipping in the Ulvesund, where she would be joined by her consort *Onslow*. The air force was to keep the enemy's heads down by making low level bombing runs against the two island garrisons. Since the fleet would approach the target through the Vaags Fjord the battery at Rugsundo was a particular concern. The air force were to mask it with smoke bombs and generally help to hold their attention until the main operation was well underway. Then the cruiser *Kenya* could engage the batteries and destroy the guns in time for the raiders to make their getaway.

The commandos sailed from Gourrock on 22 December. Mountbatten came and addressed them all immediately before their departure.

'This is the first raid against a defended port,' he said. 'This is a test, pilot run. Nobody knows quite what is going to happen, and you are the ones who are going to find out.'

The raiders sailed in two converted landing ships HMS *Prince Leopold* and *Prince Charles* with a local escort to Scapa Flow and their rendezvous with the fleet. As the little convoy cleared the northern tip of Scotland it ran full tilt into a full-blown gale. Conversion from Channel ferries to infantry landing ships had done little to enhance the seaworthy qualities of these boats, prone to roll wickedly in any kind of swell; and now, with eight heavy landing craft carried high in the superstructure, they were alarmingly top heavy. The results were frightening.

At the height of the storm while the commandos were prostrate with sea sickness, the secretary to the captain on HMS *Prince Charles* asked his master to come to his cabin. Urgently.

The cabin table fixed to the wall was moving rhythmically about six inches up and down. The captain summoned his chief engineer to pronounce upon this levitation.

The verdict was simple. The heavy seas were literally squeezing the sides of the ship; it was happening in all the outward facing cabins.

The landing ships arrived on Christmas Eve at the main anchorage in Scapa, in a very sorry condition; and neither could proceed immediately with the operation. Both had shipped so much water that their pumps could not cope. The operation was delayed for 24 hours which allowed the commandos to fraternize with the navy and enjoy a decent Christmas dinner in a secure anchorage.

The landing ships had a destroyer tied up on either side lending their pumps to the drying out operation. The *Prince Charles* had 14 feet of water in the forward hold, and over Christmas more than 145 tons of seawater were pumped from her flooded compartments.

News of the postponement was welcomed by everybody, although some believed it would never have been allowed to go ahead at that time in any case. A strong rumour was that it had been delayed 24 hours so as not to cause offence to the Pope!

The bomber crews of the Hampdens in 50 Squadron RAF had flown from their airfield in Lincolnshire north to Wick specially for this operation. Nairn Robertson was a sergeant radio operator air gunner, and his plane was detailed to attack Rugsundo Battery. He spent the first part of Christmas Day being briefed on the operation and then, along with the other air crew, serving the ground staff their Christmas Dinner in time-honoured fashion.

About 8.00 p.m. on Christmas night, Wing Commander Oxley, the squadron commander came into the temporary billet where the sergeants were changing into their flying kit. He had a fire bucket full of beer.

'Come on lads, I think you'd better have a beer on me.'

'No thank you sir. No, No, we're all flying tomorrow morning.'

'Oh, of course.' He paused.

'Well now look lads,' Oxley said, 'the operation has been postponed for twenty-four hours, so let's get pissed.'

So they did.

The delay also allowed the good people of Sör Vaagso and the German garrison to have a peaceful Christmas. The Norwegians made the best they could of their second Christmas under occupation, although most would admit that the pain and the humiliation had subsided somewhat, and the German garrison behaved correctly. The Nazi conquerors were older men, most with families at home. A priest had come to Sör Vaagso and the church had been decorated for the traditional Nordic Christmas, shared by everyone.

At the entrance of Vaags Fjord HM submarine *Tuna* surfaced at dusk to report her position. She was the navigational beacon for the task force. The crew learned that they would have to spend another 24 hours on the fjord bottom. At 1600 hours on 26 December, the force weighed anchor, to cross the North Sea out of the sunset and into the darkness of the long arctic nght.

CHAPTER TWENTY TWO

Sör Vaagso

The navigation of the task force was brilliantly accurate. HMS *Kenya* picked up the submarine exactly on time and in place.

Thereafter the force sailed quietly into Vaags Fjord, *Kenya* moved over to the southern shore screened by *Onslow* and *Offa*, while HMS *Chiddingfold* shepherded the mother ships into their secluded bay for the commandos to board their landing craft. HMS *Oribi* dropped back to the fjord entrance to act as rearguard; the last thing they needed was to be caught unawares. It was dark, and the warships hugged the mountainous shore line of the fjord, out of sight of alert eyes on the Rugsundo Battery.

But they were spotted.

At the entrance to the fjord and unbeknown to the raiders, the Germans had a small outpost which doubled as a coastguard station. The outpost radioed to its main base, the naval signalling post on Maaloy Island, that a group of enemy warships were entering Vaags Fjord.

The duty signaller left his post, ran down to the small bay on the north side of Maaloy, leapt into a boat and then rowed across to Sör Vaagso. Forty minutes later, he reported to the house which had been requisitioned by the naval commandant. It was on the main street next door to the Hagen Hotel.

The naval commandant, a fairly popular man with the local population because he made few demands, allowed them to get on with their lives, doubled as port officer and convoy controller.

The officer read the message and asked the signaller whether he had informed the battery on Maaloy.

'Oh no Sir, it's a Wehrmacht battery, and this is a naval signal addressed to you!'

The Germans are nothing, if not a methodical people.

The naval officer reached for the telephone and called the battery office. The telephone rang and rang. The duty operator was there but he wasn't answering.

It was the turn of the battery commander's servant to be telephone orderly. He had a hangover, had his master's boots to polish and wasn't in any mood to cope with more than one task at a time.

So the Wehrmacht gunners were up and about their daily chores on Maaloy Island. They had no idea what was in store for them around the corner of the fjord. The naval commandant completed his toilet and hurried across the street to the Wehrmacht headquarters.

By the time he had informed his opposite number, it was too late. The commandos had completed their transfer into the landing craft, and the task groups sorted themselves out into formation. It was past 8.30 in the morning. The first signs of the winter dawn were beginning to lighten the eastern sky.

It was time for the bombers to do their bit.

The Hampden was called the 'flying suitcase', by its crews. It was the one British aircraft which abided by the German philosophy in bomber construction – a long thin fuselage, and the crew concentrated in a single area. The idea was that physical proximity gave comfort and mutual support in action; as well as allowing the guns to provide a co-ordinated defence. The Hampden even looked as if it came out of the Dornier stable. The four-man crew compartment was three feet at its widest, so none of the positions were in tandem, and moving from one to another was exceedingly difficult.

The Hampdens came across the North Sea in darkness and low level. Formation flying was a bit too difficult. The aircraft had a single tiny blue light on the training edge of the wing, so the 12 bombers flew in a gaggle and roughly on the same course.

Nairn Robertson's pilot was a Rhodesian; his flight of four pulled away from the main group and flew up Vaags Fjord towards Rugsundo. Robertson, cramped into the upper gun turret position slid the perspex panel back and cocked the gas-operated twin 303-inch Vickers K guns.

Blurred shapes out in the water flashed by underneath, the task groups were moving into position. In the fjord there was snow on the mountain sides which reached right down to the water's edge. Rugsundo lay straight ahead. Robertson heard the wail of the air raid sirens above the roar of the engines and the howling slipstream.

The flight path took them low over the island on their first pass,

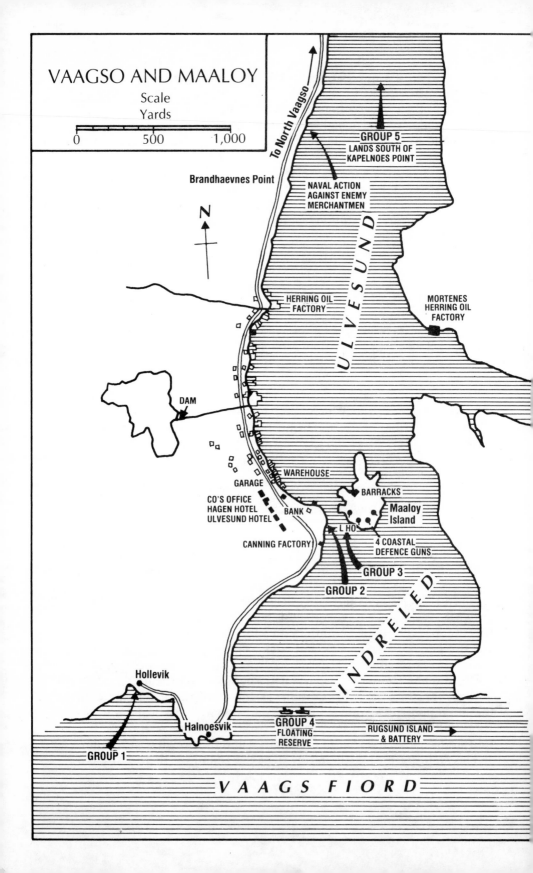

the pilot banked so that the guns (there was a second ventral position beneath Robertson), could open fire. Germans came tumbling out of their huts along the water's edge, pulling on their coats and running hard for the main batteries. While the pilot and navigator sighted the naval guns as the target, Robertson and the other gunner sprayed the enemy below.

Turning inland the pilot climbed above the fjord sides and banked to begin his diving attack on the battery. The four aircraft were to attack in echelons of two. Down they came in a steep dive, the Hampden shuddering with the speed, rocking to the turbulence of the flak, air bursting around them. The pilot was aiming for the point on the island where the three guns stuck out like sore thumbs.

Just at the aiming point, Robertson heard the navigator's voice in the headphones. With a twang that you could cut with a knife, he now sounded faint and strange, there was no preliminary voice procedure: 'Bombs gone. I've been hit, the course for home is 230.' Then silence.

At the base of the dive the plane lifted as the 500-pounders tumbled out of the bomb-bay and lighter bombs fell away from the wing racks. Then they were past the target. Robertson had time for a satisfactory burst into the open gun pits, and red balled tracer climbed lazily upwards and chased them before falling away out of range. They had no time to tell whether they had scored a hit before they raced away low down the fjord and out to the open sea. Robertson momentarily looked up at the bridge of the *Kenya* and glimpsed a few raised hands before they flashed past. Their part in the operation had taken just two minutes.

Nairn Robertson clambered forward to the navigator's position in the nose of the aircraft. He grabbed some field dressings and the first aid kit, crawled through the bulk head door under the pilot's cockpit and climbed down to the navigator. The wounded airman had released the spring on his seat back and was now flat out on the floor. The bomb-aiming panel had been shattered by cannon shell and the navigator was badly hurt. The side of his face was peppered with shrapnel and shards of perspex, and his left knee was a bloody pulp, pumping blood into his boot. Robertson rendered what first aid he could, a tourniquet stemmed the flow and a field dressing on the shattered leg seemed to do the trick. He tried to inject some morphia but the needle was far too blunt. The man had a bad wound in his wrist where a piece of shrapnel had gone right through and lodged in his wrist watch. Robertson took the needle off and allowed the fluid to drip into the open wound. He thought it might do the trick but the man was unconscious anyway. The young airman stripped off his flying jacket and

189

wrapped the injured man as best he could, for the piercing wind that came through the shattered nose was bitterly, numbingly cold.[1]

At 0842 the landing craft, in arrow head formation, began to move up the Vaags Fjord. There was little chatter or noise, the men's thoughts centred only on what lay in store for them once they rounded the corner.

Jack Churchill was in his element – the silver buttons gleaming on his battledress, his wickedly long, sharp claymore slung low on his hips, and a crossbow across his shoulders. The men loved him for his idiosyncrasies, and long since dubbed him 'Mad Jack'. The commando sergeant major had winced at the sight of his fighting major, and turned to the landing ship's bosun, as he was about to scramble into the assault boat.

'Look at that! If Robin 'ood was alive today he'd be f.....g blushing!'

The first assault group boat peeled off left and headed in shore to Hollevick. Everything was going to plan. HMS *Kenya* moved ahead to a position where the Ulvesund joined the Vaags Fjord. Broadside on, she exposed her length to Maaloy and brought all 12 6-inch guns to bear on her port beam. The range was less than 2,000 yards; point blank for her main armament.

The landing craft, shepherded by the destroyers, came skidding round the corner, turned left and headed straight up the Ulvesund.

So far, neither enemy battery had opened fire on the attacking ships. Brigadier Haydon couldn't believe their good fortune. He watched another pair of Hampdens take on Rugsundo and the flak rise to meet them. The Germans must have been convinced that all they had to contend with was an air raid.

Maaloy lay dead ahead. Sör Vaagso on the port side. Overhead the remaining Hampdens circled and waited their moment to join the attack.

HMS *Kenya* opened fire. First starshell, to illuminate the target, and then high explosive. This was the signal the Hampdens had been waiting for. Down they swooped to wave top height along the high-sided fjord towards Maaloy at the bottom. The noise was overwhelming.

The landing craft, in line abreast, moved down into the narrowing cone of fire, with the towering walls of the fjord on either side. It was for all the world like an amphibious 'Charge of the Light Brigade'.

Churchill's group had the furthest to go and his boats echeloned into the lead. The major stood high on the exposed platform at the ramp of the boat, took up his bagpipes and above the sounds of battle the men stirred to the swirling 'March of the Cameron Men'.

The cruiser deluged Maaloy with high explosives. Fifty shells a minute slammed into the island, whilst in the same mad ten minutes the destroyers bombarded the Vaagso shoreline; and it wasn't long before a number of the wooden structured buildings were ablaze.

At 0857 hours, Dunford Slater fired a sequence of Very lights into the morning sky. The warships ceased firing and the 200 men in Group 3 followed the colonel to the shore.

HMS *Kenya* turned her attention to the smoke-shrouded Rugsundo Battery, which had recovered from the air attacks and was beginning to make a nuisance of itself.

A flight of Hampdens came hurtling down the Ulvesund on one last attack, and close range anti-aircraft guns on the Sör Vaagso shore opened fire. The Hampdens were to drop a smoke screen across the beach ahead of the assault boats. The smoke screen came in the form of square 60-pound drums of liquid phosphorous which dropped out of incendiary containers. They just fell and hit the ground, burst open on impact, allowing the phosphorous to react with the air, burn, and give off smoke.

The Germans got the last aircraft in the flight. Piloted by Sergeant Smith, the port wing flamed as the navigator released the canisters. The Hampden swung out into the fjord and Smith barely had time to level out before it skidded into the water. Three of the four crew made it out before the plane sank. The air gunner in the lower ventral position never made it.[2] They had practised the 'canister run' on a number of occasions in Scotland. It required precision flying and deadly accuracy to lay the smoke screen properly. Even under the best conditions it had never really worked.

In the fjord one canister from Smith's already crippled bomber landed in a crowded landing craft, burst on impact and showered the crouching commandos with burning white phosphorous. Phosphorous fell on the explosive charges and small arms ammunition which had been stowed in the bottom of the boat.

In desperation the young Royal Marine coxswain steered his boat, which now resembled a firework display more than an assault craft, into the shore. Not surprisingly the landing craft let its ramp down early. Arthur Konrower, the troop leader, leapt ashore and stumbled on the boulders.

He slipped and fell. Before Konrower could recover, ten tons of landing craft rode up over him, bending one leg up under his back.

The commandos waded ashore, pulling their seriously hurt officer with them. Those who were on fire vaulted the ship's side and jumped into deeper water to extinguish the phosphorous by starving it of air. But phosphorous is rather like those trick birthday cake candles which light up even when they have been blown out. As soon as the commandos came out of the water the phosphorous rekindled in contact with the air, providing plenty of work for the medics, even before the men had established themselves ashore.

Colonel Dunford Slater, undaunted by the disaster to one of his boats, led the main party to the exact spot they had selected for the landing; a narrow shelf of rock below a 30-foot overhanging cliff.

The commandos stepped ashore 'dry shod' and joining their toggle ropes soon scaled the cliff, to enter Vaagso at the one place the Germans would never have expected a landing.

Meanwhile Churchill, having carefully stowed away his bagpipes, and placed them in the charge of a bemused marine, stormed ashore at Maaloy at the head of his commandos, waving his claymore and yelling awesome battle cries, in a charge through the smoke and onto the battery positions. The gun pits were deserted and the guns intact. The naval bombardment had missed their target and the gunners, mistaking the barrage for an air raid, had huddled for shelter in their bunkers.

Caught like rats in a trap, the majority surrendered to the commandos. Some tried to offer resistance and these, including their commander in his highly polished boots, were summarily shot.

Once he had secured the island, Churchill fired off a Very light. This was the signal for the two destroyers to slip past and carry out the next phase of the operation. HMS *Oribi* landed the fifth group at Kapelnoes Point and then joined her sister ship *Onslow* in sinking the ships which had gathered in convoy in the Ulvesund.

They fell upon their prey with all the gusto of a fox let loose in a hen coop. Four German manned freighters tried to beach themselves, but the 4.7-inch guns battered them into a quick submission.

One German ship, the armed trawler *Föhn*, attempted to break out on the blind side of the island. The commando spotted her and, under Churchill's direction, manned one of the coast defence guns. The *Föhn* was about 800 metres away and twice the commandos watched in utter frustration as 75mm rounds ploughed right through her without exploding. Churchill called Sergeant Vincent across. He was a real gunner, who patiently explained that if they wanted the shells to explode, then they had better set the fuses. 'Carry on Sarn't,' responded Churchill. And they opened up again on the luckless *Föhn*. But No. 3 Commando were denied the chance of claiming a trawler to their list of kills. The destroyer *Onslow* appeared on the scene and despatched *Föhn* without further delay.

At 0920 hours Churchill signalled across to the other shore and Dunford Slater, that Maaloy had fallen.

By now the main battle had developed for Sör Vaagso, and the commandos were hurting; for they were at a distinct disadvantage. The town huddled beneath a sheer rockface several hundred feet high. Its main and only street, perhaps half a mile long, had buildings on both sides, mostly made of wood. The street parallels the shoreline about, 50 yards from the water's edge. All the important buildings, warehouses, fish processing plant, canning factory etc., were at the far end of the town; and the only way to reach them was over the German garrison. Having recovered from the initial shock, the enemy reacted strongly, turning houses into strong points and fighting back with the buildings burning around them.

The company of alpine troops, élite mountain warfare specialists, who were 'visiting' Sör Vaagso for Christmas, had been taken out of town very early that morning on a route march to blow away the Christmas hangover. At the first sign of trouble they had come rushing back and some of them had found vantage points on the rugged mountainside from where they poured a volume of fire down into the streets below for as long as their ammunition lasted.

Dunford Slater lost four officers and numerous other casualties in as many minutes. His commandos were locked into a vicious street battle, and although he had no doubt they would gain the upper hand, it was all taking far too long, and once the operation ashore slipped behind schedule, the Germans would have the opportunity to retaliate; either by bringing in troops from near by or attacking the warships now bottled up in the fjord and desperately vulnerable to air attack without space to manoeuvre.

Dunford Slater called for all the assistance he could muster. The men from Group 1 who had landed at Hollevik were soon due to be on the scene, and Haydon had already sent the last of the floating reserve ashore to join the fight.

The colonel signalled to Churchill for reinforcements. On Maaloy the battery offices were being ransacked for intelligence, and the batteries' ammunition stores and other installations were being readied by the sappers for demolition. Churchill despatched Captain Peter Young and a half-troop, about 18 men, to Sör Vaagso.

In the town the civilians were caught up in the fighting. There was no escape.

Jacob Holvik, an 18-year-old boy, worked in the canning factory. He lived with his parents in a house on the edge of town and the road that led to Hollevik. His father had woken him with the news:

'Something is going on. The Englishmen are coming to liberate us from the Germans.'

Jacob quickly dressed and rushed outside where he was joined by his cousin who lived in a house just across the road. They watched the Hampdens press home the attacks and the flashes that rippled along the shadowy form of the cruiser as the *Kenya* fired her broadsides. A group of soldiers advanced down the road towards them. It was the men from Group 1 who had landed at Hollevik. At the head marched a Norwegian liaison officer.

'This is just a raid,' the Norwegian responded in his mother tongue to their question. 'The English are not coming to stay.'

The Norwegian officer asked the boys to show them where there were houses with Germans in them.

Jacob knew of one which the enemy had requisitioned. It was on the outskirts of the town, and he led the commandos straight there. Sure enough the enemy were inside and at first they put up a fierce resistance. Jacob stayed with the commandos and even helped distribute some of their ammunition. After a while, with some of their number dead, and the house on fire, the surviving enemy surrendered.

Jacob attached himself to the commando group throughout the rest of the engagement, making himself useful carrying ammunition to the firing parties and running messages. He remembered being scared stiff, but strangely exhilarated and unmoved at the sight of his town being engulfed in battle.

For a long while the enemy resistance centred on the two hotels that stood next to each other in the main street and faced out onto the Ulvesund. The Hagen Hotel had been taken over by the navy as its headquarters, while the army used the Ulvesund.

Captain Martin Linge died in the attack for the Ulvesund Hotel. The German resistance was particularly fierce, and the commando attack was in danger of losing momentum. Linge ran forward and made it into the lobby of the hotel. The roof of the building was ablaze and he called up the stairs to the Germans to surrender. They replied with a hail of fire. A Norwegian sergeant pulled Linge free of the building but he was already dead. The other Norwegian soldiers, angered by his death, kept up a sustained fusillade on the hotel while the flames took a firm hold; no defenders came out.

The battle for the Hagen Hotel was equally fierce, although the Norwegians who owned it were still inside. Anne Mor Hagen had helped her mother run the hotel ever since the German navy had taken it over. As the battle developed, the family took shelter in the cellar, together with a couple of maids and Anne Mor's brother.

When the hotel started to burn, the navy personnel surrendered and the family were able to make good their escape.

A Norwegian soldier asked if they would like to go to England but insisted they should go only if they were a complete family, otherwise those that remained in Norway risked reprisals. Anne Mor and her brother wanted to go (their livelihood had been taken away), but they had a sister who lived in Kristiansand, and their mother didn't want to leave . . .

The commandos had used the bakery across the street as a strong point to subdue the fighting Gemans in the hotels. It was owned by the parents of Anna Satren, a 14-year-old schoolgirl and one of seven children.

The family had all been up early that morning, for they had planned to take the ferry across the Ulvesund and visit their grandparents who lived in Mortenes on the mainland. Once the battle had started the family took cover in the cellar, where they were joined by friends and neighbours. They covered the only window with sacks of flour and made barricades, behind which they crowded for safety.

It was pitch dark in the cellar, the sounds of battle came ever nearer and Anna's father led them in prayer.

At the top of a loading chute there was a trap door which led directly out into the street. Somebody was tapping at the trap door. Anna's father lit an oil lamp and fearfully they opened up. In fell a German soldier. He had been severely wounded and his chest was covered in blood. He was an elderly man, and a baker in his home town. This family had befriended him. They got some water and tried to bathe the wound, but it wouldn't stop bleeding.

'The Tommies are all around us,' the man moaned. 'War is terrible.'

The bakery above them was on fire and smoke filled the cellar. Anna was sure they would die.

One of the men scrambled on top of the sacks and pulled away those which had been used to block the window. He smashed the pane of glass and called across to some commandos. They were told to come out through the trap door, and once those inside had opened it up, they threw down a rope to help them scramble up the chute to safety.

'We have a wounded German in the cellar.'

'Please don't shoot him,' pleaded Anna.

One of the commandos scrambled into the cellar and shot him. He saw Anna's accusing stare as he came out onto the street.

'I had to shoot him, love, he was too badly hurt to move, and if I left him there, he would have been burned alive.' A Norwegian soldier led them to safety, for the battle was still being waged all around them.

Colonel Dunford Slater continued to encourage his men to even greater efforts. He needed no reminding that they had been ashore long enough. German fighter aircraft were now swooping low, strafing the streets and even taking on the destroyers in the Ulvesund.

Their commanding officer was everywhere, co-ordinating the battle and seemingly oblivious to the personal risk. One German had a go at him and threw a stick grenade from the shelter of a shop doorway. Dunford Slater acrobatically threw himself to one side and escaped the blast, but his runner was badly wounded.

Directly afterwards, the German attempted to surrender, walking out of the doorway with his hands held high.

'Kamerad, Kamerad!'

The colonel had a second runner with him, a man called Mills who immediately cocked his sten-submachine gun.

'Nein, Nein!' begged the German.

'Ja, Ja,' said Mills and shot him.

'Yeah, well, Mills, shouldn't ha'done that,' was the colonel's comment, as he stepped over the body and continued with the battle.

Many of the local inhabitants had taken shelter in the town's only bank. It was a brick building, one of the very few, and the vault was just about as secure as anywhere. Peter Young's troop from Maaloy had done well in clearing the warehouses along the waterfront, and by 1145 hours had secured the buildings to the edge of town.

After about two o'clock, everything was quiet. Per Gunnar Garsen had taken shelter with many others in the cellar of a house close to the stream at the top end of town which marked the limits of the battle. He was the first to venture out of the cellar.

The ground outside was littered with German dead. Equipment and debris lay everywhere.

Hardly a house or building had escaped damage. At first, people stood in a silent group to watch the commandos prepare even that which was intact for destruction. Then they moved down through the main street and stood in shocked silence at the landing stage. To this day, those who were there could taste the profound despondency in the air. It was just a raid.

EVACUATION

By three o'clock the short arctic day was rapidly coming to a close. The final part of the operation was the evacuation of the raiders, together with those townsfolk who wanted to go with them, and the German prisoners who doubtless would have preferred to stay.

First, everything of value to the enemy had to be destroyed, and this meant the sappers putting to the torch, or demolishing the remaining factories, wharf and warehouses. Over on Maaloy, Churchill's men had found a large ammunition store which contained a consignment of sea mines. He ordered his sappers to prepare the lot for demolition and then to let him know when they were ready to detonate the charges.

The charges were set but the sappers forgot to tell the major when they blew. Churchill was drinking out of a bottle of German hock at the time, and the explosion broke his front teeth. A piece of shrapnel was blown in under his helmet and caught him in the forehead.

Badly concussed, Jack Churchill was evacuated to HMS *Kenya*.

Under Dunford Slater's guidance, the withdrawal of the commandos was masterful and orderly.

Landing craft formed up at the various jetties for the short journey down to the waiting mother ships. A couple of the destroyers steamed close inshore keeping a watchful eye on proceedings and spraying the hillside with bursts of 20mm cannon from their bridge-mounted Oerlikons.

If the evacuation for the commandos was orderly, it was chaotic for the Norwegian population.

The British were encouraging as many as they could to come with them. The Norwegian liaison officers tried to insist that only complete families should travel.

Reiddar Hoddevik was a 17-year-old seaman who, despite his youth, had already sailed around the world, and been repatriated to his native town by the Germans. He had spent the last half-hour of the evacuation helping to load stretchers into the landing craft, for Dunford Slater took his dead and his wounded home.

Reiddar followed the last stretcher onto the landing craft and stayed. He didn't speak very much English but had formed the impression that the whole town was going. His widowed mother didn't even know he had left.

It was easy enough to make mistakes and there was a fair amount of panic amongst the civilians. In the last few moments, some were simply herded on board, including a young woman and her baby. Her husband was left behind.

The people just stood and watched the soldiers they first believed had come to liberate them, leave. Some commandos were acutely embarrassed. Others, exhilarated by the battle still, or already in the after-action shock, were unaware of the feelings of the townsfolk. The Norwegian soldiers found this a time of anger and anguish, and many questioned the value of the raid.

Anna Satren and her family were taken down to a landing craft. They just followed the crowd.

A Norwegian lieutenant greeted them.

'Is this the whole family?'

Her father was missing. He had gone in search of her younger brother.

'If you haven't got the whole family with you we advise you not to go, because of German punishment.'

The last of the buildings due for demolition had been destroyed. Dunford Slater was the last raider to leave the shore. In the gathering gloom he looked back at the townsfolk who remained behind. There was no cheering, no flag waving or bantering. The crowd stood mute and still; and then followed the little boat's progress down the Ulvesund. Not out of curiosity, but because the survivors, almost by tacit consent, headed towards the undamaged hamlets of Halnoesvik and Hollevik, there to find food and shelter among their friends and relatives.

A trio of long-range Beaufighters roared in low over the Ulvesund. They marked the last of the air cover for the operation. The planes waggled their wings in salute and then climbed into the darkening sky.

One more Norwegian decided to leave Sor Vaagso: Jacob Holvik had been busy throughout the day, fetching and carrying for the commandos and now the Norwegian officer who had befriended him at the start advised him not to stay.

'Too many people have seen you help us,' he said; 'you would be safer with us.'

Jacob ran to his home in the road to Halnoesvik to bid his family farewell. His father wanted to take the whole family, but the grandfather refused to leave; and that settled it for the family.

'You can make your own choice, son,' Jacob's father said, 'But if you have done just half the things you say – then it is better for all of us that you leave.'[3]

There wasn't much time. Jacob grabbed some photographs of the family, a quick and tearful farewell, and he was out of the house and straight down to the water's edge, fearing that the assault boats had all sailed past.

One last boat came chugging down the Ulvesund. It was Dunford Slater and his command group. Jacob waved and yelled at the top of his voice, and the boat swung into the shore.

---

[1] Robertson saved his friend's life. The aircraft made it safely back to England. The navigator's leg however was too badly damaged and eventually, after months in hospital, it was amputated above the knee.

[2] The navy were too preoccupied to pick up the three swimmers, and it was more than 30 minutes before one of the destroyers fished them out of the fjord. The freezing arctic conditions had by then taken their toll. Only Smith survived.

[3] Jacob's father was arrested and sent to a concentration camp in reprisal for his son's actions.

CHAPTER TWENTY THREE

Stony Ground

Was Operation Archery and the destruction of Sör Vaagso worth the effort? It was by any scale a modest operation, in which the commandos fought with great bravery against an outnumbered but resilient foe. But for the British it proved both instructive and fruitful.

It was instructive because it showed that a combined operation, based on a genuine and unselfish integration of the three services, could pay dividends. It also showed that a defended port could be overcome with the right ingredients and firepower. It was to take Dieppe to prove that such a policy could have its limits.

Sör Vaagso was fruitful. Some 15,000 tons of German shipping, fish oil-processing plants, warehouses, stores and a small dockyard facility had all been put to the torch. A German garrison had been defeated, 100 prisoners taken. For this harvest, nevertheless, the commandos had paid a relatively high price. They suffered 19 men killed and a further 50 wounded.

The commando raid worried the Germans, and perhaps that was where its greatest value lay to the Allied cause. Hitler became increasingly concerned that the Allies would attempt to 'get at Germany' through his weak and vulnerable northern flank. There were times that Hitler did the Allies' work for them, and this was increasingly the case from early 1942 to the war's end. Had the Wehrmacht been given a free hand to wage the war, it would have been a different story.

Hitler now deployed 300,000 troops, from first-rate divisions who were destined to sit out the war in Norway, together with a significant element of the German navy and air force: the latter of course were deployed to interdict the Russian convoys.

As an exercise in 'hearts and minds', the Vaagso raid was a dismal failure; but then most raids probably were. What is instructive in this instance however is that only 71 Norwegians came home with the Allies.

Raiding did nothing to boost the morale of the Norwegian people. It resulted in their homes and livelihoods being destroyed, and was followed by a more repressive occupation by better quality troops.

The Norwegian government bitterly opposed what they saw as a short-sighted policy, and this view was reinforced when the commandos returned to the Lofotens.

It was the need to protect the convoy route to Murmansk that provided, at least in part, some of the strategic backdrop to the Lofoten raid. Initially, Moscow suggested a joint Anglo-Russian operation to expel the Germans from north Norway; but such a scheme found no favour in London. However, that northern part of Norway, beyond the Arctic Circle, was a remote area, which made it difficult for the Germans to function in a counter-insurgency role, if the Allies could operate a guerrilla base in the region. The planners spent some considerable time in 1941 examining the feasibility of Bodo on the mainland, or an offshore island serving as a guerrilla sanctuary from which naval forces and troops, even possibly supported by a modest air contingent, could operate against a long and exposed German line of communication.

Clearly none of these planners had been around during the previous Norwegian campaign, or even had bothered to check the reports properly. The scheme was only finally vetoed when the planners actually put it forward for consideration as a proposal for an operation. Wiser counsels prevailed, and the problems of resupply and reinforcement were recognized as not cost effective.

So sights were lowered, and a more modest plan took shape. A raiding force of 300 commandos were to land in the Lofotens, destroy the local industry and shipping, stay for as long as was reasonable, act as a diversion to the main attack on Sör Vaagso; and then withdraw.

No. 12 Commando, the Irish and Welsh commando formed mainly from the Northern Ireland and Welsh regiments, was chosen to provide the main force. This was to be the commandos' only 'full' operation in the war.[1] The ground forces were led by the Commando CO, Lieutenant Colonel Harrison MC, and also included 75 other soldiers, mostly demolition experts from the Sappers and 68 Norwegians.

The raiders sailed in the landing ship, HMS *Prince Albert*, and the extensive escort included eight destroyers, a dozen mine-sweepers and corvettes under the command of Rear Admiral L. H. K. Hamilton, who flew his flag in the cruiser HMS *Arethusa*. Included in the Norwegian party were a number of radio operators, trained by SOE and intended for missions behind the German lines. The Norwegians were told that the commando force and its naval covering party was to stay. Sergeant Biarne Osmundsiag was much cheered by this news, and thought it would make their mission that much easier. He was however disappointed in the British choice of the location and target for the raid. Moskenes and Reine struck him as being towns of little significance in the Moskenesoy, the southernmost island in the Lofoten group.

Nevertheless he was delighted to be home in Norway again, and lost little time in preparing for their operational role. Sergeant Osmundsiag was one of four radio operators. Their mission was to penetrate behind the German lines, make contact with the local population and gather intelligence. The commandos were to furnish escort and back-up, and, when necessary, raiding parties to attack the targets which had been identified.

Clandestine activity of this nature in Norway was ideally suited to the country's geographical characteristics. Norway's area was vast, given the small population; the long winding fjords indenting its coast provided sanctuary to the German navy, but failed to shelter them from the watchful eyes of the Resistance. The interior of the country comprised mountains, snow, waterfalls, glaciers, secluded valleys, forests, many reindeer, a few hunters and even less skiers. Few Germans dared to venture far, and as a consequence, resistance fighters had already started to hide there after operations.

The resistance also had the advantage of a long frontier with a neutral but benevolently disposed Sweden. Again the frontier was too extensive for the Germans to patrol successfully, so rebels and fugitives escaping German pursuit could easily slip across.

None of the Norwegians, for obvious security reasons, was told that their raid, codenamed Operation Anklet, was a diversion for the main attack.

It was just as well. Sergeant Osmundsiag came from Sör Vaagso, and his family, parents, brothers and sisters still lived there.

What is less easy to excuse, other than as a cynical deception to an Allied nation, is the claim that the raiding force were to establish a semi-permanent base in the area.

Twelve Commando and its Norwegian compatriots came ashore at 0600 hours on Boxing Day. There was a small German detachment at Moskenes but it surrendered without a struggle. The local people appeared in strength on the quaysides at both ports to greet these Christmas intruders, and the welcome was even warmer when the Norwegian liaison officers assured them they had come to stay. The people could regard themselves as liberated.

The commandos entered into the spirit of things. The German garrison stores were looted and Christmas delicacies distributed along with their own fare.

Admiral Hamilton, delighted at the ease of the operation, and the absence of enemy resistance or indeed activity, reported to London. Optimistically, he indicated that the force might well indeed stay for some time in the Lofotens.

On 28 December, the raiders had upped sticks and departed. A lone German reconnaissance bomber was the cause of the abrupt change of heart. The Allied presence had been detected and the plane sent out to investigate. The pilot dropped an opportunist bomb at HMS *Arethusa*; and came very close to hitting the cruiser.

Even at this midway stage in the war, British admirals still needed reminders that their warships were vulnerable without air cover. Then radio intercepts gave the impression to a now concerned task force commander that the Germans were planning some awful counter. Perhaps it was time to go home.

The Norwegian contingent were not told why they were to leave. For Sergeant Osmundsiag and his compatriots it was quite the saddest day in their lives since the capitulation of their country. They were quickly briefed on Norwegian national policy with regard to evacuation, and so, exactly as in the Vaagso raid, only complete families were encouraged to leave. The radio station, fish factories, warehouses and fishing boats, everything of value was destroyed.

The commandos re-embarked, taking with them a modest return of Quislings and recruits to the Norwegian cause, together with a few prisoners. Twenty-nine Germans and a few Quislings were taken and 226 Norwegian patriots, men, women and children. The raiders left behind considerable disillusionment and despair.

The second Lofoten raid evoked harsh reprisals. In February 1942 the Germans shot 43 people caught aboard a ship making for England. A month later, after the arrest of a group of British and Norwegians near Televaag, 300 houses in the town were burned and its citizens deported.

There was a blazing row in London. King Haakon and his government-in-exile demanded a greater say in the mounting of subsequent operations in Norway. It was eventually resolved by establishing an Anglo-Norwegian Collaboration Committee. Brigadier Colin Gubbins, now firmly ensconced in the SOE, was its first and very successful chairman.

Gubbins's involvement also pointed to the direction that future clandestine operations should take in Norway. The SOE had previously used the gallant Martin Linge as the director of operations in the country. His place was taken by a group of saboteurs in England and Norway who adopted his name in tribute to his memory.

A second resistance movement was called *Milorg* – an acronym for military organization – which typically assembled at some secret rendezvous for training and then raided a target in a surprise operation.

Milorg was led by the energetic former commander-in-chief of the regular army, General Otto Ruge. He established listening posts in five sectors of Norway and employed SIS couriers in Sweden to carry the information they collected to London. Gubbins established the principle that no operation would be conducted without close liaison with *Milorg*, which with the aid of the SOE was to have sole responsibility for sabotage operations and the training of the underground army.

These arrangements effectively removed Norway as a major happy hunting ground for the commandos and special forces; although there is no evidence to suggest that this was intentional. Geography, climate and increased enemy presence had combined to make large scale raids an even more hazardous affair. In summer, the long daylight hours and a vigilant enemy made an approach by a large naval force too dangerous. In winter the fierce storms ruled out amphibious operations.

There were still some raids, but these were on a much smaller scale and more intermittent.

On 11 September 1942, a Free French submarine sailed north from the Clyde. On board were two officers and eight commandos from 2 Commando together with a couple of Norwegian corporals who were to act as guides and interpreters. Their target was the hydro-electric station at Glomfjord, which powered an aluminium plant.

Glomfjord is north of the Arctic Circle and close to where the independent companies had fought some of the bitterest battles in the rearguard actions of 1940.

The raiders paddled ashore in folding boats and then made a long and difficult approach march to their target; the last part was across the treacherous Svartisen glacier which they negotiated at night. They successfully penetrated the defences and blew up the turbines of the power station.

The way home was via Sweden but unfortunately the Germans had guessed that would be the route. The raiders were hunted down, two were killed and six captured.[2] Three commandos and one Norwegian eventually made it to Sweden.

Other raids failed even before they began and this was invariably due to the arctic temperatures and harsh climate. In November 1942, an attempt was made to attack the heavy water plant at Vermork, part of the German nuclear programme. Two gliders, each carrying 16 Parachute Regiment raiders, were lost when their tow planes or tugs iced up and crashed.

There were to be other raids in the southern part of Norway, but it already seemed clear that for sabotage operations the Norwegian Resistance was much better suited. The SOE established a continuous liaison between their 'depot' in the Shetlands and the Norwegian islands just to their east. Materials parachuted to the Resistance in the field grew in quality and in quantity. By mid-1943, the Norwegian arm was probably the most effective of all the European resistance organizations. This was dramatically demonstrated by the destruction of the heavy water plant and with the sinking of a ferry which was carrying the last consignment of heavy water across Lake Tinnsjoe.

---

[1] The commando did provide detachments for other raids into France and Norway right through to September 1943, its last recorded operation.

[2] Those captured were later executed at the express instructions of Hitler.

CHAPTER TWENTY FOUR

Bruneval:
'Descente des Anglais'

Not all the operations which came under the heading of raiding were conducted by special forces of the type that has so far been discussed.

The Royal Marines raided German blockade runners in Bordeaux Harbour. In October 1942, five two-man canoe teams left the submarine mother ship and paddled 70 miles up the Gironde to hit at enemy ships. This raid, immortalized as the 'Cockleshell Heroes', resulted in two canoe teams reaching the port, and attacking their targets with limpet mines.

Half a dozen ships were crippled. One crew survived and eventually returned home, and another crew were captured, and shot while prisoners of the Germans.

The blockade runners were fast freighters which traded in strategic goods with Japan. The attacking Marines showed exemplary courage in the operation, but this did not cause the enemy to rethink its policy. Only the ascendancy of Allied air and sea power was eventually to smash the link with Japan.

The Second World War was a conflict of competing technologies. Radar, developed by the British, had already played a vital role on the Allied side, but by 1942 the Germans had caught up, and the anti-aircraft batteries of the Luftwaffe, combined with the increasingly effective night fighter squadrons, were being directed onto their targets, the heavy bomber stream, by ground-based radar. The code name of the German radar apparatus used in these defences was the Wurzburg Device, which allowed the ground station to track a night fighter onto the target.

Bomber Command's Thousand Bomber raids thrilled the nation at home, but achieved little and contributed less to winning the war. Throughout 1942 the loss rate (including fatal accidents in England) seldom fell below 5 per cent per month. An average of one crew in 20 was lost on operations. Bomber crews had to complete 30 missions, and it needed no statistician to calculate the chances of survival.

In January 1942 photographic interpretation specialists identified what the Air Ministry scientists recognised as the latest example of a German Wurzburg. It was located a few hundred yards from the cliff tops at Bruneval, about 12 miles north of Le Havre. The reconnaissance photograph also showed a relatively modern, pre-war villa very close by, which presumably was used to accommodate the operators.

The British needed desperately to get their hands on a Wurzburg, for only then could they really see how good German technology was, and how best it might be countered. The site at Bruneval was temptingly close and reasonably isolated. It quickly became apparent to the planners in combined operations that only an airborne operation at night was feasible. The beach defences, along this part of the French coast in the Pas de Calais, were too good and too vigilant for a force to break in, stay awhile and then break out again.

One of the prerequisites for this raid was a detailed knowledge of the local German strength and dispositions. Instructions were despatched from London to the French Resistance and a group in Le Havre plotted the positions of German strong points and numbers. They also made the important discovery that despite German notices to the contrary, the beach below Bruneval was not mined. This vital piece of information allowed the planners to complete their preparations.

French coastal maps were studied by the intelligence teams. The legend *'Descente des Anglais'* was recorded which showed that at some time in their marauding past, other British raiders had used that cove.

The intention was for a parachute descent in sufficient strength to take the radar site, hold it while the radar was dismantled, and then to break out by attacking the beach defences from behind. An amphibious group would then come in to the secured beachhead and lift the parachutists and their loot to safety.

In February 1942, Flight Sergeant Cox, an RAF radar specialist was summoned to the Air Ministry. There he was interviewed by Air Commodore Victor Tait, director of radar on the air staff, who congratulated Cox for having volunteered for a special and dangerous mission.

'I cannot tell you what it is,' said the air commodore conspiratorially, 'but you must begin by becoming proficient at parachuting.'

Cox, who before the war had been a cinema projectionist, had never been in a ship or an aeroplane in his life. He was married with a few weeks' old baby.

Cox travelled to Ringway where he learned in just a very few days to become experienced enough at parachuting to save himself from a serious injury.

Shortly afterwards the flight sergeant met up with the parachutists. A hundred and twenty men under Major Frost of C Company of the recently formed 2nd Parachute Battalion prepared and trained for the raid.

Further photographic intelligence and a scale model showed a position well defended by machine gun posts and pillboxes. It was part of Hitler's Channel defences.

There was a farm called Le Presbytère about 750 yards further inland, where intelligence estimated a company of German soldiers were billeted. The civilians had been evacuated and the farm fortified. French Resistance reports suggested that there were elements of a motorized infantry regiment and an armoured car regiment within easy striking distance. The paratroopers would all be in army uniform while Cox had only his air force blue.

The scientists who had instigated the operation did their utmost to have Cox issued with an army uniform and an army number. Otherwise it was feared that if he was captured the Germans would soon single him out for special attention by their skilled interrogators.

R. V. Jones, the leading scientist, begged, cajoled and schemed, but the Army Council remained steadfast in their obstinacy. In desperation they did give Cox a cover story but none had any faith in its credibility: if captured Cox was to claim he was the aircraft's despatcher who had fallen out of the plane!

Major Frost divided his company into four groups, each with a different mission to perform. He would lead the main assault upon the villa and thereby seize the bulk of the Germans in the barracks.

A second group was to escort Flight Sergeant Cox onto the radar site and cover him while he dismantled the vital parts. Meanwhile a blocking group was to position itself between the villa and the fortified farm, and act as rearguard.

While all this was happening, upon landing the last group was to head straight for the beach.

There was a narrow gully that covered a precipitous path down the 300-foot cliff face to the pebble beach beneath. The gully was defended by a pillbox and a complex of slit trenches. These were to be taken by the men in the beach group. Landing craft assault (LCAs), escorted by motor gun boats would stand offshore and on a given signal approach the cove. The LCAs packed some extra fire power, each had four bren light machinegun teams provided by 12 Commando, recently returned from Lofoten.

A scientist from the Telecommunications Research Establishment accompanied the naval force, in case Cox needed additional technical support.

In this truly combined operation, Bomber Command provided a dozen Whitley bombers. Ten were to carry the paratroopers; the other two were to conduct diversionary bombing raids in the area.

In order for the raid to be successful, the conditions had to be near perfect. A full moon, so that the parachutists could have visibility for landing, had to coincide with a high tide to allow the LCAs to approach the shore. The paratroopers also wanted a night with little wind, so that the drop could be accurate and injury-free.

The raiders assembled in early February, completed their training and from the 20th of the month waited . . . Inevitably they were stood by on a number of occasions, only to find the operation postponed at the very last minute. The forecasters predicted that the night 27/28 February was going to be about as close as they were going to get to ideal conditions. It was either go then or wait another month for the combination of moon and tide. The night would be cold, the French coast had a covering of snow but the night promised a clear sky and a bright moon. This would help the Whitleys in their navigation, as well as aid the paratroopers. A ground haze was also forecast which could help to mask the flotilla from the enemy coast.

Major Frost had joined the Parachute Regiment from the Cameronians. C Company were largely drawn from the Scottish regiments including the King's Own Scottish Borderers, the Black Watch, and the Seaforth Highlanders. Thus it seemed entirely appropriate that just before 10 p.m. when the raiders marched out to the airstrip, they were piped aboard the waiting Whitleys.

There had been considerable improvements in the methods of assault parachuting in the 12 months since Deane-Drummond and others had made their ill-fated drop in southern Italy.

The Whitley however had not changed. It was still cold and uncomfortable and as unsuited to parachuting as ever; the exit was still via the trap door.

It would have been remarkable if the raid had gone entirely to plan. German anti-aircraft fire over the French coast broke up the formation, and during the final critical moments as the pilots made their approach over the drop zone, two Whitleys weaved away from the flak bursts and wandered slightly off course.

Twenty men landed over a mile from the designated DZ, and were separated from the main party by a steep-sided valley and unfamiliar ground.

The remainder dropped on target and into a foot of snow, about 600 yards from the radar site. Frost quickly reduced the size of the four groups all round and sent them away on their appointed missions.

The main attack on the smart villa proved something of an anti-climax. Frost had his men screen the house to cover all the windows while he led a small group up to the front door. There wasn't a sign of life.

After a moment's hesitation, someone said, 'What do we do now?'

'Ring the bell.'

The company sergeant major noted the comedian for later and kicked the door down. Frost led the rush into the house. The ground floor was stripped of furniture and empty. A solitary German, for reasons best known to himself, tried to defend the upstairs and died quickly.

There was a spirited resistance from the radar pit, where the soldiers manning a post near by had been thoroughly alerted. Four were killed and one was captured. The latter had run away, and, in blind terror of the phantoms who materialized out of the night, threw himself over the cliff, only to land after a couple of feet on a hidden ledge. A couple of burly paratroopers lifted him by the scruff of his neck to the top. The man, almost incoherent with shock, managed to reveal, with just a little prodding, that the total German strength in the area was less than a hundred. By now thoroughly alarmed, the garrison in the fortified farm at Le Presbytère opened up with some heavy machineguns from well-concealed positions. There was little the covering force could do, depleted in numbers and lacking heavy weapons.

Although much of the German fire was coming uncomfortably close, Cox concentrated on dismantling the Wurzburg. A section of Royal Engineers, who were also trained parachutists led by Lieutenant Vernon, helped him. The group were in considerable danger and two shots actually struck a piece of apparatus in Cox's hands, but they worked quietly on until they had completed the task.

A collapsible trolley had thoughtfully been air-dropped to help them carry the dismantled pieces of radar quickly away. But the rough, uneven ground, hidden by a covering of snow, made this difficult. Lieutenant Vernon, Cox and the sappers manhandled the pieces the 600 yards to the gulley at the top of the cliff. The remainder of the paratroopers fell back in good order with the rearguard forcing the Germans to stay in their positions until the very last minute.

A voice called up from below.

'The boats are here. It's all right. Come on down.'

If the Germans in the pillbox had been more patient they could have sprung a perfect ambush, and inflicted severe casualties. Instead, they opened fire too soon and only two of the parachutists were hit. Lieutenant Ross, who had been despatched by Frost to secure the beach, called across the gulley to his company commander. 'Don't come down. The beach has not been taken.' Ross considered his force too small to tackle the beach clearance, and had decided to wait for reinforcements. Nobody bothered to check the pillbox to see whether it was manned.

Frost quickly deployed his forces. If they didn't move quickly the Germans could bottle them up between the beach and the farm until daylight, by which time reinforcements would arrive. Le Havre was only 12 miles away. Using the rearguard to provide a perimeter defence, Frost concentrated on attacking the pillbox and its slit trenches.

Like John Wayne and the Seventh Cavalry, it was at this moment the bulk of the men who had been dropped wide of the DZ appeared on the scene. Shouting the war cry of the Seaforths, 'Caber Feogh', they charged into battle. Their combined fire power quickly despatched the German defences. With the gulley and the beach now secured, Frost took the main party down into the cove while the rearguard held the cliff-top and fought off probing attacks which were now being mounted by the garrison from Le Presbytère. Flight Sergeant Cross stowed the equipment in a safe position under the cliff, and, as there was nothing else to do, sat and waited.

The signal was flashed out to sea. After about half an hour, the LCAs came crunching onto the shingle. The last of the rearguard came tumbling down taking the gulley at a run, and the force pulled out under the covering fire of the commando bren-guns, and made for home.

AFTERMATH

Bruneval was a near perfect model of a combined operation, and Mountbatten had every reason to be delighted. A British force had come ashore, taken what they wanted, and escaped with low casualties. One commando had been killed, seven wounded and a further seven were missing in action, believed taken prisoner. At the time, the raiders claimed to have inflicted very heavy casualties on the enemy, but German records show their losses as five killed, two wounded and five missing.

One of the men the paratroopers brought back as a prisoner proved to be the operator of the Wurzburg. At first the scientists were delighted, especially as the man showed every willingness to co-operate with his captors. However, his level of expertise proved to be so low as to be valueless. It would seem that Hitler's ban on short-wave radios and radio hams, in the years before the war, had deprived the Third Reich of a valuable source of recruitment into this part of the armed forces.

Analysis of the captured equipment showed British scientists where the gaps in the German radar defences lay, and this was put to good use. Bruneval gave them a firsthand knowledge of the state of German radar technology in its night fighter control system and wave lengths, and thus prepared the way for jamming.

The Prime Minister for his part was pleased but at the same time sanguine in his judgements. He responded to the report of the operation and to Mountbatten's summation that it was 'the most 100 per cent perfection of any raid I know',[1] by writing, 'I hope these small raids of yours will not have the effect of putting the whole coast line into a state of vigilance.' This proved to be a prophetic statement. The Germans heavily fortified the coast and reinforced the garrisons.

The success of Bruneval allowed the nation more cheer at a particularly difficult time. But, as Admiral James on the staff in London said: 'It seems rather silly to crow over this relatively unimportant affair when so much is going wrong elsewhere, but even a tiny success lightens up the dark clouds.'

Bruneval was not a tiny success for parachutists in the British army. The 1st Airborne Division and the 1st Parachute Brigade were immediately formed; albeit under the closest supervision of the Army Council. Bruneval is the first battle honour inscribed on the drums of the Parachute Regiment.

---

[1] After the war General Student, who had commanded the German airborne forces, congratulated Mountbatten on Bruneval. It was, he considered, 'the best example of the use of airborne forces with other forces'.

PART FIVE

ST NAZAIRE

The Sauciest Raid Since Drake

CHAPTER TWENTY FIVE

The Plan

PREPARATIONS

When Charles Newman was asked to provide additional men for the Vaagso raid, he was determined to go as well. He sailed north from Gourrock, and at Scapa persuaded the navy to give him passage on the cruiser *Kenya*. If he couldn't land at the head of his commando, he would find a spot on the bridge and have a ringside view.

The commandos were a rather informal bunch. They didn't stand much on ceremony, and military protocol was quite alien to them. If Newman wanted to see the raid and watch how his boys performed, then that was perfectly acceptable to them. And the navy had no objections either. But Newman didn't see a thing.

On Christmas Eve Brigadier Haydon summoned him to his cabin. Newman was required in London immediately and at the directorate of Combined Operations. The only consolation that Haydon could offer was that a summons of this nature, and at Christmas, could only mean a job for his commando.

An old drifter, acting as harbour picket boat, came alongside the *Kenya* and took Newman ashore. At RAF Hatston there was a De Havilland Rapide waiting to fly him to Wick. Even Newman was impressed at the speed and urgency of the system which delivered him to the mainland.

Christmas caught up with Newman at Wick. There were no planes south for three days and no trains until the morning. The Officers' Mess found him a bed and made him welcome at the bar, so he made the best of a bad job and joined in the fun. Next morning, Christmas Day, Newman caught the slowest of slow trains south. It stopped at every station and took the whole day to reach Glasgow, there was no buffet on the train, and the heating in the compartment had long since expired.

At Glasgow, the transport officer found him a bed for the night in a transit mess, and, by the time Newman had booked in, the canteen had closed.

A pub round the corner sold him a half-bottle of whisky and a cold meat pie; and these he took back to the spartan room in the mess. It was quite the most miserable Christmas of the war Newman could remember.

Boxing Day was spent in a supposedly fast train, but it still managed to take ten hours to reach Euston Station. In answer to his call, the duty officer at Combined Operations advised Newman to 'call round in the morning', and promptly rang off before he could ask for a bed.

After a third night spent in an unfamiliar mess, Newman at last reported to Richmond Terrace. And at about the time his boys were landing as reinforcements for Dunford Slater on the quayside at Sör Vaagso, Newman was ushered in to the chief of staff's office.

The chief of staff was most apologetic. Newman wasn't required after all. The operation had been given to Glendenning in No. 1 Commando.[1]

'If you care to report to the transport officer, he will give you a rail warrant back to Scotland.'

Newman caught up with Glendenning, thought about punching him on the nose, and thought better of it. Instead they both booked into the Dorchester and had one hell of a party.

Newman accompanied his aching head back to Scotland the next day. He had elicited a promise from the chief of staff at Richmond Terrace that 2 Commando would have the next raid.

The men from Vaagso returned, and Newman concentrated on getting his commando back into peak physical shape, and as battle ready as the training allowed. A team of staff officers came to see them at Ayr and briefed the officers on an operation; a raid on a new coastal battery in Normandy.

Newman increased the tempo of their training. A week later, the raid was cancelled. Morale slumped and some of the men considered applying to return to their old units.

The Japanese entry into the war had led to considerable reinforcements being shipped to the Far East. Ironically, for commandos who wanted action, the best chance now seemed to be back with their own outfits.

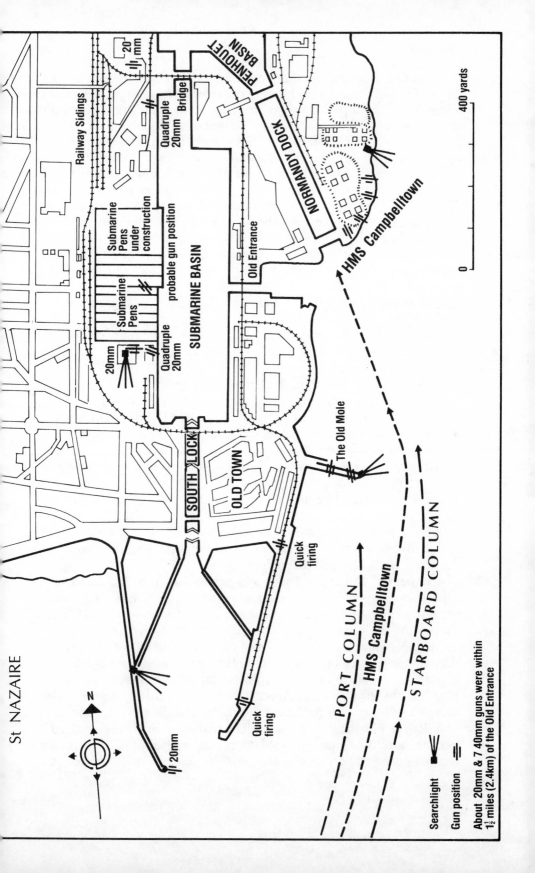

Brigadier Haydon sympathized, and compensated as best he could. He put the infantry landing ship *Prince Charles* at Newman's disposal for a couple of weeks' training in the Hebrides. It wasn't the Orient, but in a funny way the exercise did the trick. HMS *Prince Charles* was captained by Commander Fell, and she was one of the happiest ships in the 'Combined Operations Fleet'.

The weather was splendid and the commandos carried out numerous practice landings in the many lochs and coves in the Hebrides. They had a wonderful time, with hard work, good food and drink at navy prices. All the wrinkles were ironed out, and the commando returned to Ayr fit as fiddles and raring for action.

Newman was summoned to London within a couple of days of their return. Another false alarm, or was this the real thing? The commando knew of their colonel's summons almost before he did. The books were out and the odds stacked in favour of another false alarm.

Spears packed his master a bag for the usual day or two in London and drove Newman to the station in their recently acquired Hillman utility truck.

Stan Day, the adjutant, had worked a minor miracle and got Newman a berth on the night sleeper to London. He went straight from Euston to Richmond Terrace. Brigadier Haydon had not yet arrived, so one of the staff casually handed Newman an intelligence file marked *St Nazaire*.

Ushered into the brigadier's office he was to read the file while he waited for Haydon to appear.

The intelligence file, the usual War Office buff manilla folder, bulged with information about the docks at St Nazaire. There were dozens of photographs taken in the pre-war days of the dry dock, and many showed the French liner *Normandie*. Newman was none the wiser until Haydon arrived.

It appeared the commandos were going to raid the docks and 'smash them up'. Not only was this going to be the most ambitious operation yet attempted, but Newman's 2 Commando had been chosen for the job.

Once Newman had been told of the raid, the whole attitude of Richmond Terrace changed completely. He was given an office to himself, a dozen intelligence folders, large-scale maps and aerial photographs for the town. An intricate and beautifully made model of St Nazaire was brought into the room and the door locked.

A Royal Marine sentry, complete with side arm was stationed outside, and Newman was told to get on with things. Except for meals and bed, he did not stir until he had produced a general outline of his plan. Stan Day came down from Scotland to help write the orders.

Thereafter, it was a succession of meetings and conferences with the navy, air force and a myriad of specialists who inhabited Combined Headquarters. Mountbatten took a keen interest, chaired many of the sessions and put everything at Newman's disposal. Efficiency and extravagance went hand in hand. Daily the numbers of those 'in the know' grew, and Newman became increasingly concerned that secrecy might be compromised.

Meanwhile, Major Bill Copland, the second in command, brought the commando south to Falmouth where they were accommodated on board HMS *Princess Josephine Charlotte*, another unseaworthy ex-Belgian conversion.

The commando now trained in earnest and with a purpose. No details were revealed, but it didn't take a genius to realize that something was in the air; although the majority still believed it would all end in yet another cancellation. They couldn't have been more wrong. Their role in Operation Chariot, the attack on St Nazaire was to result in 83 awards for bravery, including five Victoria Crosses, and a further 51 Mentions in Despatches.

It is no wonder St Nazaire was to be called 'the greatest raid of all'.

PLANNING

The strategic setting of the raid is not too difficult to discern; although it should be remembered that the months of failure and disappointment were 'strategic impetus' enough to provide the need for a victory.

The American 'input' to the war had yet to be felt, but the lines of communications had clearly assumed greater prominence; and this was reflected in the Battle of the Atlantic.

No sacrifice appeared too great to ensure the safe conduct of convoys; although continued and heavy losses were used by those in Washington who favoured the 'Pacific first' as a further justification of their strategy.

The main thrust of the German offensive at sea was of course the U-boat. St Nazaire, by its facilities and its location in the Bay of Biscay, was an important submarine base.

Hitler had sufficient warships to unleash a couple of raiding squadrons into the Atlantic, and they could paralyse the convoy routes. The mighty *Tirpitz, Scharnhorst,* and *Gneisenau* together with the pocket battleships and heavy cruisers were more than a match for the forces the Allies could deploy in the early months of 1942 in the North Atlantic. The bulk of the German fleet stayed at home, operated in the Baltic, or lay up in Norwegian waters, where it was a constant threat.

If *Tirpitz* put to sea, St Nazaire offered the only dry dock outside her home waters that could offer full refit facilities. Destroy the dry dock and the options open to the Germans were immediately limited.

It was a nice theory but it doesn't stand up to close scrutiny. The *Bismarck* was eventually caught by the Royal Navy, making for a French port to effect repairs, but that was Brest and not St Nazaire.

The Germans had risked their squadron through the Channel mainly because it was getting hammered by the RAF; so why risk capital units in a port which was within easy range of British bombers?

However, perhaps the most telling argument was that the Germans were better off keeping their capital units in Norwegian waters. No matter how much the 'big ship' admirals in Whitehall wished, the German navy wasn't about to offer the Royal Navy a rematch after Jutland.

From Norway they could tie up large capital units of the Royal Navy in northern waters, and risk the occasional foray into the Atlantic by threatening either the Atlantic or the Russian convoy routes; and it was in these waters that *Tirpitz* and *Scharnhorst* were eventually to be destroyed.

There was a slight chance that the Germans might want the dry dock facility at St Nazaire, but the risk was interpreted as sufficiently high to warrant the extreme measures which Newman was asked to undertake. St Nazaire wasn't the easiest place to attack. The port had been on the Richmond Terrace 'hit list' during Admiral Keyes's tenure, but it had been struck off simply because it was too difficult.

The port stood on the right (or north) bank of the River Loire and was some six miles, or an hour's sailing, inland; so surprise would be exceedingly difficult to achieve. The River Loire is miles wide but much of it is shallow mud flats, and the one deep water channel was comfortably close to the coastal batteries which lined the bank. The dry dock was well known. In the years immediately before the war, it had figured prominently, if only because the French had built *Normandie* to challenge British dominance of the transatlantic luxury liner market.

St Nazaire was therefore a political symbol. It had a psychological value. Destroy the dry dock and the British public would immediately know and respond. Vaagso had been militarily brilliant, but

Norwegian fishing ports didn't mean an awful lot to the man in the High Street.

The broad expanse of treacherous mud flats were constantly shifting under powerful tidal movement, and were extremely difficult to mine.

A combination of shallow draught ships and high spring tides might provide a raiding force with an avenue of approach close to the harbour entrance which could catch an enemy unawares. Getting back of course was another matter together. Nevertheless, it did seem that there was a way to approach St Nazaire which offered some chance for success. The port of St Nazaire itself, from a close scrutiny of the aerial photographs, appeared remarkably open and very vulnerable. The analysts could find no evidence of barbed-wire entanglements ashore, neither did there appear to be any boom defences protecting the entrance to the massive lock gates; just a single anti-torpedo net.

The target for 2 Commando was the largest dry dock in the world. The *forme ecluse* at the Bassin de St Nazaire measured 480 metres by 55 metres wide, and it could comfortably accommodate ships up to 85,000 tons gross. To destroy the dock, it was necessary only to destroy the dock gates, although they were formidable – big as a block of flats and 35 metres thick.

The U-boat pens represented a secondary target. German forced labour, the Todt Organization, was already being used to provide an extension to the existing facilities. Additional U-boat pens would allow 28 submarines to have seemingly bomb-proof cover beneath massive shelters.

Headquarters combined operations came up with a plan of attack which combined the fireship tactics of the days of sail, with a variation on the Zeebrugge raid which had made Roger Keyes a public hero.

The idea was simple. A stripped-down destroyer would negotiate the shallow waters over the mud flat, and then be expended. With bow compartments packed with primed and fused high explosives, it would be rammed at high speed into the dock gates of the *forme ecluse*. Like HMS *Vindictive* at Zeebrugge, commandos would storm ashore from the destroyer and accompanying light craft, and wreak havoc before the light craft took them off and home. The destroyer would be stuck fast, with concealed high explosives on a delayed time fuse, and would then blow at the appropriate moment.

The Admiralty had been persuaded to part with an elderly Lend-Lease US destroyer. The USS *Buchanan*, a Wickes class flush-decked destroyer (DD 131), had been commissioned into the Royal Navy in September 1940 as HMS *Campbelltown*. Launched in 1919, she was one of 50 destroyers delivered in exchange for 99-year leases of sites for bases in the West Indies and British Guyana.

For two years, 'Old Buck' had hammered out the miles on the convoy routes, but now, with more modern ships available, she was past her prime. A massive refit and extensive modernization might allow her to take a front line in the anti-submarine war, but even that was doubtful. Like the commandos, the old lady was expendable.

For this her last voyage, *Campbelltown* was given a drastic and crude face-lift. Gone were the distinctively high four stacks, and in their place two smaller, raked funnels, in the hope that she would resemble a German Möwe class destroyer escort. Some armour plate was welded to the bridge and main deck to protect crew and commandos from small arms and automatic fire. Torpedo tubes and most of the guns were removed, leaving an ancient 12-pounder forward, and Oerlikons in the bridge wings.

The *Campbelltown's* main armament now became her lethal ramming bows. Below decks, 24 mark eight depth charges, each containing 400 pounds of explosives were concreted into a steel box, and behind the supporting column of the main gun. When the bow crumpled on impact, the charges should be undamaged.

Royal Navy specialists came up with an ingenious device for a delayed time fuse. The mechanism would have to be set, some time before impact, to allow the men to be clear. The fuses would also have to be sufficiently robust to survive the impact; and be on an irreversible process if discovered. The answer was to have acid burning through copper discs; the thickness of the latter determined time. They decided on eight eight-hour fuses.

A skeleton crew of 75 volunteer seamen under Lieutenant Commander S. H. Beattie RN would take HMS *Campbelltown* on her last voyage.

The German defences of St Nazaire were about as formidable as anywhere on the western seaboard of Occupied Europe. The old harbour mole had found a new lease of life as a site for batteries of multiple cannon and automatic weapons. Machinegun nests, anti-aircraft batteries and flat towers festooned the harbour area and docksides. There was a garrison of troops, naval-based personnel and crews off warships to provide trained manpower to counter any threat.

There was only one way the operation could possibly hope to succeed, which was by the time-honoured methods of *ruse de guerre*, deception and surprise.

The German navy carried out regular anti-submarine sweeps in the Bay of Biscay, using task groups of motor launches with a destroyer escort or two in support.

HMS *Campbelltown* had been disguised, and at night irrespective of flag motor launches and gun-boats look very similar. If the fleet flew the German naval ensign, as a legitimate *ruse de guerre*, then with luck they could bluff their way into the Loire Estuary.

The commandos were split between the destroyer and the accompanying motor gun-boats.

Time of year was also an important consideration. Late March, it was reckoned, produced the right combination of conditions. High spring tides and a full moon were often accompanied by a sea mist. The RAF was to lay on a raid against St Nazaire timed to coincide with the fleet's approach through the estuary. The purpose was to divert enemy attention 'skywards' and drown the noise of the warships' engines.

In the new spirit of co-operation and commitment that Mountbatten had engendered, Bomber Command diverted 70 aircraft for the operation, which at the time was a not insignificant effort.

For the operations ashore Newman had a total force of 44 officers and 233 soldiers. These included commandos with sapper experience drafted in from other special force units.

Newman divided them into three task forces. There were the assault troops, heavily armed shock groups who would charge ashore and silence or subdue the defences. Behind them were to come the protection squads, conventionally armed commandos whose task was to cover the third and most important group. Eighty commandos comprised the demolition teams. Each man had a Yukon Pack. This was a specially adapted rucksack which contained 60 to 80 pounds of explosives, and additional straps for sledge hammers, crowbars and other 'blunt instruments'.

These were 'the destroyers', their task – destruction on a grand scale. Pump rooms, machinery that powered the winding gears which opened the lock gates, raised and lowered bridges were their targets. Knock out the lock gates and the submarine pens too were neutralized. For nothing would be able to get in or out until the locks were repaired.

The task forces were divided into three groups to cover the main targets on shore. The main force, 75 men under Bill Copland, were on the *Campbelltown*. Once she had rammed, they were to attack and destroy the dock gates at the other end of the *forme ecluse*, a smaller set but which still allowed ships of up to 10,000 tons to enter.

A second group, led by Captain Mickey Burn of 6 Troop, was

to come ashore from the gunboats either side of the old harbour entrance, attack the outer harbour, blow the foot bridges which spanned the lock gates in the area and establish a defence perimeter.

Captain Bertie Hodgson was to lead the last group from the small craft and land on the north side of the Old Mole, knock out defence positions, and destroy the remaining locks that connected the submarine pens with the outer harbour. Hodgson was to hold the final defence perimeter through which the other groups would fall back and thence onto the gunboats.

Timing was critical. HMS *Campbelltown* was to hit the *forme ecluse* at 0130 hours. The air raid was vitally important, for some of the commandos would be coming ashore literally under the barrels of the enemy flak batteries. Such guns could serve equally well in an anti-ship role unless otherwise engaged.

The final phase of the operation, and it was planned to be away within two hours, was running the gauntlet of the Loire Estuary. Once at sea the gunboats would rendezvous with a couple of Hunt class destroyers, who would have escorted them from England, for the voyage home. Again, time was of the essence, since the fleet needed to put as much distance as possible away from the French coast and a doubtless avenging Luftwaffe, by daylight.

No plan is ever perfect, and this one certainly had its weaknesses. The weak link in the chain were the motor launches.

The commandos were to be carried in 16 Fairmile motor launches (MLs). These were formidable little craft in their own way, designed for inshore escort work and to counter the German E-boat menace. They were well armed and quite sturdy boats, but wooden-hulled and with no protection.

Their vulnerability was frightening. In order to make the 200-nautical-mile trip from Falmouth to St Nazaire and back, extra fuel tanks had to be bolted to the main decks. The plan was to pump the extra fuel into the main tanks and fill the auxiliary ones with sea water immediately before battle. It would have been better had they been jettisoned: pumping seawater wasn't at all successful, and the empty tanks were full of highly inflammable fumes. A motor gunboat, MGB 314, a slightly bigger brother than the Fairmiles, was the flotilla leader.

Commander R. N. Ryder RN was in charge of the naval task force and a man most suited to the role. An arctic explorer of renown, his last wartime command had been a disguised merchant ship which had been sunk. Ryder had spent four days alone in the Atlantic before rescue, and clearly was as hardy as any commando.

The last ship in the flotilla was a motor torpedo boat. Nothing was being left to chance. If the *Campbelltown* for any reason failed to ram the *forme ecluse*, MTB 74 skippered by Lieutenant R. C. M. V. Wynn RNVR was to blow up the gates. Wynn had perfected a torpedo with a delayed warhead.

While all the details of the operation were being discussed and argued through to some agreement, Bill Copland took 2 Commando through its paces. They exercised at Southampton, and practised against the dry dock in Cardiff, broadly similar, although much smaller than the *forme ecluse*. Demolition teams were able to complete their parts in the operation in ten minutes.

Newman escaped from Richmond Terrace on Friday 13 March to return to his beloved commando. The staff car was full of maps, models, wireless sets and all sorts of impedimenta, personal kit and Stan Day. They made a quick detour by way of an RAF photographic reconnaissance unit at Northolt to collect the latest shots of St Nazaire, and then headed out of London on the A4, the Great West Road.

Having stopped for the night in Tavistock, they reached the accommodation ship the next morning.

A final 'dress rehearsal' was an attack on the Devonport Naval Base to test 'the dockyard defences'. Everything except *Campbelltown* was used, and everything went wrong. The local Home Guard was jubilant at their success.

Newman could only comfort himself with the old adage that if the dress rehearsal went wrong, 'it'll be all right on the night.'

On Wednesday 25 March Newman briefed his assembled commando on the operation. They had waited for two years and trained for two years; their commando war was about to begin.

---

[1] Glendenning's operation was later cancelled.

CHAPTER TWENTY SIX

The Raid

The force sailed on the late afternoon of Thursday 26 March, 1942. In the early hours of the morning the commandos had transferred from their accommodation ship to the *Campbelltown* and small craft. Now, as the ships headed out to sea the soldiers were hidden belowdecks from curious and possibly hostile eyes. Those in the gunboats and small craft were cramped and uncomfortable, for there was precious little space below their decks; but they would have to stay until darkness.

The cover story which had been spread around the docks and pubs of Falmouth was that they were an anti-submarine task group bound for the Mediterranean. The Hunt class destroyers *Atherstone* and *Tynedale* took up station, each leading a column of small craft, while *Campbelltown* sailed in majestic isolation at the head of the force.

On Thursday night the ships hoisted German colours.

On Friday morning they sighted a German U-boat which the Hunts promptly attacked. Maybe the U-boat skipper thought there had been a coup in the Reich's Chancery in Berlin. Why the Hunts attacked has not been adequately explained. The U-boat eluded the attack, and later surfaced to signal Brest that a British mine-laying force was operating in the Bay of Biscay. Naval Headquarters immediately ordered five destroyers including the Möwe class *Jaguar* to investigate.

The German ships left St Nazaire on the Friday afternoon. Meanwhile, the British raiders plotted a course which would have them off the Loire Estuary at midnight and, blissfully unaware of the pack out after their blood, completed their final preparations for the operation. Spirits were remarkably high on board the ships. Soldiers and sailors got on extremely well, well aware that they were about to face a common danger. If any thought the operation was at all dicey, then nobody was about to admit it. Incredible optimism was abroad. One motor launch skipper had even packed a rugby ball. He thought they might have a chance for a quick knockabout ashore while they were tied up alongside the jetty at St Nazaire.

At 2300 hours on Friday 27 March, the flotilla closed to within ten miles of the Loire Estuary. Lieutenant Nigel Tibbets, a Royal Navy explosive expert set the fuses on *Campbelltown*. She was now a primed bomb, set to explode any time between 0500 and 0900 hours on the Saturday.

The motor launches pumped their extra fuel into the main tanks and filled the empty ones with sea water. The flotilla broke away from the escorting Hunts, and headed in towards the estuary. Shortly afterwards they saw the searchlights probing the night sky. The bombers were about to begin their part of the operation.

The air raid was a disaster. The bombers encountered a cloud base at 3,000 feet and were understandably loath to come in beneath it to spot their targets. St Nazaire's flak enjoyed a sinister reputation for accuracy amongst the air crews of Bomber Command. None of the bombers were prepared to unleash their bombs through the cloud base, in case they missed the docks and hit the town. St Nazaire had a population of 50,000, many of whom lived in the Old Town which intruded into the modern day dockland area.

The bombers, Whitleys and Wellingtons, stooged around for a while hoping to find a break in the clouds. Four aircraft out of the 70 planes above St Nazaire did bomb the town. The remainder, unaware of the significance of the raid, and convinced that there was going to be no break in the clouds, set course for home.

The last bomber had departed before midnight, leaving the defences suspicious and alert. The fleet moved into the Loire Estuary in two columns, one led by *Campbelltown*, and the other by the MGB 314, the flotilla flagship. Newman and Ryder were crammed into the latter's tiny open bridge, gun crews were closed up and all was set for the last lap.

They sailed in at ten knots, which appeared agonisingly slow to the men on board. For each knot faster, however, *Campbelltown* still a sprightly old lady, drew an extra foot aft.

They passed the wreck of the *Lancastrian*. Newman looked at the monster shadow of her upper works. He had come home from Norway almost two years ago in *Lancastrian*. Divebombed and sunk in June 1940, evacuating the BEF from St Nazaire, *Lancastrian* was the grave for 3,000 servicemen. At midnight, the commandos moved to their action stations. A team set up their 3-inch mortar on the foredeck of *Campbelltown*, to lend their weight, when the time came, to the 12-pounder.

At 0100 hours, the fleet was sighted by German shore defences, but the enemy were unsure if this wasn't their own destroyers returning home.

Nevertheless, the duty officer in the battery position which had made the sighting signalled the message to all positions: '*Achtung Land Gefahr*' – Beware Landings.

Fortress troops, Luftwaffe flak batteries and naval personnel returned to man those defences from which they had only just been stood down.

A searchlight probed the waters of the estuary from the shore and caught the *Campbelltown*. The beam faltered for a moment and then held the destroyer in its full glare. Everyone on board felt naked and exposed. Men tensed physically and crouched ready for the anticipated barrage.

Nothing happened. The disguise was obviously working, or was at least good enough to cause some doubt and confusion. Surprisingly, the Germans did not challenge the ship.

Thankful for small mercies, *Campbelltown* steamed on in the full glare of the searchlight. Every minute of grace meant another 400 yards nearer to the great lock gate of the *forme ecluse*.

Another light probed the night and this one settled on the small craft, whose presence of course the Germans could not explain.

The commandos heard the sound of air raid sirens and klaxons coming from the shore.

Commander Ryder had one last trick to play. He fired a sequence of red Very lights into the sky. This gave the game away. They were the wrong shade of red for German codes at night-time.

Enemy shore batteries opened fire. It was 0127 hours and *Campbelltown* had a gauntlet of a mile in length to run to the lock gates. On *Campbelltown*, they struck the German flag, and raised the most enormous Royal Navy battle ensign in its place. The 12-pounder forward opened fire and the commando team fired their mortar as if it were fed by a belt of shells. The gunboat and motor launches, white ensigns flying, all joined in the battle as they headed for their individual targets.

Beattie rang down for full speed. The engineer jammed the levers through the gates, and the old lady's stem bit deep into the water. A German flak ship proved a nasty and unexpected obstacle. Moored just a few hundred yards from the jetty, she had not been picked out on any of the photographs. The gunboat and launches smothered her in shot and shell, leaving her listing and disabled.

The shore batteries had the range, and could hardly miss. *Campbelltown* shuddered from multiple blows. The gun crews on the cruelly exposed foredeck were shot down and replaced. Commandos lay down behind their specially erected barriers but still took casualties from the shrapnel of air bursts above the ship.

The superstructure was hit repeatedly and the wheelhouse was a shambles. Coxswain and a quartermaster both died at the wheel. Lieutenant Tibbetts steered the ship in for the final few hundred yards.

The *Campbelltown* had to make it through. Everything was subordinated to this single aim. Two motor launches (they carried no commandos but were to lift the crew off *Campbelltown* and act as 'reserve'), now increased speed, moving ahead of the destroyer to take some of the fire themselves.

The German gun positions along the Old Mole, and the quaysides were firing at point-blank range. It was as if the enemy suddenly realised *Campbelltown's* intention. Even the flak towers, deeper inside the dock area, depressed their barrels and fired down onto the ship. They caused fearful casualties amongst the commandos waiting to jump ashore.

The destroyer ripped across the torpedo nets and rammed the mighty *forme ecluse*.

At the precise moment of impact, Beattie swung the stern to starboard which both left the route clear for the motor launches to get at the old entrance; and it 'skewered' the ship into the dock.

It was 0134 hours on Saturday 28 March. *Campbelltown* was four minutes late for her appointment.

It was now the turn of the motor launches to bear the brunt of the fire. Perhaps as many as 15 gun positions were within range of the dock. Some were flak towers with multiple 20mm cannons whose devastating rate and volume of fire caused havoc on the wooden decks of the motor launches now packed with commandos.

The port column headed for the Old Mole and sailed into a veritable wall of fire. The launches fired back for as long as they were able but were simply overwhelmed. Some blew up, others, literally ripped apart quickly sank. A few limped away out of the glare, their decks littered with dead and wounded. The starboard column had even further to run and suffered in consequence.

Of the total force, five motor launches made it to the quaysides and landed commandos; at least those who had survived the gauntlet.

Ryder came in under heavy fire and dropped Newman and his three-man tactical headquarters ashore. It would seem that perhaps less than a hundred of the commando force made it ashore at St Nazaire. Nevertheless, although casualties were appallingly high, the main objective of the exercise had been achieved. *Campbelltown* had rammed the *forme ecluse* and was stuck fast, acid burned through the copper discs and there was nothing the Germans could do to stop the process.

Meanwhile, assault parties, with fierce exuberance, took on the gun batteries and the flak towers with tommy guns and grenades. It was the Germans' turn to suffer and one gun position after another fell silent.

Commandos from the *Campbelltown* subdued the enemy defences as far into the docks as the Old Entrance and the bridge across the lock gates. Against the batteries on the submarine pens they had no answer and since those guns dominated the open ground, the advance stalled. The 15 small German warships tied up in the submarine basin gave the enemy added fire power.

Five demolition teams from *Campbelltown* made it ashore. One attacked the main pumping station for the *forme ecluse* and destroyed it totally.

Captain Bob Burtenshaw led another team against the smaller lock gates at the other end of the dry dock. They failed to get inside the lock but blew up the winding gear in its hut alongside, and then for good measure lowered a dozen 18-pound charges on ropes down the outside.

All of these actions were completed despite intense small-arms and automatic fire. A couple of freighters were undergoing refit in the *forme ecluse*, and they joined in the battle.

Captain Burtenshaw led an attack on one of these ships whose guns were being particularly bothersome. He led his protection group into an attack while the charges were being placed, and was killed.

Newman had established his headquarters close to the bridge over the Old Entrance, and it was here that the surviving commandos and sailors gathered. They formed a tiny defence perimeter and fought it out uncompromisingly with the Germans.

The enemy had now gathered his forces and swung into the counter-attack. Two naval flak battalions, harbour troops and crews from all the warships and U-boats in the port were mobilized. Newman had about 60 men in his perimeter defences against some 2,000 Germans. He tried and failed to contact Ryder. The army's 38 set was notoriously unreliable, and this night was no exception. They could make no radio contact.

Even if the two officers could have communicated, it would not have affected the outcome. Although Ryder had no idea of how the battle was progressing on shore, it was obvious there could be no evacuation of survivors by sea. It was a shambles in the river. The hulks of motor launches drifted on the tide, others were still burning furiously.

At about 0300 hours, Ryder took *MGB 34* alongside *Campbell-town* and lifted off a few sailors and wounded commandos. He called up the MTB whose speed alone had kept her out of trouble, and ordered Wynn to torpedo the outer lock gates of the Old Entrance. There was little else that could be achieved, and the decks of his gunboat were littered with wounded, some hit for a second and even a third time.

Loath to leave, Ryder knew he could delay the inevitable no longer. Although the sights and the sounds of battle came hot and strong from the shore, Ryder signalled the surviving ships to withdraw.

He looked back for a last time at *Campbelltown*. As he watched, the bridge Oerlikons were firing across the entrance at the Mole. Had a party crept back on board to give covering fire, or were the Germans firing at the commando perimeter?

Exhausted and drained soldiers lay along the dockside, taking what cover they could; roused only to life when an officer yelled that the Germans were coming again. The perimeter had already beaten off a number of counter attacks, but Newman could see the utter futility of a last stand.

At 0330 hours Newman ordered his men to break out. It was a strategy of despair but he couldn't stomach capitulation en masse. The best they could achieve was to get past the German lines and put as much distance as they could between themselves and St Nazaire. There was a chance they could link up with the Resistance and then be passed down the line to Spain, Gibraltar and home.

The demolition men had landed armed only with side arms. While the wounded manned the perimeter and hoped to deceive the attacking enemy, with assault and protection men covering them, they slipped away.

Most did not get very far. The Germans had all the foot-bridges covered, and there was no other way off the dock. Some died in the attempt to run the gauntlet of fire, others surrendered when their ammunition had been exhausted.

Those commandos who did succeed in getting past the Germans and into the Old Town found cellars and hideaways before daylight. They were flushed out next morning and forced to surrender.

Whilst the last act ashore was being played out for the

commandos, the surviving naval units had to run their own gauntlet of fire; six miles of the River Loire to the sea. Lieutenant Wynn in his motor torpedo boat had a top speed of 40 knots and more. He should have made it with relative ease, had he not stopped to rescue some survivors clinging to a Carley float. A crippled motor launch was nearby; the German batteries waited until the torpedo boat had stopped, before they opened fire. There were 36 sailors including the men in the water. Four survived.

Motor launch No. 14 still had her full complement of commandos. She had been heavily damaged early in the operation, her youthful skipper and commando leader were both casualties when the bridge took a direct hit. Temporarily leaderless and damaged, she had taken no further part in the operation, until now.

The German destroyer flotilla was returning home. Three miles into the Loire Estuary they encountered ML14. The flotilla leader left one ship to deal with this impudent little intruder, whilst he hurried on ahead to provide reinforcement for a battle which might still be waging. The escort *Jaguar*, 1400 tons and armed with three 4.1-inch guns took an hour to sink the motor launch. The latter put up the stoutest resistance and refused to surrender until her last gun was silenced and she sank from under her few surviving sailors and commandos.

The *Jaguar* picked up the survivors. The German officers and sailors treated their prisoners with the utmost kindness and consideration.

Ryder's gunboat and two MLs made the rendezvous with the destroyers, although one launch was so badly damaged that it had to be abandoned and sunk. Four other MLs missed the rendezvous and sailed home independently, in what must have been epic voyages in their own right.

Operation Chariot totalled 611 commandos and sailors; 242 returned to England.

HMS *Campbelltown* blew up at 1030 hours on Saturday morning. An added and unexpected bonus was the large number of souvenir hunters that were on board at the time. The German navy lost a number of senior and very valuable staff officers because their curiosity got the better of them. The explosion burst the dry dock gate or *caisson*. Sea water flooded in and the *forme ecluse* was rendered useless.

The French in St Nazaire have no reason to love the British. It was 1950 before the dry dock was repaired, and they suffered a repressive occupation after the raid. They will tell you, however, that a British officer remained hidden on board HMS *Campbelltown* and sacrificed his life to blow the charges. It is more likely that the acid took longer to burn through the copper disc than had originally been calculated.

Lieutenant Wynn survived the sinking of his torpedo boat, although he lost an eye, and spent the rest of the war as a prisoner. His torpedos didn't explode until the Monday morning; completely blocking the Old Entrance to the submarine basin. By that time, Lieutenant Colonel Charles Newman and Lieutenant Commander Beattie were marching their men out of St Nazaire and into captivity.

There is no comparison with the Zeebrugge raid. Sir Roger Keyes, who became a national hero and a household name, lost 200 men out of 1800 and the Germans had that port working within four days.

At St Nazaire 169 commandos and sailors were killed. Newman and Beattie were among 200 prisoners. Was the raid worth the price and the sacrifice?

Any judgement on St Nazaire has to be clouded by the sheer heroism and gallantry of those who took part. Newman had spent two years training a force of élite troops who were decimated in a single action.

In September 1943, 2 Commando went into action again, this time at Salerno. There were just two officers who had fought at St Nazaire.

Nobody can claim that the destruction of the *forme ecluse* was so important as to have materially affected the outcome or indeed have shortened the war. Neither did its loss for the Germans reduce the threat of the rest of their fleet. The capital ships *Tirpitz, Scharnhorst* and others in the Norwegian fjords remained a menace until they were sunk. Even if the destruction of the *forme ecluse* did affect German naval strategy, its destruction was effected by the Royal Navy. The commandos showed incredible bravery, and increased the level of collateral damage with the pumping houses and machinery which they destroyed. However, it was the act of ramming *Campbelltown* into the lock and the high explosives which then ruptured the huge *caissons*, which caused the damage.

At the time of the raid, Major Jack Churchill was attending a senior officers' course at Earlstead Park in Wiltshire. It was a sort of wartime emergency staff college course for army officers destined to command. Churchill was still convalescing after the wound he had received on Maaloy Island, and this seemed as good a way as any to spend the time.

One morning he was called to the telephone.

It was Brigadier Haydon. 'Jack, we're going to reform 2 Commando. It was badly knocked about at St Nazaire. As you know, Charles Newman and Bill Copland, his second, were both captured.'

'Yes I know, Brigadier.'

'Jack, how would you like to take command?'

Churchill rebuilt the commando, and took it to the Mediterranean. They took part in the amphibious operations as the Allied shock troops, spearheading landings in 1943 at both Sicily and Salerno.

By this time, although there were other raids in Europe, this had become the main commitment for combined operations and the commandos.

For 2 Commando, their raiding days were not quite over. Later they were switched to the Balkans to fight alongside Tito's partisans in a true and prolonged guerrilla war.

CHAPTER TWENTY SEVEN

Reflections

IT'S ALL IN THE MIND AND IN THE HEART.

On 4 March 1942, Mountbatten was summoned to luncheon at Downing Street. The Prime Minister told him he was to be, 'Chief of Combined Operations, to sit as the fourth Chief of Staff, and have the acting ranks of Vice Admiral, Lieutenant General and Air Marshal.'

Winston Churchill had insisted on this elevation in the face of entrenched opposition from his most senior service advisers. The Admiralty looked with horror at such accelerated promotion for a junior captain in a shore appointment, where there wasn't even the saving grace of a fleet action which had devasted the admirals in command. Alan Brooke at the War Office cared little about the honours and titles conferred, but he did care about having Mountbatten foisted onto the Chiefs of Staff Committee.

The Prime Minister allowed for little discussion and indeed, in a handwritten postscript appended to the memorandum to the chiefs which spelled out the appointment, added 'I trust they will find themelves generally able to agree.'

Mountbatten could take personal satisfaction that he had suddenly become the youngest vice admiral in the Royal Navy since Nelson, while the power and prestige of his office was now way beyond even the wildest dreams of Sir Roger Keyes.

By this time combined operations headquarters had been expanded to over 400 officers, men and women. It was one of the first headquarters where the 'silk stocking brigade' was very much in evidence.

The chief's promotion was greeted with joy at Richmond Terrace. Combined operations enjoyed a virtual monopoly of the ways and means of amphibious warfare, and now, at a single step, the organization had penetrated into the very centre of the war's direction.

Mountbatten was excited at the work, amused by the oddballs Richmond Terrace and special forces attracted, and ensured that he remained the centre of attraction, supported and advised by those whom he liked and trusted.

Increasingly, he saw his main task as being to 'develop the training and tactical doctrines applying to the assault echelon'. This required an equal emphasis on special craft and specialist troops to spearhead the assault.

In February 1942 Charles Haydon established a new Commando Training Centre at Achnacarry. This was the castle and clan seat of Sir Donald Cameron of Lochiel, the chief of the clan Camerons, located in a remote glen some 15 miles from Fort William.

Lieutenant Colonel Charles Vaughan was the first commandant, and it was largely due to his skill and leadership, that it was to become one of the finest battle schools in the world. Known variously as 'Laird of Achnacarry' or the 'Rommel of the North', this bull of a man began his military service as a private soldier in the Buffs, and thence worked his way through the ranks and a commission.

Achnacarry was a ritualized and specialized business.

Success to its recruits, officers and soldiers, meant membership into an exclusive club. Failure was RTU, the return to conventional soldiering knowing that one was second best.

The Commando Training Centre was trial by ordeal, a test of endurance, requiring ready acceptance of pain and danger. Under Vaughan's tutelage, everything in the three-month basic course, which both officers and soldiers had to complete usually in the most awful weather, had a purpose. Cliff climbing, speed marching and unarmed combat, together with the devilish variations in good, old-fashioned physical training, instilled resilience and stamina.

The exercise of skills such as street and house-to-house fighting, assault courses and the like, where only live ammunition was used, helped to produce soldiers whose fieldcraft tactical skills and weapons' handling were second to none. They were indeed recognized as the finest shock troops in the Allied armies. Achnacarry indoctrinated them with the notion they were expendable, and thus operations all carried this hallmark of a raw and terrible courage.

The course reflected the characteristic qualities of the special forces – proud discipline and extreme violence.

Achnacarry taught young men, from quiet domestic backgrounds, its own form of total war. They learned to kill with anything that came to hand – from a matchbox to a coin. They used knuckledusters, flick-knives and other weapons of the street. They were taught to slit throats, gouge eyes, break necks, backs, limbs, crack skulls and crush testicles.

Achnacarry was an experience none of them would ever forget, not one aching moment.

Later in the war such training was to earn dividends in the commando contribution to the great amphibious operations, where the men lived up to the finest traditions of the light infantry of a bygone age.

Inevitably, special forces also attracted the oddballs. Army psychology had made significant progress since the Great War, but was still quite unable to cope with some of the strange characters.

One story, probably apocryphal but illustrative, is told of one selection process, where the officer would interview volunteers sitting at a table with a bowl of eggs between them. If the potential recruit had not taken at least one egg in the ten-minute session then he was penalized.

An army is a reflection of its own society; and a civilian army in war mirrors precisely its own society at that time. There were psychopaths, homosexuals and many who would today be adjudged the criminally insane. There were criminals, thugs and bullies. The special forces undoubtedly attracted those who lived by their wits and on both sides of the law.

When Mountbatten assumed command of combined operations in October 1941, Churchill had ordered him to prepare for the coming invasion of Europe and to mount raids; but the priorities were never defined.

So far as the European War was concerned, the belated entry of the United States meant that the question was no longer *if* there could be a Second Front but *when*. This in turn provoked a shift of direction for combined operations. More and more time was devoted to the amphibious aspects of the Second Front.

In April 1942, General Marshal, the United States chief of staff, was in London for high level talks. He was invited to visit the Service Ministries and responded by placing Richmond Terrace at the head of the list. It was a great success and within a month Brigadier General Lucian Truscott and a team of eight American officers had joined the headquarters.

The Prime Minister too was pleased with the performance of his protégé. At the same time he maintained and rekindled enthusiasm for the commando concept.

He wrote to the Secretary of State for War, 'It occurs to me that the Lovat Scouts, by reason of their origin, traditions and composition might with advantage be added to the existing Commandos, to take the place of the three Commandos which were sent to the Middle East in 1940 and there disbanded. Pray put me up proposals.'

The reasons for this fresh enthusiasm for a commando policy are not difficult to discern.

Beginning in December 1941, and stretching through into the autumn of 1942, Britain experienced a pretty dismal time. The entry of Japan into the war, although it brought confidence in ultimate victory through the American as well as the Russian alliance, introduced a string of appalling disasters in the Far East, culminating in the fall of Singapore and the loss of Burma. At the same time, it triggered a whole series of German and Italian successes. Three British battleships were knocked out in the Mediterranean, and Rommel romped across the Western Desert to take Tobruk with comparative ease, making fools out of British generals. When the German capital ships *Scharnhorst, Gneisenau*, the heavy cruiser *Prince Eugene*, and their numerous escorts sailed up the English Channel in broad daylight, there was a public outcry. The infamous 'Channel Dash' in February 1942 was a national humiliation.

In these months of failure and unbroken disappointments, Bomber Command's gathering offensive received full publicity and the real truth was carefully hidden from view. The commando raids were in turn given a prominence which far outweighed their military contribution. Together Bomber Command and commando raids went some way to satisfy public demand for success and helped offset some of the worst conventional military disasters.

In order to complement the larger and less frequent raids, Mountbatten determined to maintain the pressure with smaller operations against the French coast. Originally, it had been planned a mount a raid every two weeks but this was impossible. So they occurred with less frequency; but even then the policy of raiding for raiding's sake against a coastline which the Germans had fortified and garrisoned could have little value.

'Trench raids across a watery no-man's land', were dangerous, especially if only to gather odd bits of intelligence and the occasional act of sabotage. Even so a number of raids were planned, a few launched, but none proved really successful.

There were, even in adversity, some lighter moments. Lieutenant

Philip Pinkney, Berkshire Yeomanry, became a popular commando officer and a leading light in raiding. He was an exemplary exponent of living off the land, and on exercises his men had to exist on a diet of berries, snails and baked hedgehogs. The fact that they would follow him anywhere demonstrates his leadership skills.

During one night raid on the tiny Channel Island of Sark, Pinkney lost his bearings and climbed in through the bedroom window of the house belonging to the Dame of Sark. Seemingly unperturbed at this nocturnal visitor, and recognizing the blackened face of a British soldier, the redoubtable Dame sat up in bed and exclaimed, 'Thank God to see a decent-sized man at last.' [1]

An exception to the comparative failures of the Channel operations was the Small Scale Raiding Force (SSRF), founded by three commando officers, Majors March-Philips and Appleyard, and Captain Hayes. They formed the unit back in March 1941, and raided in small parties of around eight to ten men against targets chosen at random, with the broad objective of killing Germans.

March-Philips established his headquarters in Anderson Manor near Wareham, where they used the surrounding Dorset countryside for training, and set up an advanced base in the Antelope Inn in Poole Harbour.

Later the SSRF came under the operational direction of the Special Operations Executive where their prime tasks were to deliver agents and gather intelligence. They used an old wooden-hulled Brixham trawler called the *Maid Honour* as their mother ship. Small parties would slip ashore in a variety of folding boats, canoes and other small craft.

Intelligence gathering sometimes took the form of abducting an enemy soldier or two for interrogation in England. One such incident, again on the island of Sark was to have tragic circumstances.

A raiding group took some prisoners, who were manacled and hurried down to the beach. The alarm had been raised, however, and they ran into an ambush. In the ensuing fire fight two of the manacled prisoners were killed, although the rest of the party were able to make good their escape. A report of the incident infuriated Hitler.

In October 1942 a Führer Directive ordered that 'all enemy troops taking part in the so called Commando Operations . . . in uniform or not . . . whether in battle or whilst escaping . . . will be destroyed to the last man.'

Even without a German army hell-bent on revenge and bloody reprisal, small-scale raiding across the Channel was a desperately risky affair, and none of the leading members of the SSRF or their men entertained thoughts of a long life.

Nevertheless, these courageous men continued with their work until, inevitably, the enemy were in the right place at the wrong time.

On the night of 7 September 1942, March-Philips, Appleyard and Hayes with nine soldiers raided St Honorine on the Normandy coast, again after prisoners and intelligence. The Germans were alert to the threat and forced the raiders to withdraw under heavy fire which killed March-Philips. Captain Appleyard had remained with the boat and he made it back to Portsmouth. Hayes eluded the Germans and sought shelter with the French Resistance, who passed him 'down the line' to Spain. Franco's police caught him and he was handed over to the Germans. After nine months in solitary confinement Major Hayes was executed for being a commando.[2]

Mountbatten's tenure of office at Richmond Terrace was also tinged with tragedy and controversy. It was called Dieppe.

Operation Rutter which was launched on 19 August 1942 was an out and out disaster. The Canadian troops took 68 per cent casualties in their frontal assault while the commandos tasked with the flank attacks suffered a 20 per cent loss. At the end of the operation 1,000 dead littered the beaches and a further 2,000, stranded ashore, were taken prisoner.

Dieppe was never intended as a raid in the sense that the term has been applied through this book. Indeed the controversy continues to this day as to the true purpose and intentions. A 'reconnaissance in force' is what both Churchill and Brooke were to dub it with the benefit of hindsight. Perhaps too it was a compensation to the Americans for our failure to launch a full invasion in 1942, and a sop to the Soviets who continually complained that they were having to bear the brunt of the fighting.

Dieppe certainly pointed starkly to the real priority for Richmond Terrace; that was combined operations and the need to produce more and better commandos with special forces to spearhead the amphibious assault.

The Americans created the Ranger Battalions in the commando image and the Royal Marine Infantry became commandos too. The latter had volunteered to be marines but were not volunteer commandos, although belatedly they recognised the new requirements of naval infantry.

Some US Rangers, all the Royal Marines and even more Army Commandos, passed through Achnacarry, which was now geared to the needs of amphibious assault.

Achnacarry also had another purpose. It centralized and rationalized commando training, producing a uniform standard, and thereby further reducing 'the freebooter image', the power and latitude of the independently minded commanding officers.

The image of Churchill's Private Armies, in so far as the European theatre was concerned, was fading fast. The Prime Minister was losing interest, and the memoranda dwindled as he grappled with the burdens of Alliance Warfare in which Britain progressively became the junior partner.

The young leopards were a thing of the past.

All of this was very agreeable to the Army Council, and the military hierarchy demonstrated a determination to ensure that these special forces should remain a wartime contingency. Shoulder flashes were given grudging approval, but any attempts to establish *esprit de corps* by allowing a single commando cap badge were stubbornly blocked.

As early as the summer of 1941, when Sir Roger Keyes raised the question, in the proper manner for once, the response was predictable: 'The Army Council feels that the men would rather carry the badge of their own Regiments.'

The distinctive green beret appeared, more by chance, in late 1942, when 1 Commando had some made locally and the idea spread.

We have seen too that these commandos formed, trained and fought their war with the opposition of many senior members of the hierarchy. Men like General Sir Alan Brooke were convinced that special forces, and the talents they attracted, denuded the field army of the best of its junior command. Those the commandos rejected had their confidence undermined by failure.

In some instances, commandos could have achieved high rank in the conventional army. But in the European Theatre, in France and in Italy, as in North Africa earlier, the British army was most severely tested by its weakness at platoon and company level. The weakness could not have been drastically changed had there been no special forces.

In Britain, Churchill had called for ten commandos each of 500 men. Most commandos in the period covered in this book rarely were made up of more than 380 men, and had to borrow heavily when it came to mounting an operation. The average size of a troop in 1942 was about 36 men.

By the war's end the army had raised 14 commandos, and the Royal Marines a further eight. Some army commandos existed for just a short period before being amalgamated or disbanded, and for a variety of reasons.

Had these men been 'released' for conventional military service, perhaps they could have exerted some local influence, but many, it must be said, only performed so outstandingly because of the commando.

Special forces have been the scapegoat for a weakness which the British army would not confront and therefore could not overcome. In large measure the solution to its ills lay within its own gift, since, as the army expanded, it also distorted the proportion of service troops to combat or *teeth* arms.

Other features were beyond their control. In the competition for human resources the army lost out to the air force and in particular the Bomber barons, with their ravenous consumption of the finest talent available.

Bomber Command absorbed an estimated 7 per cent of the nation's manpower. The air crews which flew the bombing missions, in a series of campaigns whose value to the war effort has been consistently questioned since, suffered 60,000 casualties. The British army commissioned 200,000 officers into its service during the Second World War, so the loss in terms of those with potential who served in the special forces, could hardly have exerted a profound influence.

Churchill's Private Armies did not have the detrimental effect on military performance which was claimed by their detractors. Indeed their misuse in operations later in the war, in a continuous infantry role, both squandered manpower, and compensated on so many occasions for the indifferent performance by line battalions. It was their exemplary courage, and *esprit de corps* which marked them out as élite units.

That had been the original intention behind Winston Churchill's Private Armies.

---

[1] Lieutenant Pinkney later transferred to the Special Air Service Regiment, and many of his commandos followed him. In 1943 he was captured in Italy and later executed.

[2] The independent role of the SSRF ceased in early 1943. Appleyard joined the SAS and was killed later that year in the Middle East.

Bibliography

BUCKLEY, Christopher	Norway The Commandos Dieppe	*HMSO 1977*
CHURCHILL, Winston S	The Second World War	*Penguin Books 1985*
CLARKE, Dudley	Seven Assignments	*Jonathan Cape 1948*
COLVILLE, John	The Fringes of Power	*Hodder & Stoughton 1985*
COOK, Graeme	Commandos in Action	*Hart-Davis MacGibbon 1973*
FRASER, David	And We Shall Shock Them	*Hodder & Stoughton 1983*
GILBERT, Martin	Finest Hour	*Heinemann 1983*
LADD, James D	Commandos & Rangers of World War II	*MacDonald & Janes*
LEWIN, Ronald	Ultra Goes to War	*Hutchinson 1978*
LOVATT, The Lord	March Past	*Weidenfeld & Nicholson 1978*
LUCAS, James	Kommando	*Arms & Armour 1985*
McDOUGALL, Murdoch C	Swiftly They Struck	*Odham Press 1984*
MILLAR, George	The Bruneval Raid	*The Bodley Head 1974*
MILLER, Russell	The Commandos	*Time Life Books 1981*
SAUNDERS, Hilary St George	The Green Beret	*Michael Joseph 1949*
YOUNG, Peter	Storm From the Sea	*William Kimber 1958*
ZIEGLER, Philip	Mountbatten	*Collins 1985*

Index

This is WAR!

" Attack when the enemy thinks its won! "

" Think creatively and strategically.

" Dont let people know what you intend to
do, - until its done.

" Give misinformation!

" Small can conquer Big, - if strategy &
good planning involved.

" Dont say too much - (keep them guessing)

"Conserve your energy, - dont waste it "